BASIC
ACCOUNTING

J. Randall Stott is a chartered accountant and former lecturer in accounting at Boston College of Further Education and Cannock Chase Technical College. He is the author of ten textbooks and workbooks on accounts and commercial subjects, including *Introduction to Accounts* and *Mastering Principles of Accounts*.

TEACH YOURSELF BOOKS

BASIC
ACCOUNTING

J. Randall Stott FCA

TEACH YOURSELF BOOKS

Hodder and Stoughton

First published 1985
Sixth impression 1990

British Library Cataloguing in Publication Data
Stott, J. Randall
Basic accounting. – (Teach yourself books)
1. Accounting
I. Title
657'.024658   HF5635
ISBN 0 340 36513 7

Printed in Great Britain for
Hodder and Stoughton Educational,
a division of Hodder and Stoughton Ltd,
Mill Road, Dunton Green, Sevenoaks, Kent,
by Richard Clay Ltd, Bungay, Suffolk
Photoset by Rowland Phototypesetting Ltd,
Bury St Edmunds, Suffolk

Contents

1

Introduction

There is nothing magical about book-keeping and accounting. The *keeping of accounts* simply involves the routine recording of business transactions, the exchange and the payment for both goods and services being identified by money values.

The accounting device and method explained in this textbook is called 'double entry book-keeping'. Sometimes referred to as the *arithmetic of commerce*, it is a form of simple arithmetic – that is all.

The purpose of accounting

We live in a world of credit. Without some form of accounting record, indecision and confusion would result. Not only is it businesslike to keep accounts as a check on suppliers and credit customers, but the financial statements made up from these accounting records keep management informed, from time to time, of the progress of their businesses.

These financial statements are scrutinised and verified when:

(*a*) a business is sold or a new partner is admitted to an existing firm;
(*b*) a bank loan or a substantial overdraft is needed by the business;
(*c*) the local Inspector of Taxes assesses the income tax liability on the trading results of the business.

Business transactions involving all aspects of production, trade and distribution are varied and voluminous in every town and village. The bulk of these transactions are on credit, the settlement for the merchandise bought or for the services used often being delayed for a few days or a few weeks. It is important that there is printed or written evidence of the original terms and money values agreed upon between producer and consumer, vendor and credit customer, or the professional man and his client.

In double entry book-keeping, the money values of all transactions with suppliers of goods on credit (the creditors) and the sales to credit customers (the debtors) are recorded, and the details of all money received and money paid, whether by cheque or in cash, are also recorded in a manner, which, with practice, becomes routine and easy to comprehend.

Some of our existing terms take on a different meaning when used in the accounting sense. A few of these terms are now introduced.

Assets refer to the property and possessions of a business, which may be owned by an individual (a sole trader or one-person business), a firm or partnership, or perhaps a limited company. In this elementary textbook, book-keeping is explained as it would be adapted to the financial accounting side of a sole trader's business. Nevertheless, basic principles of double entry, throughout the world of commerce, remain the same.

Fixed assets are those assets which are retained for the benefit and permanent use of the business, such as premises, machinery and plant, vehicles, fixtures and fittings. These assets are not for re-sale in the trading sense.

Current or circulating assets change their form in the course of trading, common examples being stock of goods for sale, the trade debts of customers, money in the bank and office cash.

Liabilities are the debts and obligations of the business, the external and trade liabilities falling into two main categories:

(a) *fixed liabilities* such as a mortgage or a long-term loan,
(b) *current liabilities* comprising outstanding accounts owing to trade and expense creditors, and sometimes a bank overdraft.

In addition to the external debts and obligations of the business, there is generally a large internal debt owing by the business to its proprietor under the heading of **capital**. This, in the case of a sole trader, would be regarded, on the basis of the account book figures, as the equity of the proprietor or the net worth of the business.

Balance sheet: an introduction

The main consideration, normally, to be given to any new business venture, even one based at home, is that of finance, money or financial backing. A trading business needs substantial funds or extended credit facilities from the outset. A place has to be found for the storage and safety of merchandise, and thought needs to be given to deliveries (involving transport), communications (post and telephone), and the recording of cash and credit dealings (the book work and accounts). In addition, at least some small reserve of finance is required to maintain oneself during the initial period of creating or developing the business.

Before we start on the routine book work of a typical small trader, we shall take a glimpse at one of the targets and main end-products of this short course in elementary accounting. This is a financial statement called the *balance sheet*.

Suppose your great-aunt Sarah recently bequeathed you a legacy of £500. You decide to be 'your own boss' and work up some kind of small trading connection from your home address.

With effect from 1 June, this £500 is allocated to your new business venture to become the sole asset and property of the business in your name. The business, regarded as a unit and entity separate from you personally, acknowledges its debt and obligation to you, as owner and proprietor, in this commencing balance sheet, thus:

Balance Sheet as at 1 June

Assets employed		You may have other sources of income and property of your own, but that is your private affair, quite distinct from this new trading venture now being financed by your investment of £500.
	£	
Cash in hand	500	
Financed by		
	£	
Proprietary capital	500	

The proprietor's holding or control over the net assets of a business is sometimes referred to as the *owner's equity*.

The routine business dealings of a small retail trader are called transactions. Generally, they involve the purchase and sale of merchandise for cash and/or credit (where payment is delayed), the settlement of trade and expense accounts for goods bought and for services used, and occasionally the purchase of a 'fixed asset' for the retention and permanent use of the business.

During the first week of June a number of transactions take place, and in this particular instance a separate balance sheet has been drawn up simply to illustrate how this financial statement is *affected in two ways by each transaction*. Normally, though, the listing and grouping of assets and liabilities on a balance sheet would be made in greater detail at the end of the trading period, perhaps every six months or only once a year.

2 June   You pay £130 for two large storage cupboards and some strong shelving.

N.B. The four stages of these elementary balance sheets are explained by simple arithmetic. The routine debit/credit procedure starts in Chapter 4.

Balance Sheet as at 2 June

Assets employed		Property has been acquired for permanent use by the business. This purchase is shown as a 'fixed asset'. Cash is decreased by the sum paid out.
Fixed assets	£	
Fittings/fixtures	130	
Current assets		
Cash in hand	370	
	500	The payment for the fixed asset does not affect the holding of the proprietor (his capital) nor current liabilities, as the business at this stage has no outside debts.
Financed by		
	£	
Proprietary capital	500	
Current liabilities	—	
	500	

3 June You buy merchandise on credit priced at £200 from Wholesalers Ltd, arranging to pay for the goods bought later in the month.

Balance Sheet as at 3 June

Assets employed		£		Goods to the value of £200 have been taken into stock at *cost price*, increasing current assets to £570. These goods have been bought on credit (no money has been paid). So cash remains at £370.
Fixed assets				
Fittings/fixtures		130		
Current assets	£			
Stock	200			
Cash in hand	370	570		
				There is still no change in the owner's capital account. However, an outside liability has been incurred of £200. The individual names of trade creditors do not appear on the balance sheet.
		700		
Financed by				
		£		
Proprietary capital		500		
Current liabilities				
Trade creditors		200		
		700		

4 June   You sell goods priced at £60 to a cash customer, and further goods priced at £40 to a credit customer (to be paid at the end of the month).

Say profit mark-up is 25% on cost, i.e. 20% on the selling price. The cost of the goods sold is thus £80.

Balance Sheet as at 4 June

Assets employed			£80 of stock (at cost) is sold for £100. This leaves stock balance in hand at £120.
Fixed assets		£	
Fittings/fixtures		130	
Current assets	£		The cash position is now £370 + £60 = £430.
Stock	120		
Trade debtors	40		Amount due from credit customer (£40) is shown under 'trade debtors'.
Cash	430	590	
		720	The difference between cost price £80 and the selling price of £100 is the trading profit. This is added to the proprietor's capital as the reward for his investment.
Financed by			
	£		
Capital 1 June	500		
Add profit	20	520	
Current liabilities			
Trade creditors		200	
		720	

5 June   You pay £50 off your supplier's account for the goods bought on 3 June, and then withdraw £25 cash for your own private and personal use.

Balance Sheet as at 5 June

Assets employed				The £50 paid off trade creditor's account reduces *both* the business cash and the amount of the trade liabilities total. The stock figure is not affected by this payment.
Fixed assets		£		
Fittings/fixtures		130		
Current assets	£			
Stock	120			
Trade debtors	40			The sum of £25 withdrawn for the proprietor's own use is called 'drawings'. Business cash is reduced and also the proprietor's holding or net assets as shown by his capital account.
Cash	355	515		
		645		
Financed by				
	£	£		
Capital 1 June	500			
Add profit	20			
	520			
Less drawings	25	495		
Current liabilities				
Trade creditors		150		
		645		

Note how the proprietor's capital account of this small business remains constant until affected by:

(*a*) business profits or losses;
(*b*) withdrawals by the proprietor (and it would of course be increased by additional private capital paid into the business).

Some elementary accounting concepts have been touched upon in this short balance-sheet preamble. At each stage there is the emphasis upon total assets equalling total liabilities (including the capital). The accounting equation $A = C + L$ applies all the way through, where:

A represents the total assets of the business;
C the proprietary capital; and
L the external debts and liabilities of the business.

Practical work

Like typewriting, book-keeping is a 'doing' subject. The progress of the student is geared to his capacity and inclination for work. At the beginning, a fair amount of repetition is necessary to encourage the development of correct habits. Attention to detail is continually stressed, and once the basic principles have been established, new procedures are built in stage by stage.

In the classroom, the teacher will probably supplement the textbook explanation by simple blackboard illustration, and students will then work through similar exercises from the textbook.

At this stage the text should be re-read, and then the remaining exercises of the chapter completed and checked against the brief answers at the back of the book. There are also additional problems at the end of the book for those who proceed in advance of the class or require further practice.

2

The Ledger System

The ledger system of double entry book-keeping entails the use of a number of account-ruled books (known as a set of books) for the purpose of recording accurate information, in money values, of the day-to-day trading operations of a business. From these permanent records, periodical statements are prepared to show the trading profit or loss made by the business and its estimated net worth, at any given date.

Ledger accounts

The record of trading transactions is kept, in money value, on the folios or pages of these account books, called *ledgers*. The ledger folios have special rulings to suit the needs of the business. The bank statement style (page 58) lends itself to modern mechanised accounting, but for the time being double entry will be explained by the older traditional method, using the ledger rulings still adopted by many small businessmen. This is the ordinary ruling for the older style of ledger account:

Name of Account

Debit *or left-hand side*			£	**Credit** *or right-hand side*			£
Date	**Value COMING IN**			*Date*	**Value GOING OUT**		

In practice, separate ledgers are kept for the different classes of accounts (customers, suppliers, business property, trading revenue and expense, etc.). Batches or groups of similar accounts are kept together, and ledgers are indexed so that information with regard to any particular account may quickly be obtained.

However, when learning the first principles of elementary book-keeping, and for economy of paper, it is customary for the student to use only one ledger-ruled exercise book in the early stages, to be followed by a cash book and a journal after a week or two.

The cash account

The cash account is first explained as *part of the ledger system*. Some students may already be familiar with the simple recording of receipts and payments of money.

Assume that you start in business (a small retail shop) on 1 June with *£200 cash as your commencing capital*. At present we shall only deal in currency notes and coin: cheque and bank transactions will be explained later.

During the month of June all your business dealings are for cash. The details of your trading transactions are listed below, and then posted or entered in your *cash account* for the month of June as the first stage of a book-keeping exercise involving the *receipt and payment of money only*. Note that at this stage there are no credit transactions.

June		£
2	Goods bought for re-sale	75.00
5	Money received for goods sold	45.80
12	Paid for advertising	7.30
18	Cash takings (i.e. cash sales)	56.20
20	Bought further goods for cash	85.00
24	Cash sales	110.50
30	Paid salary to temporary assistant	60.00
	Withdrew cash for private use (this is called *drawings*)	50.00

The cash account is now made up for the month of June, all money *received* being *debited*, and all money *paid* being *credited*. Note the one-word description of all the credit entries, and the complete absence of the words 'cash' and 'paid' on this side, because all these entries refer to *cash payments*.

Dr. *(debit)* **Cash Account** *(credit)* Cr.

Date	Money COMING IN	£		Date	Money PAID OUT	£	
June				June			
1	Balance in hand	200	00	2	Purchases	75	00
5	Cash sales	45	80	12	Advertising	7	30
18	Cash sales	56	20	20	Purchases	85	00
24	Cash sales	110	50	30	Salary	60	00
				30	Drawings	50	00

Explanatory notes

1 The cash in hand, a debit balance at 1 June, is your commencing capital in this particular instance, being the sole asset and property possessed by the business on this date. In later exercises it will be seen that business property *in money* is normally *only part of the proprietor's capital.*

2 Cash takings or cash sales refer to the normal and continuous 'across the counter' sales of the small retailer, in contrast to his **credit sales** where the possession of the goods passes from vendor to buyer at the time of the sale, with the settlement and payment being deferred until later. In these early exercises we are concerned only with cash purchases and cash sales.

3 The narrow column on the left of each cash column is used for cross-referencing to the appropriate and corresponding account of the double entry (explained in Chapter 4).

4 Goods and merchandise bought by the business to be re-sold are identified by the word **purchases**, distinguishing this heavy prime cost from the other many and varied expenses of trading, and also to show a clear distinction between this basic trading expense and the acquisition cost of property and assets such as machinery and fixtures, bought for the retention and permanent use of the business.

5 The one-word description, as far as possible, of each entry, is important, as this serves to identify the opposite and corresponding double entry, normally in another ledger.

6 The posting of all amounts *coming into* an account on the *debit side*, and all amounts *paid or going out* of an account on the *credit side*, avoids the necessity for continual addition and subtraction until the balancing-up stage, generally at the end of the month.

Assignments

Key Points

1   Centre the heading of the cash account and leave a blank space between the heading and the details within the account.

2   The name of the month need not be repeated when once placed at the top of the date column, but the date of each transaction must be given.

3   The £ sign need only be shown at the top of each cash column, and should not appear against the individual receipts and payments.

4   As far as possible, use a single one-word explanation of the entry in the details part of the account.

5   The words 'received' and 'paid' are superfluous in the details section, and the word 'cash' need only appear on the debit in order to distinguish cash sales from any sales on credit (which are not posted to the cash account).

6   The correct and *vertical* alignment of the figures in the money columns will make additions easier at the balancing-up stage.

7   The main rule for all cash accounts is:

   (*a*)   Debit money *coming in*
   (*b*)   Credit money *paid out*.

2.1   You are required to post up the transactions listed below in a cash account for the first week of March:

March		£
1	Balance of cash in hand	40.00
3	Cash takings	26.44
4	Paid for further goods	14.80
	Paid advertising account	10.50
5	Cash sales	46.02
	Bought further supplies	16.60
6	Wages paid for temporary assistance	25.00

2.2   Give three good reasons for the permanent recording of business transactions.

3

Balancing the Cash Book

In book-keeping the term 'balancing' simply means adding up both the debit and the credit sides of an account, and deducting the smaller side (of less total value) from the larger side. The difference between the two sides is called the **balance** of the account.

Later it will be seen that the cash account is kept in a special ledger called the cash book, which, in practice, would probably be balanced weekly, and certainly at the end of every month.

The cash account on page 11 is reproduced here and balanced up in the ordinary way. Study the illustration and then read carefully the following instructions on balancing.

Dr. *(debit)*   **Cash Account** (1)   *(credit)* Cr.

Date	Money COMING IN		£		Date	Money PAID OUT		£	
June					June				
1	Balance in hand	2	200	00	2	Purchases	5	75	00
5	Cash sales	15	45	80	12	Advertising	8	7	30
18	Cash sales	15	56	20	20	Purchases	5	85	00
24	Cash sales	15	110	50	30	Salary	9	60	00
					30	Drawings	4	50	00
					30	Balance c/d		135	20
			412	50				412	50
July									
1	Balance b/d		135	20					

Note that there are fewer items on the debit of this cash account, and spaces have been left blank to allow for neatness and to ensure that the *corresponding totals are on the same horizontal.*

The *folio* or page numbers relating to the opposite and corresponding double entry have been inserted in the narrow folio column in front of each amount, prior to the posting of the double entry in the separate ledger accounts as shown in the next chapter. For clarity, the folio or page number is shown in brackets after the name of each ledger account in these early stages.

The balance of cash in hand at 30 June (£135.20) is the difference between the debit total of £412.50 and the total of the payments (£277.30). This balancing figure of £135.20 is inserted as an additional item on the *credit side above the total*. The two totals now agree and are ruled off in the manner shown. The total of the payments (£277.30) before balancing may be noted in pencil, but *is not inked-in* as a permanent feature.

The difference or balance on an account should never be left suspended in mid-air. In the case of the cash account, the balance will be entered as the last item on the credit side above the total, and then *brought down below the debit total on the opposite side*. The two totals are ruled off neatly on the same horizontal, the lower line of the total being double ruled.

The abbreviations c/d and b/d signify 'carried down' and 'brought down', and where balances or totals are sometimes carried forward from one folio to another, the abbreviations c/f and b/f denote 'carried forward' and 'brought forward'.

The physical cash balance must always be a *debit balance* as money can only be paid out of an available fund or balance in hand.

Assignments

Key points
1 First make your additions in pencil and ink-in afterwards. In balancing, remember to deduct the total of the payments from the total of the receipts, only inserting the *difference* (which is the balance) on the *credit side above the total* on the right-hand side of the cash account.
2 Bring down the same amount shown on the credit side above as a *debit balance now below the total on the left-hand side* of the account. This debit balance is simply the excess receipts over payments.
3 Cash account totals must be on the same horizontal, and the lower line should be double-ruled to indicate a total.
4 With a little concentration, these simple cash book exercises will quickly teach you how to record elementary cash transactions, leading on to the routine of ledger posting.
5 In assignment 3.3, although payments are mentioned to a supplier and by two credit customers, we are only concerned at this stage with how the money received and the money paid affects your cash position. The earlier part of this kind of transaction (the credit purchase and the credit sales) is explained later in the text.

3.1 What is the purpose of the two columns on the left and the right of the ledger, debit always being on the left and credit always being on the right?

What kind of receipts and payments would be found in the cash book of:

a confectioner	a plumber
a dentist	an accountant?

3.2   Post up the transactions shown in a cash account for the month of September, rule off the account, and bring down the new balance as at 1 October:

Sept.		£
1	Cash balance	200.00
2	Bought goods for cash	35.60
4	Receipts from customers	42.10
8	Paid rent for month	30.00
10	Cash takings	10.50
	Paid advertising account	16.40
12	Cash sales to date	38.28
	Stationery supplies bought	12.60
18	Cash takings	28.48
20	Further purchases for re-sale	19.36
22	Paid carriage on purchases	2.25
	Paid part-time typist	56.00
28	Withdrew for private expenses	30.00

3.3   At the close of business on 30 June you have £300 in cash, your only asset and commencing cash balance for the month of July.

Your daily cash sales for July total £168.50. Two old customers pay their outstanding accounts (Marcia Moore £23.40 and Leslie Lane £35.60) on 5 July. You pay your own supplier Robert Reese & Son £52.50 on 20 July for deliveries during June. Other payments made in July were:

July		£
3	Rent	40.00
11	Petrol/oil	12.50
15	Stationery	8.36
28	Salaries	48.00

On 25 July you withdrew £50 from the business to go on a fishing trip. From this information, you are asked to post up a cash account for the month of July bringing down your cash balance on 1 August.

4

Double Entry Theory and Practice

The cash account shown in Chapter 3 is two-sided like all ledger accounts, but this is not the meaning of double entry book-keeping. Each entry in the cash account, whether receipt or payment, has only one aspect.

The cash account itself is a useful device for the recording of money received and money paid, and periodical balancing up will reveal and check the physical cash in hand, but the cash book figures alone cannot be used as a true guide to finding out the trading profit or loss of a business.

With the ascertainment of business profit in view, we now identify and record the opposite or dual aspect of each cash account entry as it is posted to another ledger account.

First principles of double entry

In all business transactions there are *two separate and distinct aspects* to be recorded within the same accounting period. Two separate accounts are involved in each transaction, one account recording the debit (receiving) aspect, the other recording the credit (giving or paying) aspect.

The account *receiving value or benefit is debited.*
The account *giving, paying or relinquishing benefit is credited.*

Sometimes it is easier to decide or identify the account (or person) giving up something of value. This will determine the *credit part* of the two aspects and at the same time serve to identify the *related debit.*

Dr.						Name of first account			Cr.
Date	**Debit what comes into the account** (value received)		£		*Date*	**Credit what goes out** (value paid or relinquished)		£	

Dr.						Name of second account			Cr.
Date	**Debit what comes into the account** (value received)		£		*Date*	**Credit what goes out** (value paid or relinquished)		£	

Practical book-keeping

Only one aspect of double entry has been recorded with regard to each item in the cash account in the previous chapter. The opposite and dual aspect of each entry is now shown on the related ledger accounts.

The reason for the one-word description of most of the postings in the cash account will now be understood, as these are the *names and headings of the new ledger accounts.*

In practice, the postings from the cash account to the related ledger accounts would be made in date order, but for ease in explanation, all debit items will be dealt with first, and then the credit items.

Capital and net worth

The first entry in your cash account is the commencing cash in hand, a balance of £200 at 1 June. You have given or loaned this business £200, which from this date becomes the sole asset and property of the business. This is also your own *personal contribution* to the business, and in consequence will be credited to your **capital account** to show that you now have a financial stake or holding in this business of the net worth of £200 at 1 June.

Thus the posting of this first item of £200 to the credit of capital account initiates the double entry to the opposite side of another ledger account.

Dr.						Capital Account (2)			Cr.	
					June 1	Cash	CB1	£ 200	00	

Cash sales or daily takings

The remaining three entries on the debit side of the cash account are all for cash sales or daily cash takings. These individual daily sales are posted to the *credit of sales account* for the month of June, and in due course this grouped information will be used to work out the trading profit for the month. In practice, the postings would be made day by day.

Dr.   **Sales Account** (15)   Cr.

					June			£	
					5	Cash	CB1	45	80
					18	Cash	CB1	56	20
					24	Cash	CB1	110	50

Now we turn to the *credit* side of the cash account where the nature of the entries is a little more varied. All items on this side refer to payments for merchandise bought, trading expenses incurred, whilst 'drawings' indicates that some money has been withdrawn by the proprietor for his own private use.

Goods bought for re-sale

Goods may be bought for stock or conversion into merchandise for sale to the general public. In any event, a clear distinction must be made between goods and merchandise bought as the stock in trade of a business and the property (assets) and every-day trading expenses of the business. Merchandise bought for re-sale is termed 'purchases' and thus the payments made on 2 June and 20 June are posted to the *debit* of Purchases Account.

Dr.   **Purchases Account** (5)   Cr.

June			£						
2	Cash	CB1	75	00					
20	Cash	CB1	85	00					

Trading expenses

The various trading expenses for the month of June (in this instance only advertising and salaries) are debited to *separate accounts*, thus completing their double entry.

Dr.   **Advertising Account** (8)   Cr.

June 12	Cash	CB1	£ 7	30						

Dr.   **Salaries Account** (9)   Cr.

June 30	Cash	CB1	£ 60	00						

Money withdrawn for private use

The remaining credit item of £50 for drawings is not a business expense. It is a withdrawal by the proprietor of part of the money invested in the business, although in the case of profitable businesses the owner would regard his withdrawals to be in anticipation of excess revenue or profit. Nevertheless, since part of the business assets (cash) is reduced, there is also a reduction of the proprietor's holding, i.e. his capital account. Sums withdrawn will temporarily be debited to drawings account, and at the end of the trading period be *transferred* to the debit of capital account.

Dr.   **Drawings Account** (4)   Cr.

June 30	Cash	CB1	£ 50	00						

In this small exercise and introduction to double entry the word 'cash' has been used throughout in the body of each account, simply indicating that the original posting or entry has come from the cash account (or cash book as it will shortly be called). At this elementary stage, the cash book is our main and only *book of original entry*, but as we proceed through the various phases of accounting procedures, it will be seen that the initiation stage is not always from the cash book.

In the practical world of commerce, financial transactions are varied and voluminous, and systems vary greatly to suit the needs of particular trades, industries and organisations. Nevertheless, the basic principles of double entry accounting remain the same.

Pause for thought

(a) Consider now the use and purpose of the folio columns, those narrow columns in front of the main cash columns. What is the accounting term used for entering or making the dual entry from one account to another?

(b) How would you decide which account should be debited and which account should be credited?

(c) Is it possible to finish with the cash balance *brought down underneath* the total on the credit side of the cash columns?

Assignments

Key Points

1 Financial information is being grouped at this stage, in total form, for the use of the accountant and management. By this means, the task of the accounts department is made easier in the preparation of various financial statements.

2 Do not cramp the writing up of your ledger accounts in trying to economise too much on paper. Leave a space of several lines between accounts, allowing perhaps for 4 to 6 ledger accounts per page of the standard exercise book.

   Again, remember to leave a space between each ledger account heading and the details in the account.

3 Do not scratch out or try to rub out any wrong figures. Simply rule through incorrect amounts, inserting the correct figure above the error.

4 As far as possible, reduce the description of the money value received or paid to one word, as this will be the heading of the opposite or contra account as a rule.

5 Use the £ sign only at the top of the cash columns, and do not repeat the name of the month once inserted at the top of the debit or credit columns within the same account.

6 Number the various ledger accounts in assignment 4.2 and give some thought to the cross-referencing procedure between cash book and ledger.

4.1   Study the cash account of Mark Clark now shown, and then answer the questions underneath:

Dr.   **Cash Account**   Cr.

June			£		June			£	
1	Balance b/f		175	00	2	Purchases		120	00
9	Cash sales		39	80	5	Adverts.		15	60
14	Cash sales		66	45	9	Garage a/c		12	85
22	Cash sales		52	35	18	Self		30	00
28	Cash sales		84	40	25	Salaries		112	25
					30	Rent for June		35	00

- (*a*)   What is meant by 'Balance b/f'?
- (*b*)   Explain each item in date order.
- (*c*)   Distinguish between cash sales and the sales to credit customers.
- (*d*)   Why is information about purchases shown separately from other expenses?
- (*e*)   Again, why are the payments for salaries and 'drawings for self' not combined?
- (*f*)   Balance up this cash account, and post up the double entry to the corresponding ledger accounts.

4.2   Make up the cash account of Janina Jones from her cash transactions, shown below, for the month of January:

Jan.		£
1	Cash in hand	250.00
2	Bought goods to be sold	66.60
	Paid for stationery/stamps	8.20
5	Cash takings	54.48
12	Paid salaries	64.00
	Withdrew for 'self'	30.00
14	Sundry expenses	14.15
18	Cash takings	84.94
	Paid insurance	12.50
22	Drawings	30.00
28	Paid salaries	64.00
30	Telephoned Thomas Hudson for urgent delivery of stock. Consignment received the next day, invoiced at £44.50.	

After balancing up Miss Jones' cash account for January, post the double entry to the related accounts in her ledger.

5

The Trial Balance

The next stage, after the completion of the postings, is the extraction from the books of all balances on a statement called the *trial balance*. It is *not* an account.

The financial information, classified and grouped on the various ledger accounts in the last chapter, is now totalled on each account, and the debit and credit *balances* listed on the trial balance, including the *final balance of the cash account*.

Trial Balance   30 June

		Debit £	Credit £
Cash balance	CB1	135.20	
Capital	L2		200.00
Sales	15		212.50
Purchases	5	160.00	
Advertising	8	7.30	
Salaries	9	60.00	
Drawings	4	50.00	
		412.50	412.50

The trial balance is made up on journal-ruled paper, usually at the back of the student's exercise book called the **Journal**. There is no particular order for the grouping of the account balances, but to avoid omission it is suggested that the final cash balance should be extracted first, and the remainder of the ledger balances may then be listed in either page or book sequence.

There is no complication about double entry here, as this has been completed. Debit balances are merely listed on the debit of the trial balance, and credit balances on the credit.

Purpose of the trial balance

It is emphasised that the trial balance is not an account. It is not part of the double entry, but merely a list of debit and credit balances taken from the books, normally at the end of a specific trading period (which may be a month, six months or often one year) for the purpose of:

(*a*)   checking the arithmetical accuracy of the postings, and
(*b*)   rendering the work of the accountant or book-keeper easier in the making up of financial summaries, often with a view to the preparation of revenue trading accounts, together with a balance sheet.

Note that only the balances of the accounts are brought on to the trial balance. For example, the debit balance of £135.20 is extracted from the cash account, and *not the two totals* for receipts and payments.

The sales account is totalled to show total sales of £212.50 for the month, which in effect is the credit balance taken to the trial balance. Similarly with the purchases, and so on.

If no mistakes have been made in posting the cash book to the various ledger accounts (debit for credit and vice versa), the sum total of the debit balances on the trial balance should equal the sum total of the credit balances.

Pause for thought

(*a*)   What is a trial balance and what does it prove?
(*b*)   When your trial balance totals do not agree, what steps do you take to find the difference?

Assignments

Key Points

1 With practice you will acquire an automatic thinking habit of 'debit this account' and 'credit that account' and comprehension will become as easy as simple arithmetic.

2 The trial balance is *not* an account. It is simply a list of debit and credit balances assembled by the book-keeper to prove the arithmetical accuracy of his postings.

3 Every *account balance* in the books is brought on to the trial balance, including the *closing balance of cash in hand.*

4 When the trial balance does not balance:

  (*a*) Check the trial balance additions again. Your figures may be out of alignment.

  (*b*) Check all additions again, in particular those in the cash book, and those of the purchases and sales accounts.

  (*c*) Make sure that the *closing cash balance* has been brought to the *debit* of the trial balance.

  (*d*) Check the double entry of all postings in the books, *debit for credit*, and re-check the extraction of the balances to their correct side of the trial balance.

5.1 Assemble the information shown below in trial balance form, and ascertain the capital or net worth of this business at 31 December by deducting the total credit balances from the total debit balances:

	£
Cash in hand 31 Dec.	225
Advertising expenses	65
Purchases for December	4500
Sales for December	5750
Rent and rates paid	360
Stationery bought	40
Salaries paid	880
Drawings for month	400

5.2   Enter up the transactions shown below in your cash book and post the double entry to the ledger accounts. Balance the accounts where necessary, and prove the arithmetical accuracy of your postings by taking out a trial balance at 31 January.

Jan.		£
1	Cash in hand	300.00
2	Paid insurance	15.50
	Bought goods	120.00
6	Paid rent	30.00
8	Cash sales	38.80
11	Advertising	10.50
15	Paid salaries	60.00
	Bought stamps	5.00
18	Cash sales	56.20
22	Purchases	84.00
24	Petrol/oil	18.30
	Cash sales	42.10
28	Salaries	60.00
31	Drawings	50.00
	Cash sales	64.40

5.3   Explain the difference between salaries and drawings. Why is the Inland Revenue very much concerned about this distinction when checking the sole trader's year-end accounts?

Revision Exercise 1

In this exercise you start with £400 cash as the sole asset or property of the business financed by you. The following transactions take place during the month of September.

Sept.		£
1	Arranged to pay a rent of £25 for the use of a small lock-up shop, and paid the landlord a month's rent in advance	25.00
3	Bought miscellaneous goods for sale	75.50
	Purchased stamps from Post Office	5.00
	Cash sales	55.74
6	Hired a part-time assistant and paid wages	30.00
	Paid for advertising in local paper	12.20
8	Cash sales	64.82
	Bought further goods for sale	45.40
	Paid carriage on purchases	4.50
10	Cash purchases	15.66
	Withdrew cash for household expenses	50.00
14	Paid wages	30.00
	Cash sales	54.30
18	Paid insurance premium for fire risk	16.60
	Cash sales	68.78
20	Paid wages	30.00
	Bought invoice stationery etc.	9.98
25	Cash takings for past three days	82.20
	Further purchases for stock	26.50
28	Paid wages	30.00
30	Cash withdrawn to pay private bills	50.00

Enter up these cash receipts and payments in your cash book for September, post up the corresponding double entry to the ledger accounts and take out a trial balance as at 30 September.

At what stage and date of the month was your cash balance, in its circulatory flow, at its highest and lowest ebb?

6

Gross Profit and Stock

This small arithmetical problem explains how basic costs (including the adjustment for stocks) influence the selling price of commodities.

Say you have 10 articles which have cost you £1 each. You buy 20 more, also at £1, and sell 25 articles at £1.40 each. What profit have you made? Quickly, by mental arithmetic, you might say £5 profit (the excess of your sales receipts £35 over the total cost of the available stock you had for sale).

But what about the stock of articles not yet sold? This stock presumably has a very definite value and must be taken into account in working out your profit. It is valued at its cost price of £5 (i.e. 5 articles not yet sold which you bought at £1 each).

Arithmetically, the true profit is worked out thus:

		£
Total sales (25 articles at £1.40 each)		35.00
Add stock unsold (5 valued at £1 cost)		5.00
		40.00
Less stock at start (10 articles at £1)	£10.00	
and additional purchases (20 at £1)	20.00	30.00
Showing a final profit of		10.00

Another illustration is now shown, both arithmetically and in a proper accounting manner, leading on to the business trading account and gross profit.

A small trader, on 1 April, has a stock of 200 articles bought at the average cost of £1 each. Early in April he buys 100 more of these articles, now priced at £1.10 each. During the month of April he sells 240 articles at £1.50 each.

The trader's true profit is first worked out arithmetically in this way:

		£
Total sales (240 at £1.50)		360.00
Add stock unsold (60 at cost of £1.10)		66.00
		426.00
Less stock at start (200 at £1	£200.00	
plus purchases during April		
(100 at £1.10)	110.00	310.00
To show a trading profit of		116.00

In accounting, the money values of this arithmetical problem would be set out in this way:

Trading Account for the month ended 30 April

	£		£
Opening stock 1 April	200.00	Net sales	360.00
Purchases for month	110.00	Closing stock 30 April	66.00
Gross profit	116.00		
	426.00		426.00

The older style of trading account shown above has now been superseded by a more modern style, disclosing the *cost of sales figure*, thus:

Trading Account for the month ended 30 April

	£		£
Stock 1 April	200.00	Net sales	360.00
Add purchases	110.00		
	310.00		
Less stock 30 April	66.00		
Cost of sales	244.00		
Gross profit	116.00		
	360.00		360.00

Note that the gross profit is unchanged by the variation in style.

Cost of sales

The cost of the goods sold (commonly called the cost of sales) is found by adding purchases to the opening stock, and then deducting the closing stock at its valuation.

The purpose of the trading account is to find the main or gross profit (or loss) on trading for a certain stated period. The gross profit is simply the balance of the account, the difference between the net sales and the cost of sales.

Valuation of stock

In the commercial world, the valuation of the stock not yet sold at the close of an accounting period is taken to be either at its cost price (the price at which it was bought) or at the current market price, *whichever is the lower*. When working elementary exercises, students are given the closing stock figure as a rule, unless the problem is specifically based upon the calculation of stock.

The stock account

The commencing stock of an established business is already a debit balance in the books at the beginning of a new accounting period. It will have been debited to stock account at its valuation at the close of the previous accounting period. Consequently the *old stock figure* of an established business is taken to the debit of the trial balance when final accounts are being prepared for the current trading period.

In examination papers, the new closing stock figure can always be identified by its date. Generally, the closing stock is brought into the books *after the trial balance stage*, by a new debit to stock account and with its corresponding credit to the newly prepared trading account.

Note how the stock account below is made up from the information given earlier in this chaper. The opening stock (£200) at 1 April will be *transferred* from the debit of stock account to the debit of trading account. This transfer is shown on the credit of the stock account, squaring off this part of the old account as at 30 April. At the same time, the £66 debit for the more recent valuation of closing stock at 30 April is now brought into the books for the first time by *creating a new debit* on this account and with its corresponding double entry being credited to trading account, or, alternatively being deducted on the debit side of the trading account.

Dr.	Stock Account					Cr.	
Apl. 1	Opening stock at beginning of month	£ 200	00	Apl. 30	Transfer of old stock to trading account	£ 200	00
30	Trading account (closing stock now brought into the books)	66	00				

Assignments

Key Points

1 The period covered by a trading account should always be given in its heading.

2 The dates of the two stocks (at the beginning and at the close of the trading period) should be shown, so that there is no confusion.

3 Assignment 6.1 simply involves a little arithmetic in finding the physical amount of closing stock. This will be valued at its last price, i.e. the price of the latest or most recent purchase. It is assumed that earlier stock bought is sold first.

4 Items of *prime cost* will be found on the debit of trading account, the commencing stock figure, the net purchases, and the wages of production or of preparing the goods for sale. Also debited to trading account will be expense items which vary with the turnover, such as carriage inwards or carriage on purchases.

5 On the credit of trading account will be found the net sales and the closing stock, although the latter is more often shown as a deduction on the debit side to give the *cost of sales figure*.

6.1   Make up the trading account of Edwina Ewing, showing her cost of sales figure from the information given below:

May
At the beginning of the month there was a stock of certain articles on hand of 1800 items, bought at the average cost of £1 each.
The total net purchases for May comprised 3400 articles bought at an average cost of £1.25.
Total net sales of 3800 articles realised £7300 from cash customers.

Ascertain Miss Ewing's final stock figure, place a valuation on it, and make up her trading account for May.

6.2   Extract the information you need from the trial balance below, to make up the trading account of Miss Vivette Green for the month of October.

Trial Balance of Vivette Green

31 October	£	£
Capital account 1 Oct.		2500
Drawings for month	180	
Net purchases	4800	
Net sales		6800
Carriage on purchases	50	
Warehousing expenses	220	
Stock 1 Oct.	1150	
Cash balance 31 Oct	2900	
	9300	9300
Miss Green valued her closing stock on 31 October at £1550.		

6.3   What is the cost of sales figure in the preceding problem? Explain why, although recent purchases will comprise much of the closing stock valuation, the figure for net purchases is quite a different amount than the cost of goods sold.

7

Trading and Profit and Loss Account

In the preparation of the final accounts, the profit element is split, for convenience, into two parts:

(*a*) The *gross profit*, already described as the difference between the cost of sales and the actual sales total.

(*b*) The *net profit*, which is the final trading profit of a business, after all office, general and distribution expenses have been charged against the gross profit brought down from trading account.

Illustration by arithmetic

Another arithmetical example is shown. Say a trader buys £500 of goods for sale. He pays £10 delivery costs and sells the whole consignment for £780, after incurring office and distribution expenses of £120. Arithmetically, his gross and net profit would be worked out in this way:

		£
Net sales on the whole consignment		780
Less purchases and	£500	
delivery costs	10	510
To give a gross profit of		270
Less office and distribution expenses		120
To show a final net profit of		150

In this illustration the commencing and closing stocks have been omitted for the sake of simplicity.

Making up the final accounts

Let us now refer back to the trial balance in Chapter 5 and make up a trading and profit and loss account from those details which relate specifically to the revenue income or expenditure of the business, namely purchases, sales, advertising and salaries.

Since this business was started from scratch, there is no opening stock, but it would be reasonable to assume that some stock would be unsold at the end of the first month's trading. If we place a valuation on the stock of purchases not yet sold of £80, the trading and profit and loss account will be made up on these lines:

Trading and Profit and Loss Account
for the month ended 30 June

	£		£
Stock 1 June	nil	Sales for month	212.50
Purchases for month	160.00	Stock 30 June	80.00
Gross profit c/d	132.50		
	292.50		292.50
Advertising	7.30	Gross profit b/d	132.50
Salaries	60.00		
Net profit	65.20		
	132.50		132.50

The trading and profit and loss account is really two separate accounts with a combined heading. These are the main revenue accounts of the business, the excess sales revenue (in the form of gross profit) being taken down to the credit of the lower account, an appendage or extension of the trading account. The gross trading profit is reduced, often substantially, in the profit and loss account, by the varied office, selling and administrative expenses of the business, the resultant figure being the net profit (and occasionally a net loss). Note that *net profit is a credit balance* of this lower account, whereas a *net loss would be a debit balance*.

Business revenue and expense

The only figures extracted from the trial balance in Chapter 5 to make up the revenue account were those figures affecting the firm's trading profits. Three important balances were excluded in working out the business profit, namely *capital, drawings and cash*. A simple illustration will explain this:

Suppose you have £10 in your pocket. You buy £8 worth of goods, incur selling expenses of £3, and then dispose of your entire stock for £15. Your profit is £4 (£15 sales less £8 purchases plus £3 expenses).

Total sales		£15.00	
Less purchases	£8.00		
and expenses	3.00	11.00	= £4.00 profit

Now if you consider this problem carefully, it will be seen that your original capital of £10 has not figured in your profit calculation, and neither has your final cash balance entered into it.

Also, if you had withdrawn £1 cash to buy your small sister a birthday present, this sum would certainly have reduced your cash balance, but it would have *no effect upon the profit already made*.

Two kinds of carriage

Carriage on purchases *(carriage inwards)* is an additional expense on the goods bought, increasing the cost of the materials or com- modities, and, as such, is a trading account expense.

Carriage on sales *(carriage outwards)* is a selling and distribution expense and is debited to the profit and loss section along with the many and varied administration and distribution expenses.

Note that both aspects of carriage are *debits*, and must not be confused with returns inwards and returns outwards explained in Chapter 15.

Production wages and office salaries

The wages of production or of warehousing (where merchandise is prepared for sale) vary with the turnover of the business, and are debited to the trading account as part of the cost of the goods produced.

The salaries of the office and administrative staff are charged to profit and loss account. Like other routine expenses such as rent, rates and insurance, salaries are a more constant figure and not so much affected by short term variation of production volume.

On no account must the amounts spent upon the purchase of fixed assets and business property such as machinery, motor vehicles, fixtures and equipment be debited to either of these revenue accounts. Later, though, it will be explained that a kind of 'wear and tear' allowance called *depreciation* is sometimes agreed upon by the Inland Revenue.

Credits on the revenue accounts

Few items appear on the credit of either the trading or the profit and loss account. Generally, when they do, they often refer to small and miscellaneous profits and are usually taken to the lower account, and are identified by the words 'received' or 'recovered' as in the instances of discounts received, commissions received, rents received and bad debts recovered.

Bringing closing stock into the books

When the new valuation figure for closing stock is credited to trading account, a corresponding debit must be made on stock account to sustain the full principles of double entry.

Since we are now reaching the final stage of the illustration commenced in Chapter 2, and the closing stock at 30 June has been valued at £80 and already taken to the credit of the trading account at the beginning of this chapter, we must now open a new stock account and debit this same amount to complete the double entry.

Dr.			**Stock Account** (20)				Cr.
June 30	Trading account		£ 80 00				

Pause for thought

(*a*)   What is meant by the terms: revenue accounts, cost of sales, gross profit and net profit?

(*b*)   Why is the main revenue account of the business split into two parts or sections?

Assignments

Key Points

1 The heading of a revenue account should show the period covered and the date to which the account is made up.

2 Unless stated to the contrary, wages are normally taken to the trading account, and salaries to the profit and loss account. Some discretion should be used, as wages paid to office cleaners are chargeable to the lower account.

3 In the beginners' trial balances commencing stock is a debit, but closing stock (only just valued at the end of the period) does *not become a book entry until it is credited first to trading account.*

4 Carriage inwards (on purchases, i.e. goods coming in) joins the purchases debit in trading account, whereas carriage outwards (on sales, i.e. goods sent out) is a selling and delivery expense to be debited to profit and loss account. *Both are debits.*

5 Neither assets (other than stocks) nor capital expenditure appear in revenue accounts.

6 Occasionally a business sustains a net loss. The effect on the trader's capital is explained in the next chapter.

7.1 Re-draft the statement below to show clearly the correct gross and net profit of this business:

**Trade and Profit Account of Annabel Royle on
31 December**

	£		£
Stock 31 Dec.	300	Sales	6200
Purchases	2850	Carriage	
Salaries	200	outwards	30
Gross profit c/d	3300	Stock 1 Dec.	420
	6650		6650
Carr. inwards	60	Gross profit	
Warehouse wages	1600	b/d	3300
Travelling	45		
Insurance	35		
Rent	80		
Drawings	100		
Net profit	1380		
	3300		3300

7.2   Extract the necessary information from this trial balance and make up the trading and profit and loss account of Wilfred Brazenbit, master plumber, for the month of June:

Trial Balance   30 June

	£	£
Capital W.B. 1 June		6 000
Drawings for month	400	
Van at valuation	1 750	
Office fittings at cost	350	
Purchases and sales	5 200	8 800
Carriage inwards	52	
Carriage outwards	46	
Advertising	108	
Insurance	30	
Petrol/oil	24	
Heating/lighting (workshop)	34	
Heating/lighting (office)	14	
Wages (workshop)	1 444	
Office salaries	420	
Stamps/stationery	8	
Stock 1 June	1 850	
Cash balance 30 June	3 070	
	14 800	14 800

Stock valuation at 30 June £2350

Show the cost of sales figure in the trading account of Mr Brazenbit.

8

The Balance Sheet

The balance sheet takes care of the remaining 'open' balances in the books. After incorporating the retained profit (or loss) on trading, it depicts the assets, capital and liabilities at what should be their true or estimated net worth on a certain date.

The balance sheet is *not an account* but a financial statement, grouping and listing the business property and the capital and liabilities on *that certain* date. The date is important as the value of property, commodities, debts and obligations changes day by day.

Methods of presentation

This is the final stage of the illustration commenced in Chapter 2. First shown in the modern vertical style, adopted by all limited companies and most big organisations, it would be presented in this way:

Balance Sheet as at 30 June

	£	£
Assets employed		
Stock on hand 30 June	80.00	
Cash in hand	135.20	215.20
Financed by		
Proprietor's capital 1 June	200.00	
Retained profit	15.20	215.20

'Retained profit' is that balance of profit remaining after all appropriations (or withdrawals in the case of a sole trader) have been deducted.

If this vertical statement is tilted over to the right, the older horizontal 'T' style balance sheet is shown, still in use by many smaller firms.

Balance Sheet as at 30 June

Capital and liabilities		£	Property and assets		£
Capital 1 June	£200.00		Stock 30 June	£80.00	
Add net profit	65.20		Cash in hand	135.20	215.20
	265.20				
Less drawings	50.00	215.20			
		215.20			215.20

Note that in horizontal presentation the proprietor's capital account is generally shown in fuller detail; in effect, it becomes a vertical copy of his own personal ledger account (see page 41).

There should be no confusion between *debit and credit* at this stage. Double entry has already served its purpose and does not apply to the balance sheet. Again it is emphasised that the balance sheet is *not an account*, but a financial statement listing assets and liabilities at a certain date.

In this simple illustration there are only two assets and one liability at the balancing date, but even this small balance sheet has a story to tell. You started in business a month ago, made a small trading profit of £65.20, withdrew £50 on account of profits (thereby relinquishing part of your capital holding), and finally finished up with £15.20 more in asset value than when you started. Your capital or net worth at the end of the month of June is represented by the two assets, stock or merchandise not yet sold valued at £80.00, and £135.20 cash in hand; your net assets have thus increased by £15.20 since the beginning of June.

Net loss on trading

Occasionally a net loss might result through adverse or unfortunate trading conditions. The *debit balance* on profit and loss account would be transferred to the *debit* of the proprietor's capital account in addition to his drawings for the period. The net loss on trading would be reflected on the assets side of the balance sheet by a corresponding decrease in total net assets.

Capital and drawings

The capital account of the sole trader is an internal obligation of the business towards its owner, and must be kept quite distinct from the outside liabilities (trade and expense creditors to be introduced a little later). The business capital, now represented in the form of assets-in-trade, continues to finance the day to day trading operations of the business, but any withdrawals of money (or goods) for the private and family use of the proprietor involve a corresponding reduction of the capital account. Bear in mind, though, that we are in no way concerned how or in what manner the owner of a business disposes of the cash or the goods he has withdrawn.

Closing of ledger accounts

In the exercise just completed, the proprietor's capital account is brought up to date by transferring the net profit (a credit balance of excess sales revenue) to the credit of that account, and also by transferring the debit balance on drawings account to the debit of capital account, as now shown:

Dr.						**Drawings Account (4)**			Cr.
June 30	Cash		CB1	£ 50	00	June 30	Transfer to capital account	2	£ 50	00

Capital Account (2)

June 30	Transfer from drawings account	4		£ 50	00	June 1	Cash	CB1	£ 200	00
30	Balance c/d			215	20		Net trading profit for month		65	20
				265	20				265	20
						July 1	Balance b/d		215	20

The recently created stock account remains open with its new debit balance of £80 at 30 June, but the remainder of the old revenue accounts is now *closed by transfer* either to trading or profit and loss account.

Dr.   **Sales Account** (15)   Cr.

June 30	Transfer to trading account		£ 212 50	June 5 18 24	Cash Cash Cash	CB1 CB1 CB1	£ 45 80 56 20 110 50
			212 50				212 50

Purchases Account (5)

June 2 20	Cash Cash	CB1 CB1	£ 75 00 85 00	June 30	Transfer to trading account		£ 160 00
			160 00				160 00

Advertising Account (8)

June 12	Cash	CB1	£ 7 30	June 30	Transfer to P&L a/c		£ 7 30

Salaries Account (9)

June 30	Cash	CB1	£ 60 00	June 30	Transfer to P&L a/c		£ 60 00

Assignments

> **Key Points**
> 1 Assignment 8.1 is simple arithmetic. Remember, though, to *add back drawings* to the difference in capital values between the beginning and the end of the trading period. The sum withdrawn is part of the true profit made.
> 2 One main feature about vertical presentation of the balance sheet is that the figures take on a more positive and realistic meaning, with the capital shown as representing the holding and value of net assets.
>
> The vertical style balance sheet has superseded the old horizontal 'T' style in all forms of trading and professional firms in addition to limited companies.
>
> The vertical style trading and profit and loss account has also become an accepted feature with most large organisations. For the time being, however, the revenue accounts will be presented in the older and more closely related two-sided accounts, probably easier to comprehend from a beginner's viewpoint with the similarity to the double entry ledger system itself.
> 3 In elementary book-keeping examinations, although arithmetical accuracy is important, even more important is the correct grouping and presentation of the figures, in particular on the balance sheet.

8.1 Davidia Kneale started in business a year ago with £5000 cash as capital.

Her present capital, at 31 December, after one year's trading, cash transactions only, is represented by:

	£
Furniture/fittings	840
Stock of goods unsold	2680
Money in hand	3150

Miss Kneale has withdrawn £3180 on account of profits during the year. Can you work out her trading profit?

8.2   You are required to assemble Martin Kent's ledger balances (shown below) in trial balance form, with a view to finding out his opening capital.

In making out his final accounts for the month ended 31 May, show the cost of sales figure on his trading account:

	£
Stock 1 May	740
Purchases	3330
Sales	4650
Rent/rates proportion	136
Drawings	200
Salaries	400
Cash balance 31 May	1780
Insurance	12
Warehousing expense	30
Carriage inwards	7
Advertising	15

Martin Kent valued his closing stock at £530.

8.3   Enumerate some of the fixed and current assets you would expect to see on the balance sheet of:

(*a*)   a small retail grocer,
(*b*)   a village garage,
(*c*)   an estate agent.

9

Illustrative Example

As a basis for revision we take over the final balances shown on the balance sheet at 30 June in Chapter 8, and continue with a few further cash transactions for the month of July.

This means that we start the new period with the two debit balances of cash in hand £135.20 and stock £80.00, and one credit balance of £215.20, now our opening capital at 1 July.

As from the beginning of this new period our total debits equal our total credits. By simple equation $A = C + L$, where A is the symbol for the assets, C for the capital and L for the liabilities.

The trading transactions for the month of July are now listed:

July		£
2	Bought further goods for re-sale	75.10
	Carriage on purchases	5.00
4	Cash sales	37.50
8	Paid for stationery	8.60
9	Cash sales	118.20
14	Bought new counter (*see text below*)	75.00
15	Received cash for goods sold	82.30
24	Cash sales	135.70
	Carriage on sales	2.00
	Paid for further purchases	54.00
25	Withdrew for family expenses	125.00
28	Paid salary to part-time assistant	86.00
30	Postages bought during month	8.00

The closing stock at 31 July was valued at £38.

Note that the transaction on 14 July is a special purchase of a *fixed asset*, bought for the permanent retention of the business and not for re-sale in the trading sense. The cost of this asset (£75) will be debited to a separate ledger account called fittings account to appear ultimately under its own heading on the assets side of the balance sheet at 31 July.

The various accounts are now written up:

Dr.						**Cash Account** (2)				Cr.
July			£		July				£	
1	Balance brought				2	Purchases	6		75	10
	forward from June	CB1	135	20		Carriage inwards	17		5	00
4	Cash sales	16	37	50	8	Stationery	22		8	60
9	Cash sales	16	118	20	14	Fittings	3		75	00
15	Cash sales	16	82	30	24	Carriage outwards	18		2	00
24	Cash sales	16	135	70		Purchases	6		54	00
					25	Drawings	4		125	00
					28	Salaries	9		86	00
					30	Postages	24		8	00
					31	Balance c/d			70	20
			508	90					508	90
Aug.										
1	Balance b/d		70	20						

It will be seen that the balance of cash in hand on 1 July is *only part of the business capital*, the other part being invested in stock, as now depicted by the stock account as at 30 June brought forward.

Dr.				**Stock Account** (20)				Cr.
June			£					
30	Trading account		80	00				

The capital account is also brought forward to show clearly all the ledger accounts as from the beginning of the new period.

Dr.					**Capital Account** (2)			Cr.
				July			£	
			£	1	Balance b/f		215	20

The remainder of the ledger accounts for the new period, to the completion stage of the double entry from the cash account, are now shown:

Dr.					**Purchases Account** (6)				Cr.
July			£						
2	Cash	CB2	75	10					
24	Cash	CB2	54	00					

Dr.   **Sales Account** (16)   Cr.

				July			£	
				4	Cash	CB2	37	50
				9	Cash	CB2	118	20
				15	Cash	CB2	82	30
				24	Cash	CB2	135	70
							373	70

Carriage Inwards (17)

July			£					
2	Cash	CB2	5	00				

Stationery (22)

July			£					
8	Cash	CB2	8	60				

Carriage Outwards (18)

July			£					
24	Cash	CB2	2	00				

Salaries (9)

July			£					
28	Cash	CB2	86	00				

Postages (24)

July			£					
30	Cash	CB2	8	00				

Drawings (4)

July			£					
25	Cash	CB2	125	00				

Fittings Account (3)

July			£					
14	Cash	CB2	75	00				

The postings have now been completed for the month of July. A trial balance will be taken out at this stage to prove the accuracy of the postings.

Trial Balance   31 July

	£	£
Cash in hand 31 July	70.20	
Capital 1 July		215.20
Drawings	125.00	
Fittings	75.00	
Purchases	129 10	
Sales		373 70
Carriage inwards	5 00	
Carriage outwards	2 00	
Stationery	8 60	
Salaries	86 00	
Postages	8 00	
Stock 1 July	80 00	
	588 90	588 90

Note that the opening stock at 1 July is debited to this general form of trial balance, but that the *closing stock of £38 at 31 July is not yet a balance in the books until the trading account is made up.*

All the revenue accounts for July are now closed (sales, purchases, carriage inwards and outwards, stationery, salaries and postages) by transfer of their balances either to the trading account or to the profit and loss section of this combined revenue account.

**Trading and Profit and Loss Account
for the month ended 31 July**

	£		£
Stock 1 July	80.00	Sales for July	373.70
Purchases	129.10		
Carriage inwards	5.00		
	214.10		
Less stock 31 July	38.00		
Cost of sales	176.10		
Gross profit c/d	197.60		
	373.70		373.70
Carriage outwards	2.00	Gross profit b/d	197.60
Stationery	8.60		
Salaries	86.00		
Postages	8.00		
Net profit for July	93.00		
	197.60		197.60

The commencing stock at 1 July (£80.00) has now served its purpose by transfer of its debit balance to trading account. That part of the stock account may now be ruled off. At this stage, too, the new valuation for closing stock at 31 July (£38.00) is *brought into the books for the first time by a credit to trading account* (shown as a deduction on the debit side). The double entry and corresponding debit to stock account is now shown:

Dr. **Stock Account** (20) Cr.

		£				£	
June 30	Trading account	80	00	July 31	Transfer of old stock to debit of trading a/c	80	00
July 31	Trading a/c (new stock brought into books)	38	00				

At this final stage the assets are listed on the balance sheet in order of permanency, fittings being regarded as more permanent than stock, and stock thought to be rather more permanent than cash, with which it has been bought. The listing of the assets in order of permanency *as opposed to that of liquidity and realisation into cash* is simply a question of preference, generally followed by the majority of industrial, commercial and professional organisations, with big exceptions in the world of banking and finance whose huge enterprises like to display their formidable array of liquidity to the general public.

The balance sheet is now drawn up for the second month of the illustration started in the second chapter of the book. Note that the proprietor's equity and capital holding has decreased since 1 July by £32, the amount of the withdrawals in excess of the profit made during the month of July.

Balance Sheet as at 31 July

		£
Assets employed		
Fixed assets		
Fittings		75.00
Current assets		
Stock at 31 July	£38.00	
Cash in hand	70.20	108.20
		183.20
Financed by		
Capital 1 July	£215.20	
Add net profit	93.00	
	308.20	
Less drawings	125.00	183.20
		183.20

Assignment

> **Checkpoints**
> Before starting Assignment 9, check yourself on the following routine, which, by this stage, should be becoming automatic:
>
> 1 Are your worked exercises reasonably neat and tidy, with the correct alignment of figures in the total columns?
> 2 Occasionally mistakes will occur. Instead of scratching out, simply rule through the error and insert the correct amount over the top.
> 3 Never rule free-hand. Always use a good ruler and keep any corresponding totals on the same horizontal.
> 4 Are your headings clear and bold with a space for neatness between the ledger account heading and the details within the account?
> 5 Do you confine the use of the £ sign to the top of the amount column only, and write in the name of the month only at the top of the date column?

9 You start in business on 1 January with an opening capital of £1500 comprising these assets:

	£
Second-hand fittings (counters and shelving) valued at	500
Stock of goods bought at the special price of	200
Available cash for business use	800
	1500

First record these details in your financial books as follows:

Debit £500 to fittings account	and credit £1500
Debit £200 to stock account	to your opening
Debit £800 to cash account	capital account.

Note that these three assets totalling £1500 is your *commencing capital* in this instance. *The £800 cash is only part of your capital.*

After recording the opening entries, open the cash book and the ledger and post up the following transactions for the month of January. Take out a trial balance at 31 January, and make up the trading and profit and loss account and a balance sheet as at 31 January. The valuation of your closing stock is £375.

Jan.		£
2	Bought a second-hand van. Paid cash	650
	(debit van account – credit cash)	
3	Cash sales	162
	Bought stationery	8
	Paid rent for month	35
5	Bought goods for re-sale	188
	Cash takings	154
8	Paid fire/theft insurance	25
	Cash sales	107
	Drew for 'self'	50
10	Paid wages for warehousing	30
	(see note on wages in Chapter 7)	
	Travelling expenses of staff	14
	Bought a filing cabinet for office	85
14	Cash sales	76
16	Cash sales	166
	Paid wages	30
22	Paid for advertising	27
	Bought postage stamps	8
	Paid wages	30
23	Cash sales	148
	Further purchases to replenish stocks	155
	Paid carriage on goods bought	12
25	Cash sales	78
	Paid petrol account	22
	Repairs to van	24
	Cash purchases	186
28	Drew for 'self'	50
	Paid wages	30
31	Cash sales	72

Show as two distinct accounts, van account and fittings account, and debit the purchase of the filing cabinet (£85) to the latter. These *fixed asset* accounts are shown under their own headings at the top of the assets on the balance sheet.

10

Cash and Bank Transactions

All transactions up to this stage have been on a cash basis. Money has been received for cash sales, and all purchases and expenses of the business have been paid in cash, i.e. in currency notes and coin. Only a single-column type of cash account has been needed.

This may suit a small shop-keeper with his sales across the counter for cash, but in most businesses these days there is a certain amount of credit dealing, and settlement by cheque or credit transfer has become both necessary and convenient.

The bank account

It has been emphasised that the cash account is part of the ledger system. It still remains an integral part of the old system, but with the introduction of banking facilities, a specially ruled ledger, called the cash book, now supersedes the former cash account.

The cash book has additional columns for bank transactions, and the two accounts for *both cash and bank* are balanced up independently. The account columns for cash and bank (cheques) are simply *kept side by side* for convenience, as quite often money (both cash and cheques) is paid out of the office cash surplus into the bank, and vice-versa cash is withdrawn from the bank by cheque for the needs of the office.

Generally, both accounts have debit balances, but the bank account, unlike the cash account, could have a credit balance if the money at the bank was overdrawn. It would then be referred to as an 'overdraft'.

In these early cash and bank exercises it is usual for the student to assume that cheques from customers are banked on the same day that they are received. In practice, however, the firm's cashier often pays his surplus cash together with customers' cheques into the business current account at the Bank only once or twice a week.

An illustration is now shown of the two-column cash book.

Note that the cash and bank columns are two separate accounts and are balanced up independently of each other. The bank columns in these early exercises relate entirely (on the debit side) to cheques received from customers and surplus cash paid into the bank and (on the credit side) to cheques drawn by the firm, withdrawing cash from the bank or in settlement of creditors' accounts.

Two-column Cash Book

Date			Cash	Bank	Date			Cash	Bank
Oct.			£	£	Oct.			£	£
1	Balance b/f		5 00	200 00	2	Contra	c		20 00
2	Contra	c	20 00		4	Rent			30 00
8	Cash sales		62 80		6	Purchases			88 50
12	L. Harris		22 70			Cleaning		12 50	
18	Cash sales		110 20		9	Stationery		4 80	
	Contra	c		100 00		Stamps		5 20	
22	P. Marsden Ltd			180 00	12	Purchases			66 60
28	Cash sales		82 50			Advertising			8 40
30	S. Roberts			78 90	16	T. Jones			42 30
31	Contra	c		150 00	18	Contra	c	100 00	
					19	Petrol/oil		8 20	
					24	Cleaning		12 50	
					28	G. Rawson & Son			55 50
					30	Salaries			185 00
					31	Contra	c	150 00	
						Drawings			55 00
						Balance c/d		10 00	157 60
			303 20	708 90				303 20	708 90
Nov.									
1	Balances b/d		10 00	157 60					

The small letter 'c' in the folio columns indicates *contra* entries, or transfers between office cash and bank and vice-versa. These postings, shown on both sides of the cash book, debit in one column for the corresponding credit on the other side, cancel themselves out, so that *ledger postings are unnecessary.*

Any charges made by the Bank (interest on overdrafts etc.) are shown as deductions on the bank statement sent to the customer at the end of the month or sometimes quarterly. The firm's cashier, on checking the bank statement against his own cash book bank columns, will enter any bank charges of this nature on the *credit side* of his cash book bank column. Later the ledger clerk will complete the double entry by posting the amount to the *debit* of Bank charges account in the nominal or expense ledger.

Cash or cheque?

Sometimes, in an examination question, it may not be clear whether a receipt or a payment is to be entered in the cash or the bank column. In the absence of instructions, make it a rule to treat all payments from customers, and all payments to suppliers, as *cheque payments* (even a small amount of under £1 owing to a creditor residing a distance away would be sent through the post by cheque). As a general rule, too, all expense accounts to local tradesmen for over £2 would probably be paid by cheque; this would apply to advertising, car repairs, stationery etc. Remember, too, that postages and parcels taken to the Post Office are generally paid in cash. Wages also are usually paid in cash, but a cheque may be drawn specifically for the payment of wages.

The important thing is to avoid the complication of an overdrawn cash balance which, strictly, should not be possible. *When in doubt, pay by cheque.*

Primary records

The entries on the debit side of the cash book originate from the daily till rolls of cash registers, duplicate receipt books and from the listed amounts on the bank paying-in slips.

Entries on the credit side of the cash book originate from the official receipts from suppliers, cash memos from sundry small purchases, and the counterfoil stubs of the firm's cheque books.

Pause for thought

In this short course on elementary accounting only the practical use of cheques and certain banking procedures are explained. The student is recommended, however, to read (in a book on commerce or office practice) about the purpose and use of cheques, the different types of crossings, the safeguards against theft and misappropriation of cheques, and why 'order' cheques are far more common than 'bearer' cheques.

Assignments

Key Points

1   Check the contra items to ensure that there is a debit to correspond with every credit. Do not guess with regard to contras. Think which account has increased or received benefit (cash or bank?). Debit cash and credit bank or vice-versa as the case may be.

2   Generally there are more items and lengthier columns to add up in the firm's cash book. The importance of correct alignment cannot be over-emphasised.

3   Usually there are more entries on the credit or payments side of the cash book. This means leaving a few blank spaces on the debit, when balancing up, as the totals must be on the same horizontal. Remember, too, that allowance must be made on the credit side of the cash columns (and generally bank columns too) for the cash and bank balances.

4   Where personal names are given (the names of people and firms), these names should be recorded in the details column of the cash book. Generally the receipt or payment refers to the settlement of a credit account already posted up from an original invoice to a customer's or supplier's ledger account.

5   It is not necessary to record the names of suppliers or customers *where goods are bought or sold for cash or cheque payment* at the time the goods are handed over in completion of the transaction, i.e. cash sales and cash purchases transactions.

10.1   Enter the following cash and cheque transactions in a two-column cash book for the month of April, balancing up both cash and bank columns at 30 April.

April		£
1	Cash in office	40.00
	Cash at bank	560.00
3	Cash sales	56.28
	Paid cash into bank	50.00
	Paid rent by cheque	35.00
8	Paid Jim Lord by cheque	28.40
	Cash purchases	12.70
14	Cheque from R. Davies	25.60
	Cash sales	54.84
	Cash paid into bank	50.00
18	Bought stamps	3.00
	Drew cheque for 'self'	60.00
25	Paid Ossie Pye by cheque	48.80
30	Bought some shelving from	
	A.B.C. Services Ltd	36.30

10.2 On 1 September Charmain Wade's cash and bank balances were £10 and £640. Her transactions during the month are listed below. Write up her Cash Book for September, bringing down her cash and bank balances as at 1 October.

Sept.		£
1	Cheque drawn for office cash	40.00
3	Bought goods from Bob West	80.00
5	Paid Sam Ronson's account	24.20
	Paid office cleaner (cash)	18.00
8	Cash sales	78.80
	Paid cash into bank	50.00
12	Bought stamps	3.00
	Paid rates by cheque	135.50
15	Cash sales	68.70
18	Cash sales	72.30
	Paid wages out of cash	55.00
	Drew cheque for 'self'	80.00
22	Paid Josh Brown's account	36.40
	Leslie Frost paid by cheque	66.60
24	Cash sales	94.90
	Paid cash into bank	50.00
26	Cash purchases	15.20
	Paid wages	55.00
	Bought stamps	5.00
27	Paid advertising account	22.50
29	Sarah Raven sent cheque	
	in payment of old account	25.00
30	Miss Wade paid all surplus	
	cash over £10 into the bank	

11

Bank Reconciliation

In this chapter we concern ourselves solely with the bank columns of the cash book and the agreement or reconciliation of these columns with the Bank's own ledger statement forwarded monthly, or to bank customers on request.

It is seldom that the bank balance according to the cash book agrees with the balance according to the Bank's own statement on the same date. This is due to the time lag between the receipt of cheques from the firm's customers, and their actual settlement or collection from the bank accounts of the debtors. Again, there is a similar delay between the handing over or posting of cheques drawn in favour of the suppliers or creditors, and their collection, via their bankers, from the account of the paying firm.

Checking the bank statement

Apart from the delay in clearing, presenting and collection of cheques, there are often other bank debits for charges and expenses that appear periodically on the bank statement. Instances of these are the interest charged by the bank on loans and overdrafts, and sometimes charges per cheque drawn when the bank balance falls below a certain figure. Occasionally there are debits for standing orders in compliance with the instructions of the customer for the Bank to make certain direct transfers of money (such as insurance premiums).

Dividends from investments owned by the business are often paid direct to the Bank, and it is only when credited to the firm's current account and checked through reconciliation by the cashier that these amounts will be entered in the cash book. The cash book in this way is brought up to date as far as possible before the final reconciliation takes place, which involves ticking, item for item, all the debits in the cash book against all the credits on the Bank statement, and all the credits in the cash book against all the debits on the Bank statement.

A note is made of *all amounts remaining unticked* in either the cash book or the bank statement. It is these unticked items which form the basis for the reconciliation.

Dr.   **Cash Book** (bank columns only)   Cr.

June		Cash £	Bank £	June		Cash £	Bank £
1	Balance b/f	✓	300 00	2	Cheque to X	✓	16 20
8	Cash paid in	✓	70 20	5	Rates		44 00
10	Cheque from A	✓	24 50	12	Wages	✓	60 00
15	Cheque from B	✓	36 30	15	Advertising	✓	8 50
25	Cash banked	✓	66 10	24	Wages	✓	60 00
28	Cheque from C		55 50	28	Cheque to Y		9 70
				30	Cheque to Z		36 40
					Balance c/d		317 80
			552 60				552 60
July							
1	Balance b/d		317 80				

Bank Statement

June				Debit £	Credit £	Balance £
1	Balance b/f					✓ 300.00
4	X			✓ 16.20		283.80
8	Cash receipts				✓ 70.20	354.00
9	Rates			✓ 44.00		310.00
12	Wages			✓ 60.00		250.00
	A				✓ 24.50	274.50
18	B				✓ 36.30	310.80
19	Chq. no. 22643			✓ 8.50		302.30
24	Wages			✓ 60.00		242.30
25	Cash receipts				✓ 66.10	308.40
28	TS dividend				50.00	358.40
	Standing order			10.50		347.90
30	Charges			4.00		343.90

Procedure for reconciliation

Note that all items in the firm's cash book have been ticked off with the exception of:

(*a*)   C's cheque for £55.50 not yet cleared by the Bank.
(*b*)   The cheques made out to Y and Z for £9.70 and £36.40 not yet presented for payment.

All items on the bank statement have been ticked off except for the debits against the firm for £10.50 and £4.00, and the dividend of £50 paid direct to the Bank.

The firm's cashier now brings his Cash Book up to date as far as possible, to show an *amended bank balance* of £353.30, thus:

Dr.	**Cash Book** (continuation)					Cr.
June 30	Balance b/d Treasury stock div. Paid direct to bank	£ 317 80 50 00	June 30	Standing order Bank charges Balance c/d	£ 10 50 4 00 353.30
		367 80			367 80
July 1	Balance b/d	353.30			

The cheque not yet cleared and the cheques not yet presented for payment are adjusted on the reconciliation statement as follows:

Bank Reconciliation Statement   30 June

		£	£
Amended balance as per cash book			353.30
Add cheques drawn but not yet presented for payment	Y Z	9.70 36.40	46.10
			399.40
Deduct cheque not yet cleared (i.e. not yet credited to the firm's current account)			55.50
Balance according to bank statement			£343.90

Assignments

Key Points

1   You will probably comprehend, at this stage, that a 'debit' bank balance in the firm's cash book means that there is money (perhaps a fairly adequate reserve) at the Bank.

   From the Bank's accounting aspect, however, you are *in credit*, i.e. the Bank owes you money.

   When you pay cash and cheques into your bank account, your current account is credited, thereby increasing your bank balance; but when you withdraw money or make a payment by cheque, your bank current account is debited, thereby reducing your bank balance.

2   'Cheques not presented yet for payment' are those cheques given or sent to creditors who have not yet claimed or collected payment from your Bank.

   'Cheques and cash not yet cleared' refers to remittances (currency and cheques) paid into your own Bank, but not yet shown on your bank statement. Often this is the total of the last paying-in slip handed in to the Bank on the last day of half-yearly balancing.

3   The reverse of the conventional procedure applies when dealing with a bank overdraft, your bank account perhaps temporarily being 'in the red'.

   Cash and cheques paid into the account reduce the overdraft, whereas further cheques drawn increase it.

4   The correct figure for the business bank balance to be taken to the trial balance and also to the balance sheet is always the *adjusted or amended figure according to the Cash Book*.

11.1 The cash book bank balance of Alan Jones on 30 June shows a debit balance of £728.24, whereas the statement given to him by his bank on the same date shows a credit balance in his favour of £696.93.

Checking the bank statement against his cash book, Mr Jones finds that cash and cheques paid into his bank on 30 June, totalling £224.75, had not been credited to his current account; and two cheques for £82.64 and £110.80 sent to Holt Bros Ltd and Eric Hardwick on 28 June had not yet been presented to his bank for payment.

You are required to draw up a reconciliation statement showing the difference between the two balances mentioned in the first paragraph above.

11.2 The bank statement of Linda Owen made up to 31 December, received early in the New Year, showed her current account overdrawn by £24.54.

Checking the statement against the bank columns of her cash book, she noted the following:

(*a*) Cash and cheques totalling £178.28 paid into the Bank on 31 December had not been credited to her account.

(*b*) A cheque for £83.40 sent to her supplier on 29 December had not yet been presented for payment.

(*c*) A dividend of £60 Treasury Stock had been credited direct to her account.

(*d*) Bank charges of £12.50 had been debited to her account by the Bank.

What was the bank balance shown by Miss Owen's Cash Book on 31 December?

12

The Petty Cash Book

Under what is known as the *imprest system* of keeping petty cash, a round sum of money (say £20) is handed over to a junior clerk or typist, who becomes responsible for the payment of small expenses of the office.

At the end of the week or the month, the *exact amount of money paid out* (the total disbursements) is refunded by the main cashier to the petty cashier, so that the balance of petty cash in hand is brought back again to the original amount of the imprest, i.e. £20.

An analysis cash book, with columns specially ruled to suit the needs of the particular office and the general expense payments, is used for this purpose of relieving the main cashier of some of the routine work. This book is called the *petty cash book*.

Posting of the petty cash expense totals

The petty cash book is part of the double entry system because the imprest amount is transferred from the credit of the main cash book to the petty cashier. The totals of the various expense columns of the petty cash book are extracted and debited to the relative expense accounts in the nominal ledger, and at the end of the trading period the balance of petty cash in hand is included or absorbed into the main cash balance.

Illustration

A simple style of petty cash ruling is shown on p.63 with analysis columns for four classes of routine expense. The commencing balance of petty cash on hand, the imprest amount, at the beginning of the month of January is £20. The expense payments are listed for the first week of the New Year, and this page of the petty cash book balanced up on 6 January.

Disbursements for the first week of January:

Jan.		£
1	Paid bus fares	0.68
2	Bought postage stamps	2.00
	Paid for office cleaning	4.00
3	Bought tea and milk for week	1.64
4	Paid for carbon paper	0.76
	Bought more stamps	1.00
5	Taxi fare to station	2.25
	Donation to Oxfam	1.00
6	String and sealing wax	0.65

Petty Cash Book

Rec'd from cashier	Date	Details of expense	Voucher no.	Total	Stamps Stat'y	Travel	Cleaning	Sundries
£	Jan.			£	£	£	£	£
20.00	1	Imprest b/f						
	1	Bus fares	–	0.68		0.68		
	2	Stamps	1	2.00	2.00			
		Cleaning	2	4.00			4.00	
	3	Tea/milk	3	1.64				1.64
	4	Carbon paper	4	0.76	0.76			
		Stamps	5	1.00	1.00			
	5	Taxi fare	–	2.25		2.25		
		Oxfam donation	6	1.00				1.00
	6	String	7	0.65				0.65
				13.98	3.76	2.93	4.00	3.29
	6	Balance c/d		6.02				
20.00				20.00				
6.02	8	Balance b/d						
13.98	8	Imprest refund						

Note that each item of expense in the petty cash book is shown both in the total column and in the appropriate analysis column. The totals of the combined analysis columns agree with the addition of the main total column (£13.98). This is the total petty cash expenditure for the week, and, when deducted from the original imprest amount of £20.00, leaves a balance of £6.02 petty cash in hand at 6 January.

At the end of the week the main cashier will refund to the petty cashier the sum of £13.98 (his total disbursements) so that the balance of the imprest for the commencement of the second week is made up to the original sum of £20.00.

As far as possible, vouchers and receipts for payment of these small expenses should be asked for, so that they can be verified by the main cashier. It should be possible to obtain a receipt from the cleaner, and the Post Office counter clerk will date-stamp a petty cash disbursement slip when stamps are bought.

Assignments

Key Points

1   The word 'imprest' means loan. The imprest amount is loaned or advanced by the main cashier to the petty cashier.

2   The analysis columns in use refer to regular routine expenses, often office expenses.

   A 'sundries' or 'miscellaneous' column takes care of casual and incidental expenses.

3   Sometimes an extra column is brought into use for the payment of small and occasional payments to a few creditors' accounts in the bought (suppliers) ledger.

4   Where a full length exercise includes a petty cash book, remember to bring the petty cash balance on to the trial balance at the close of the trading period, and again on the assets side of the balance sheet.

5   Remember, too, that all the *analysis expense totals* must be taken to the *debit of* nominal ledger accounts, and brought to the debit of the trial balance. This would not apply, though, to the settlement of small bought ledger accounts (see KP 3 above).

12.1 Willie Woodbine is the petty cashier of a small textile manufacturer. He is responsible for a weekly imprest of £30. During
his absence on holiday, you are required to write up his petty
cash book for the first week of March, using four analysis
expense columns. Show the amount of the imprest refund at
the end of the week.

March		£
1	Petty cash imprest in hand	30.00
	Bought stamps	3.00
2	Paid for travelling	3.20
	Tea and milk for office	0.82
3	Newspapers	0.65
	Typewriter ribbons	2.50
4	Bought stamps	3.00
	Paid bus fares	1.28
	Donation to charity	0.50
5	Wrapping paper and string	1.48

12.2 Rule up a petty cash book with five analysis columns and
enter up the routine expenses shown below. Show the imprest
refund at the end of the first week in May.

May
1 Petty cash in hand £35
2 Bought stamps £4; paid £3.85 for stationery; and 75p for tea and
milk.
3 Paid cleaner £5; 52p for a parcel and £2.50 taxi fare for a sick
employee.
4 Bought £4 stamps; refunded 36p bus fare to newly engaged
typist.
5 Window cleaner £2.35; ribbon for typewriter £2.26; donation to
police charity £2.

12.3 Explain what is meant by 'petty cash imprest'.
Rule up a petty cash book with four analysis columns and
with an imprest of £50. Make up your own headings and
expense details for two weeks, balance up, and show the
imprest refund.

13

Credit Transactions and Suppliers' Accounts

All trading transactions, up to this stage, have been on a cash (or cheque) immediate payment basis. Modern business, however, is built up upon credit, buying and obtaining the possession and use of the goods or services today, but delaying the payment and settlement for a few weeks or even a month or two. This means that permanent records must be kept of these credit transactions, and also of debtors and creditors.

A debtor is a customer who has bought goods or obtained a service *on credit*, i.e. he has not yet paid for the goods or the service he has received. *Money is owed by a debtor.*

A creditor, in the business sense, is the supplier of goods or services, who has not yet been paid. *Money is owing to a creditor.*

Day books or journals

Subsidiary books called day books or journals are used for the initiation of credit transactions in connection with the purchase and sale of merchandise on credit. These books, referred to as original records of entry, are used as aids for posting the ledger accounts. Generally, after the extraction of essential information the books are stored away, to be produced for checking by the firm's auditor when requested.

The significance of the term 'set of books' may gradually be becoming recognised with the introduction of these additional account books, and as the ledger, particularly with the larger businesses, becomes sectionised and split up to suit the requirements of the firm or the industry to which it belongs. The different aspects of the ledger (bought ledger and nominal ledger, etc.) are briefly explained in Chapter 17.

An illustration is now given of this new procedure as applied to the purchases side of the business and the trade creditors' accounts.

The purchases day book

The primary accounting document for merchandise bought on credit is the supplier's bill or *invoice*, handed over to the purchaser by the vendor at the time of the purchase or sent to his address by post.

An invoice is shown first, the essential information then being extracted from it and posted to part of a folio of the purchases day book, or bought journal as it is sometimes called.

	INVOICE			
Samuel Smith		No. 876		
South Parade	**BOUGHT OF**	3 Feb. 19. .		
Seatown	**DAVID BROWN 5 Eastgate Stafford**			
Stock Ref.		£		£
Y 38	½ doz. white cotton vests			
	size 16 @ £3.60	21 60		16 20
	Less 25% trade discount	5 40		
P 54	3 doz. pair Nustyle			
	socks @ £1	36 00		28 80
	Less 20% trade discount	7 20		
	E.&O.E.	Net		45 00

The ruling of the purchases day book is similar to that of the Journal, the exercise book generally used by students for trial balances.

Purchases Day Book (36)

Feb. 3	Invoices from suppliers David Brown Stafford	BL 52			£ 45 00

The postings from another three invoices are now added to the purchases day book (PDB), to allow the illustration of the double entry procedure between the day book and the personal and nominal ledger accounts:

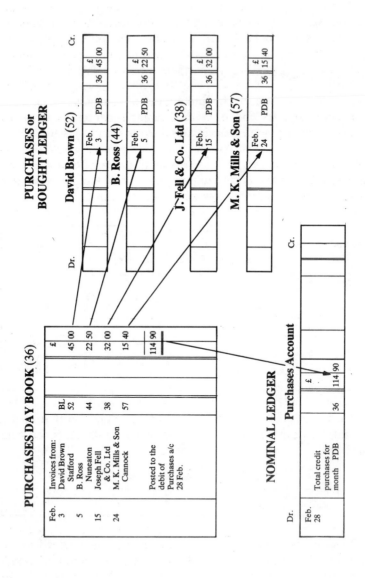

PURCHASES or BOUGHT LEDGER

PURCHASES DAY BOOK (36)

Feb.	Invoices from:	BL		£	
3	David Brown Stafford	52		45	00
5	B. Ross Nuneaton	44		22	50
15	Joseph Fell & Co. Ltd	38		32	00
24	M. K. Mills & Son Cannock	57		15	40
				114	90
	Posted to the debit of Purchases a/c 28 Feb.				

Dr.   **David Brown (52)**   Cr.

			Feb. 3	PDB	36	£ 45	00

B. Ross (44)

			Feb. 5	PDB	36	£ 22	50

J. Fell & Co. Ltd (38)

			Feb. 15	PDB	36	£ 32	00

M. K. Mills & Son (57)

			Feb. 24	PDB	36	£ 15	40

NOMINAL LEDGER

Purchases Account

Dr.   Cr.

Feb. 28	Total credit purchases for month PDB	36	£ 114	90		

Each invoice is certified and approved for payment before being entered in the purchases day book. The details on the invoice are checked against the daily records of goods received by the receipts storeman, and he initials the debit note prior to its approval for payment by the buying office. After the price and the correctness of the trade discount has been confirmed, the only essential detail to be recorded in the day book is the date of the invoice, its official number, the name of the supplier and the net amount to be paid.

Where value added tax is applicable, separate columns are needed in the day book. This is explained in Chapter 16.

The purchases day book is used only for goods bought on credit for re-sale, or for re-sale after conversion. *Permanent assets acquired such as fittings and office equipment are not posted in the day book*: if these are bought on credit, they are debited direct to the asset account and credited to the personal account of the supplier.

Cash purchases (which may also be paid for by cheque) are taken direct from the credit of the cash book to the debit of a separate nominal ledger account, and the cash memo details filed in a separate folder for easy access by the auditor.

Trade discount

Trade discount is a special trade allowance generally recognised between firms within the same trade or industry, and operating between manufacturers, wholesalers and retailers. The discount is normally a percentage ranging between 10 and 35%, and is always deducted from the supplier's invoice. *Only the net amount of the invoice is posted to the day book and to the creditor's account.*

Trade discount is not recorded in any account under its own heading.

Purchases account

The same purchases account is used for both cash and credit purchases, but now there is a slight change of procedure for credit purchases. The individual debits (invoice totals) are not posted to the nominal ledger at the time they are entered in the day book, but are allowed to accumulate day by day and are *posted in one total for the month* to the purchases account at the end of each month.

The individual supplier's (creditor's) account, however, is posted up immediately direct from the day book, so that at any time the amount owing to any creditor may quickly be ascertained.

Creditors' accounts

The balances outstanding (unpaid) on all suppliers' accounts are listed at the end of the trading period. The total for 'trade creditors' is taken to the credit side of the trial balance, its final destination being under the heading of current liabilities on the balance sheet.

Payments made to creditors in settlement of their accounts *in no way affect the purchases total* on the debit of purchases account.

Cash or credit?

Students sometimes experience a little difficulty in deciding whether a transaction is for cash or on credit. These rules will help:

(*a*)   Unless instructed to the contrary, assume that all transactions for the purchase or the sale of goods are on credit when a personal name or the name of a firm is mentioned in the question. There should be no need to mention the name of buyer or vendor in the case of a cash purchase or a cash sale, as money is simply exchanged for the goods handed over.

(*b*)   Assets and office equipment are often bought on credit, and again this should be assumed when the name of the supplier is mentioned, but remember that the cost of the asset should be credited direct to the supplier's account and the debit taken direct to the asset account.

(*c*)   Cash purchases, cash sales and all transactions where the word 'paid' is mentioned are obviously cash transactions.

The buyer's records

Accounting systems and rulings vary a good deal, but the general principles involved in the purchase and sale of goods remains basically the same. On the purchase side, illustrated opposite, start with the official order placed with the supplier and follow through (*a*) the initiation of the storehouse procedure, and then (*b*) the invoicing process and the various aspects of documentation.

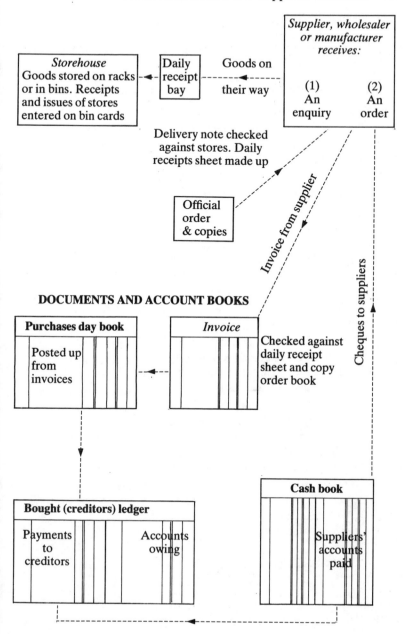

Pause for thought

What is a book of prime or original entry? Does the cash book fall into this category?

What kind of purchases are entered up in the bought journal?

Would you expect to find the purchase of a new car posted to the bought journal? If not, how would you deal with this acquisition?

What is another name for the bought journal?

Assignments

Key Points

1   Money is *owing to* trade creditors. Their ledger accounts kept in the bought ledger, for merchandise supplied on credit, have *not yet been paid*.

2   The purchases or bought day book is a book of prime entry, used for recording invoices of credit purchases (goods to be re-sold or material bought with a view to reconditioning it for sale). Other books of prime entry are the cash book, the sales day book and the returns books.

3   Suppliers' accounts, kept in the bought ledger, have *credit balances*. The individual credits have been posted to these accounts day by day from the bought day book. The day book totals are carried forward until the end of the month, and then the monthly total is taken to the *debit* of purchases account in the nominal ledger, thus completing the double entry.

4   Trade discount is an allowance made from the vendor's price list or catalogue. The deduction is made from the invoice and the net amount due to the creditor is posted *net* to the credit of the supplier's account in the bought ledger.

5   Payments made to creditors in no way affect the day book or the total taken to purchases account. These payments concern only the cash book and the personal accounts of creditors.

13.1 Enter up the bought day book of Maree Lyritis from the details below, and post up the double entry to the bought ledger:

July
  4 Bought £80 of goods from Adrian Shaw less 20% trade discount.
  9 Received delivery of £28.50 goods from Samuel Swift. This included £2.50 transport costs.
 18 Bought another £60 of goods from Adrian Shaw less usual T.D.
 24 Ordered by telephone £45 of goods from W. H. T. Suppliers Ltd. Forwarded and invoiced the following day.
 30 Received a debit note for £18 from Samuel Swift for goods delivered and checked the previous day.

Assuming Miss Lyritis settled the two earlier accounts of Shaw and Swift on 20 July, show all ledger accounts in full detail and balance up on 31 July.

13.2 Garry Hall commenced trading with £800 in the bank and a stock of goods valued at £200 on 1 April. His transactions during April are listed below:

April		£
2	Cashed cheque for office	50.00
	Bought goods from Tom Wynne £60 (gross) arranging for trade discount of 25% on all purchases	
4	Cash sales	126.30
	Paid for stationery (cash)	8.40
	Bought stamps	4.00
6	Bought goods from Fred Maples	36.60
	Cash sales	156.80
	Paid cash into bank	200.00
	Bought goods from Wynne (gross)	80.00
12	Paid Maples on account	20.00
	Paid insurance	15.50
	Sent cheque for advertising	12.20
18	Cash sales	162.70
	Paid into bank	100.00
	Cash purchases (cheques)	18.25
	Paid Wynne's April account	105.00
30	Cheque for month's wages	320.00
	Cash for 'self'	60.00

Post all transactions through original records to the ledger accounts. Balance all accounts and take out a trial balance at 30 April.

14

The Accounts of Credit Customers

When merchandise is sold on credit, the ownership of the goods passes immediately to the buyer who, at the time of purchase or perhaps a few days later, receives an invoice from the vendor showing the full details of the sale, with trade discount deducted if this is applicable, and the net amount to be paid in due course.

Sales day book

In the books of the vendor, credit sales follow a similar procedure to that already outlined on the purchase side in the previous chapter, another book of original entry being brought into use called the sales day book (abbreviation SDB).

The larger organisations, most of them on fully mechanised accounting, make several copies of each invoice sent to their credit customers, one copy being taken by the accounts department and used for the making up of the sales day book, which again, like the purchase day book, serves as an aid towards the accuracy and mechanical efficiency of modern accounting methods.

The essential details (date, name of customer, and net amount) are taken from the copy of the invoice sent to the credit customer and entered in the sales day book, trade discount being deducted (if allowable) to show the net charge to the customer. Only this *net amount* is posted to the debit of the customer's sales ledger account.

The daily sales total is carried forward and at the end of the month the total gross sales are credited to sales account in the nominal ledger. The illustration shows the posting procedure between the day book and the personal and nominal ledgers.

Illustration

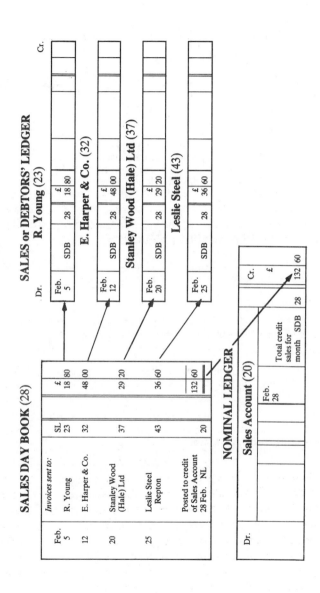

SALES DAY BOOK (28)

	Invoices sent to:	SL		£	
Feb. 5	R. Young	23		18	80
12	E. Harper & Co.	32		48	00
20	Stanley Wood (Hale) Ltd	37		29	20
25	Leslie Steel Repton	43		36	60
	Posted to credit of Sales Account 28 Feb. NL	20		132	60

SALES or DEBTORS' LEDGER

R. Young (23)

Dr.						Cr.
Feb. 5	SDB	28	£ 18	80		

E. Harper & Co. (32)

			£		
Feb. 12	SDB	28	48	00	

Stanley Wood (Hale) Ltd (37)

			£		
Feb. 20	SDB	28	29	20	

Leslie Steel (43)

			£		
Feb. 25	SDB	28	36	60	

NOMINAL LEDGER

Sales Account (20)

Dr.					Cr.
			Feb. 28	Total credit sales for month SDB	28	£ 132	60

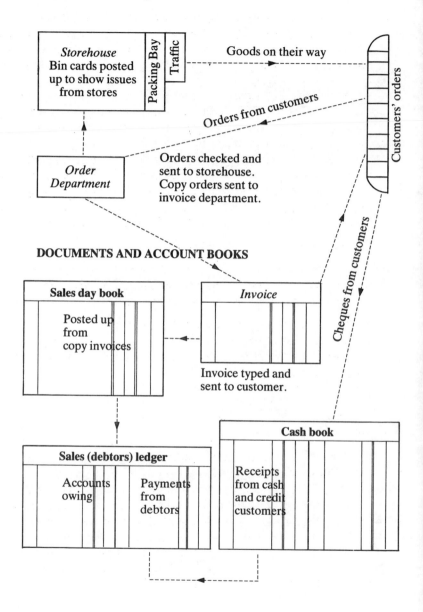

Storehouse
Bin cards posted
up to show issues
from stores

Packing Bay

Traffic

Goods on their way

Customers' orders

Orders from customers

Order
Department

Orders checked and
sent to storehouse.
Copy orders sent to
invoice department.

DOCUMENTS AND ACCOUNT BOOKS

Sales day book

Posted up
from
copy invoices

Invoice

Invoice typed and
sent to customer.

Cheques from customers

Sales (debtors) ledger

Accounts
owing

Payments
from
debtors

Cash book

Receipts
from cash
and credit
customers

The sales day book is used only for *credit sales*. Cash sales and miscellaneous receipts are taken to the credit of a nominal ledger account unless in connection with the sale of assets (money received from the sale of old fittings would be debited to cash and credited to fittings account).

The same sales account in the nominal ledger is used for both the total cash sales and the total credit sales in elementary textbook exercises, the latter being the transfer of the monthly total from the sales day book, as shown on page 75.

Emphasis is again laid upon the fact that payments in settlement of personal accounts *in no way affect the monthly total of sales*. Payments by debtors simply involve the cash book and the personal accounts of the credit customers.

The sales records

The *copy invoice* is the basis for the financial accounting entries on the sales side of the business. In mechanised accounting at least five copies of the customer's invoice are needed for processing:

(*a*)   the original to the credit customer (the debtor),
(*b*)   a sales departmental copy,
(*c*)   the advice/delivery note (without financial detail),
(*d*)   a despatch copy for traffic office,
(*e*)   the accounts departmental copy.

Columnar book-keeping

Day books may be designed and adapted to suit the needs and purposes of the business. If there are several departments the original books of entry for credit purchases and credit sales can be ruled to show a detailed analysis of costs and the revenue for each department. Separate trading accounts can then be made up, with stocks attributable to each department. Comparisons may then be made between the departments, or between the different lines of merchandise, and the non-profit-making lines discarded, or economies put into effect to improve profitability.

A break-down of the merchanting costs on the purchase side of a business with three separate departments might take the following form, in so far as the bought journal is concerned (VAT is ignored for ease of comprehension).

Date	Supplier	Inv. No.	BL folio	Total	Dept. X	Dept. Y	Dept. Z
June				£	£	£	£
1	S. Adams	36	24	120	55	65	–
3	L. H. Dale	45	16	14			14
	Guy Lord	46	176	240	150	40	50
6	Jay & Lee	47	82	72		48	24

Assignments

Key Points

1 Money is *owing by* debtors. The listed total for trade debtors is taken to the debit of the trial balance and shown under the heading of 'current assets' on the balance sheet.

2 Brief details are taken from copies of the invoices sent to customers, to make up the sales day book.

   Some firms make up the spare copies of customers' invoices into book form, and this becomes their day book, the daily totals being carried forward and at the end of the month these accumulated totals are posted in one big total to the credit of sales account.

3 Neither the sales day book nor the sales account are affected by the individual payments from debtors, the accounting entries involved simply concerning only the cash book and the customer's personal ledger account in the sales or debtors' ledger.

14.1   What is another name for the sales day book?

What kind of sales are posted to the sales day book? How would you deal with daily cash sales across the counter?

Which books or records are indicated by these abbreviations?

PDB   SDB   BJ   PCB   BL   SL

14.2 Felicity Jones commenced business on 1 October with £500 in the bank and a stock of goods valued at £200. These are her recorded transactions for the month of October:

Oct.		£
1	Cashed cheque for the office	50.00
	Ordered £40 of goods from Sarah Gosling subject to 20% trade discount. The merchandise was delivered the next day.	
3	General expenses paid in cash	6.00
	Paid for some advertising by cheque	15.50
	Cash sales	72.40
9	Cash purchases	9.10
	Cheque drawn for 'self'	30.00
12	Cash sales	87.20
	Paid cash into bank	100.00
	Sold goods (on credit) to Tom Lister	25.80
15	Bought £60 of goods from Roy Morris less 10%, and sold £45 of goods to Ted Batten making him an allowance also of 10%.	
18	Cash sales	66.70
	Paid Sarah Gosling's account	
20	Received cheque from Tom Lister	25.80
	Sold £30 of goods to Ted Batten, invoiced gross less 10%.	
25	Drew cheque to pay salary of part-time typist	90.00
	Withdrew cash for private use	50.00
30	Cash sales	58.60
31	Paid all surplus cash into bank except for a cash float of £20.	

You are required to post up all the original records, balance up all ledger accounts, and take out a trial balance on 31 October.

15

Purchases and Sales Returns

Goods are returned to suppliers for a variety of reasons. They may have been damaged in transit; they may not be what was ordered; the wrong size or another colour may have been consigned in error.

Credit note
The vendor (the supplier) will be expected to make an allowance or rebate from the amount on the original invoice, where certain merchandise is returned. This allowance applies also when returnable crates, packages and containers are sent back to the supplier.

The vendor's document agreeing or certifying the rebate is called a *credit note*. It is similar to the invoice but is normally printed or written in red to distinguish it from the debit note (the invoice).

Accounting for returns

The accounting procedure is not complicated. It simply involves putting the whole or part of the original transaction in reverse. When goods are returned to your supplier, your *total purchases are thereby reduced*, and, if bought on credit, you do *not owe your creditor so much*. The original transaction or part of it is reversed by debiting your supplier's account and crediting purchases with the value of the goods returned.

Similarly on the sales side. When a credit customer returns some goods to his supplier, the figure for the *recorded sales is reduced* (in the books of the vendor) and the *debtor does not owe so much*. The book-keeping procedure is a debit to sales account and a credit to the personal account of the customer (debtor) for the value of the goods returned.

One important thing to remember about the return of goods is that any *trade discount* deducted on the original purchase or sale must also apply and be *deducted from the gross value* of the goods which are returned.

In practice, when a trader's returns of goods sold are few and infrequent, brief details of the returns are often recorded at the back of the ordinary purchases and sales day books.

In the larger firms, and particularly where returns are more numerous, separate returns day books are brought into operation. These are known as the returns outwards book (purchase returns) and the returns inwards book (sales returns).

The ultimate destination of the returns is to the credit of the purchases account or the debit of the sales account, but in the meantime the trial balance may be made up. Assuming that the returns have already been taken in reduction of purchases and sales account, the *net purchases* and the *net sales* figures are debited and credited to the trial balance, but it would not be incorrect to show the gross figures for the purchases and the sales, together with separate amounts for the returns, i.e. a debit for returns inwards (sales returns) and a credit for returns outwards (purchase returns).

Illustration
Let us assume that two of the white cotton vests invoiced by David Brown on 3 February (Chapter 13) were torn in transit, and that a claim is made by the buyer Samuel Smith against the full charge shown on the original invoice no. 876 dated 3 February.

David Brown would investigate his customer's complaint and examine the faulty merchandise. He acknowledges the claim by sending a credit note, say on 8 February, to Samuel Smith, for the value of the two vests already charged, i.e. £7.20 *less trade discount* at 25% which was deducted from the original invoice.

In Samuel Smith's books (the purchaser's books) the posting from the returns outwards book to the creditor's bought ledger account is now shown, which reduces the balance due to this supplier by £5.40. The purchases account total for the month is also reduced by the same amount by a credit for these returns which is posted from the returns outwards book at the end of February.

In the illustration shown, the returns outwards book total for February has been taken direct to the credit of purchases account at the end of the month. In some instances an account might be opened for these purchase returns called purchase returns account or returns outwards account and the credit total for the month posted to this intermediary account, and then a *transfer* made of the returns to the credit of purchases account when the trading account is made up. In any event, the returns will ultimately be deducted from the purchases total in trading account, so that the figure for *purchases will be shown net*.

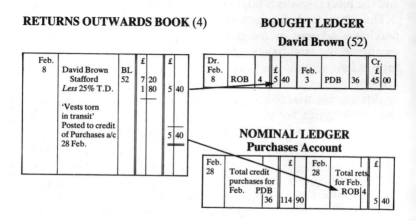

RETURNS OUTWARDS BOOK (4)   **BOUGHT LEDGER**

David Brown (52)

NOMINAL LEDGER
Purchases Account

A similar procedure is adopted with the sales returns. The net value of the goods returned is taken straight from the returns inwards book to the credit of the customer's personal account in the sales (debtors) ledger, thereby reducing his indebtedness. The total of the returns inwards book for the month will be taken to the debit of sales account (or an intermediary returns inwards account if one is in use), and the turnover figure on trading account will be shown *net*, i.e. total sales less returns inwards.

Where VAT is applicable, again there will be the need for additional columns in the returns books (see the next chapter).

Assignments

Key Points

1 The writing up of ledger accounts is fairly simple, as long as you establish, from the outset, whether the account to be written up is in the bought ledger or the sales ledger.

Be careful where contra sales take place (as in the problem below). Put yourself in the place of the business owner and *balance up his books for him*.

2 As with credit purchases and credit sales, the cash book is not affected by the physical return of goods and crates. The book-keeping entries simply entail a reversal of the original transaction, or at least part of it.

Sometimes, though, cash sales are returned, and then the money would be refunded via the cash book.

3 In any return of goods, ask yourself immediately, 'Has trade discount been deducted from the original transaction?'

4 The treatment of returns may affect the trial balance totals. Check whether purchases and sales have been shown as *gross or net*, and whether returns appear under *their own heading* on the trial balance. This could account for the difference between the textbook answer and your own TB total (which may not be wrong, after all).

15.1 Write up the account of Julian Morton in the books of The Midland Agency from this information for the month of March:

March		£
1	Balance brought forward	84.40
3	Credit sales to Morton	56.20
	He paid his February account	
12	Further sales to Morton	36.30
	Allowance for returns	2.50
22	Bought some special fittings and equipment from Morton	22.60
25	Returned some damaged parts bought on 22 March.	
	Morton sent credit note to adjust	4.80
31	Balanced the account	

15.2   The purchases and sales accounts of Kate Danson are shown, balanced to 30 June:

Purchases Account

June 30	PDB total to date Cash purchases		£ 3880 250	June 30	ROB total to date		£ 85

Sales Account

June 30	RIB total to date		£ 225	June 30	SDB total to date Cash sales		£ 8960 515

During the month of July these transactions affecting the above accounts, took place:

July
2   Bought goods from Percy Henson £160 less trade discount of 25%.
4   Cash sales £34. Goods gross value of £16 returned to Henson.
9   Sales to Sue Wheeler £90 less 20%.
12 Cash purchases £14.
18 Credit sale to Bert Dench £86.
22 Dench returned £4 of goods.
    Cash sales £26.
26 Further sales to Miss Wheeler £75 less 20% TD.
30 Bought goods from Will Thomson £110 less 20% trade discount.

Make up the original records of entry, complete the above purchases and sales accounts, bringing down balances at 31 July.

16

Value Added Tax

VAT is a government sales tax paid by the consumer, applicable to most trades and professions, and levied at all stages of distribution. The tax is a straight percentage (15% at present (1984)) on the net sales price of the merchandise or the charges made or the fees payable for the services.

Certain exemptions include the postal services, insurance, education and food, but generally most trades, manufacturers and professional firms with an annual turnover above £18000 are liable for registration with the Customs and Excise Department.

Proper records must be kept of purchases and sales affected by VAT, and the registration number allotted by the government department must be shown clearly on all invoices and bill-heads.

The tax due to the government is added to the basic cost of each invoice, with the full amount being payable by the customer. This means that the day books of credit traders registered for VAT need additional extension columns to record the tax on every purchase and sale.

On the purchase side the supplier's invoice is divided, on entry into the day book, between the net cost of the goods (after deduction of trade discount) and the VAT charge, the amounts being shown in separate columns.

The combined amount of *net cost plus tax* is posted to the credit of the supplier's account, to be paid in due course by the buyer of the merchandise.

At the end of the month, the separate totals accumulated day by day, of the basic invoice costs and the related tax, are *debited* respectively to the purchases account and the customs and excise account in the nominal ledger of the purchasing firm.

PURCHASES DAY BOOK (36)

Feb.	Invoices from:		Net £	VAT £	Total £
3	David Brown Stafford	BL 52	45.00	4.50	49.50
5	B. Ross Nuneaton	44	22.50	2.25	24.75
15	J. Fell & Co. Ltd	38	32.00	3.20	35.20
24	M. K. Mills Cannock	57	15.40	1.54	16.94
	Posted to debit of Purchases a/c and Customs Excise a/c 28 Feb.		114.90	11.49	126.39

BOUGHT LEDGER

Dr.   Cr.

David Brown (52)

Feb. 8	ROB	5 94	Feb. 3	PDB	36	49 50	£

B. Ross (44)

			Feb. 5	PDB	36	24 75

J. Fell & Co. Ltd (38)

			Feb. 15	PDB	36	35 20

M. K. Mills (57)

			Feb. 24	PDB	36	16 94

NOMINAL LEDGER

Purchases Account

Feb. 28	Total credit purchases for month PDB 36	£ 114 90	Feb. 28	ROB	5 40

Customs & Excise Account

Feb. 28	Total VAT for month PDB 36 11 49	Feb. 28	ROB	0 54

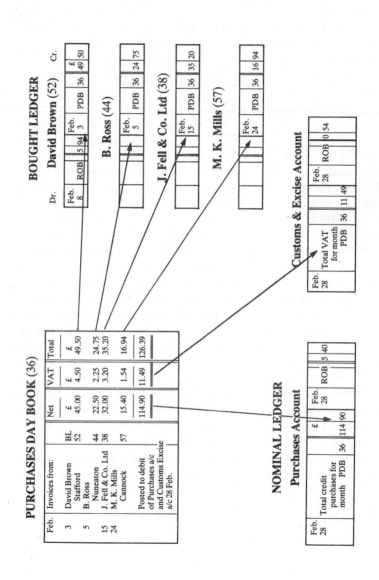

On the sales side, too, the net amount of the invoice (after deduction of trade discount, but including VAT charged) is debited to the sales ledger account of the credit customer, and the separate cumulative totals for the individual invoice charges and the VAT column are, at the end of the month, credited respectively to the sales account and the *same* customs and excise account already in use in the nominal ledger.

Reverting to the illustration of the purchases day book procedure in Chapter 13, the same figures and accounts are now reproduced, with the *inclusion of VAT at 10%*, and allowing for the 10% adjustment of VAT for the returns outwards to David Brown.

Note that the figure for net purchases remains constant at £114.90, but the additional 10% VAT on invoices from suppliers together with the net invoice cost is taken immediately to the credit of the suppliers' accounts in the bought ledger. When the creditors' accounts are paid, probably early in March, the *settlements will include the VAT* to be adjusted on the periodic return made to Customs and Excise in due course.

The sales side is dealt with in a similar way. Now refer back to the accounts of credit customers, in Chapter 14. Additional columns would be required for VAT in the sales day book, which would show the net charge for each individual invoice, the VAT liability of each customer, and a total column for the *combined amount* to be debited to the account of each credit customer.

At the end of the month the total sales will be posted from the day book to the credit of sales account (£132.60 as before), but the debtors' accounts in the sales ledger will now be increased by ten per cent VAT to show a net total increase of £13.26.

This same amount (£13.26) will also be the accumulated total for the VAT column in the day book for the month of February, and is posted at the end of the month to the credit of the *same* customs and excise account brought forward:

Dr.								Customs and Excise Account				Cr.		
Feb. 28	VAT input total for February	PDB	36	£ 11 49		Feb. 28	28	Returns outward book VAT output total for February				£ 0 54 13 26		
28	Balance due to H.M. Customs c/d			2 31										
				13 80								13 80		
Mar. 1	Cheque in settlement			2 31		Mar. 1		Balance b/d				2 31		

The customs and excise account is a kind of adjustment account for VAT liability, as the tax payable (on the merchandise bought or the services used) is offset against the tax collected on the sales to customers, generally showing a balance in favour of the government department, otherwise there would be no point in adopting this extremely lucrative form of taxation.

Note the wording 'input' and 'output' in the last account. These have become general terms for the VAT debits and credits. The output totals in the long run are substantially the greater, otherwise trading profitability would be negligible.

VAT settlements take place at intervals of three to four months, and occasionally there is a refund from the government to the unofficial tax collector. The ledger statement shown below is more indicative of value added tax being collected for the customs and excise department, probably by one of many thousands of small or medium-sized firms.

Customs and Excise Account
for the four months ended 31 December

Dec. 31	VAT input totals from PDB	£	£	Dec. 31	VAT output totals from SDB	£	£
	Sept.	2 260			Sept.	4 250	
	Oct.	2 540			Oct.	5 720	
	Nov.	3 120			Nov.	3 860	
	Dec.	1 880	9 800		Dec.	2 970	16 800
	Due to Customs	c/d	7 000				
			16 800				16 800
Jan. 1	Cheque in settlement		7 000	Dec. 31	Balance b/d		7 000

Similar rulings are adopted in the returns books or that particular section of the purchases and sales day books which applies to returns, and the tax is adjusted on returns inwards and returns outwards when making up the customs and excise account.

PAYE and NIC

'Pay as you Earn' refers to a person's income tax deducted on behalf of the government by the employer from the salary or wage earned by that employee. Individuals are given code numbers according to tax allowances and reliefs to which they are entitled, and the tax due from them is calculated by reference to official tax and code tables issued by the Inland Revenue.

A person's national insurance contribution is more of a fixed and regular amount of additional tax, also deducted by the employer when salaries and wages are paid; at the same time a supplementary amount, rather more than that to be deducted from the employee, is contributed by the employer for each member of his work-force.

Both these forms of taxation have to be accounted for by the employer, to the Inland Revenue and to the Department of Health and Social Security.

The wages and salaries sheets applicable to every form of paid employment are made up each week or month to show the gross pay earned (including bonuses and overtime) of every employee. Deductions are made by the employer for PAYE and NIC and then the net 'take home' pay for each individual is put into a pay packet or is credited direct to the employee's bank account.

The gross wages bill for a firm may, for example, be £50000 in one month; the amount of deductible PAYE tax is £10000; the NIC for the entire labour force is £4000, and the employer's NIC contribution is £4500.

The total 'take home' pay of work-people would amount to £36000, and the employer would have to account to the Inland Revenue for £10000 tax collected, and to the Department of Health and Social Security for £8500 of NI contributions.

The total sum chargeable against this firm's profits would be £54500 (the gross wages plus the firm's own contribution of £4500).

In the case of a sole trader or a partnership, though, neither the *personal* PAYE nor the NIC liability of the proprietor(s) is allowable as a charge against the profits of the firm.

Pause for thought

What does VAT mean and how is this form of taxation collected from the ordinary consumer?

Explain how a plumber subject to VAT regulations would deal with this aspect of taxation on his invoices and in his accounting records.

Assignments

16.1 On 5 July, George Lomas, a cycle and general dealer of 115 Deepdale Road, Preston telephoned his supplier The Rapid Supply Stores of Bolton for an urgent delivery of two dozen garden spades, Cyclops Brand ZX, and also one dozen garden forks of the same brand.

The Rapid Supply Stores made the delivery the following day, their invoice number 643 (VAT registration 56/218/14) giving full details of the credit sale.

The catalogue price of the garden spades was £6.40 each and of the garden forks £5.20 each, with a full allowance made of 25% trade discount in both instances.

The whole consignment was subject to 10% VAT.

You are required to make up the supplier's invoice in all detail, and enter up the purchases day book of the purchaser, and then post up the creditor's account in the bought ledger of George Lomas.

16.2 The information given below is extracted from the various day books of The Rapid Supply Stores by the accountant on 30 June. The net costs of the invoices as listed are shown *after the deduction of trade discount but before charging VAT at ten per cent.*

Day Book monthly totals	PDB	PRB	SDB	SRB
	£	£	£	£
March	5840	–	7200	80
April	4330	50	6840	50
May	5780	120	8160	60
June	4450	30	8700	110

You are required to make up the HM Customs and Excise account showing the net VAT liability of the firm and the settlement of the value added tax on 1 July.

17

Classification of Ledger Accounts

The ultimate and permanent destination of the financial aspect of all business transactions is in the ledger. This is not just one book recording many and varied accounts, but a series of books, cards or files often kept in visible index cabinets and occupying a substantial floor area of the accounting department and the modern office of a large organisation.

A 'full set of books' would comprise at least the cash book, separate ledgers for customers (debtors) and suppliers (creditors) where credit trading is involved, and a general, nominal or expense ledger, split up according to the views of management. Sometimes, too, a private ledger might be kept by a small family-type business to record matters of a fairly confidential nature such as loans made to or by the firm, and perhaps details of the proprietor's or partners' drawings. In addition, the private ledger might be used to record fixed assets, additional purchases of fixed assets, and details of disposals and replacements.

Again, the rulings of these ledgers might differ considerably, according to the needs of the particular business. The explanation of elementary book-keeping in this book is based upon the traditional methods still in general use among small merchants and sole traders, although many of these, during the past two decades, have been introduced, by their accountants, to the bank statement form of ledger account, illustrated in Chapter 11, and now often superseding the 'T' form used in this textbook.

Even though systems and rulings vary with different businesses, the general rule applicable to all ledger accounts is still:

(*a*)   debit the receiving side of one account, and
(*b*)   credit the giving or paying side of the related account.

Types of ledger accounts

There are two main divisions of ledger accounts:

1   Personal accounts of people, firms and companies relating in the main to the credit accounts of suppliers and customers.
2   Impersonal accounts, subdivided into:

   (*a*)   Real and property accounts, comprising 'fixed assets' such as premises, machinery, motor vans, furniture and fittings, and 'current assets' of stock on hand, money at the bank and in the office.

   (*b*)   Nominal accounts, relating to the firm's sales revenue and the expenditure incurred in creating that revenue. These accounts include profits and gains (sales, commissions earned, rents and discounts received); and also losses and expenses such as wages and salaries, advertising, rent and rates payable, repairs, lighting and heating, insurance, and miscellaneous expenses.

General rules for posting

	Personal accounts	*Real/Property accounts*	*Nominal accounts*
Debit:	Who receives	Asset value coming in	Losses and expenses
Credit:	Who gives or pays	Asset value going out	Profits and gains

It is customary for all personal ledger accounts to be balanced at the end of the month, the *new balance being brought down* showing the exact amount owing to each creditor or due by each debtor. When, however, an account shows a single posting, it need not be balanced, as the *amount shown is the balance*.

In large firms credit customers' accounts are often so numerous that further sub-division of the sales ledger is necessary. It could be divided into three or more separate parts, alphabetically or geographically, for instance.

Common forms of ledger accounts

Dr.   **Andrew White** (debtor's personal account)   Cr.

June			£		June			£	
1	Balance b/f		10	50	3	Cheque	CB	10	50
15	Sales	SDB	18	20	17	Returns	SRB	2	20
					30	Balance c/d		16	00
			28	70				28	70
July									
1	Balance b/d		16	00					

John Norton (creditor's personal account)

June			£		June			£	
2	Cheque	CB	22	90	1	Balance b/f		22	90
6	Returns	PRB	3	60	5	Purchases	PDB	65	60
30	Balance c/d		96	20	18	Purchases	PDB	34	20
			122	70				122	70
					July				
					1	Balance b/d		96	20

Furniture & Fittings (a *real* account)

June			£						
1	Balance b/forward		200	00					
8	Cheque (new cabinet)	CB	60	00					

Motor vans (a *real* account)

June			£		June			£	
1	Balance b/f		600	00	10	Sale of old van	CB	550	00
20	Cheque for new van	CB	2800	00	30	Loss on sale			
						(P&L a/c)		50	00
					30	Balance c/d		2800	00
			3400	00				3400	00
July									
1	Balance b/d		2800	00					

Rates (a nominal expense account)

June 24	Cheque for ½ yr's rates	CB	£ 320	00					

Insurance (nominal expense account)

June 5	Fire & General	CB	£ 88	00					
29	Employers' Liab.	CB	54	00					

Commissions Received (nominal gains account)

					June 28	Cheque from WB Agency	CB	£ 40	00

The destination of these ledger accounts between the trial balance and the balance sheet is now shown:

	Trial Balance		T&P&L a/c		Balance Sheet	
	Debit	Credit	Debit	Credit	Assets	Liabs.
A. White, debtor	16.00				16.00	
J. Norton, creditor		96.20				96.20
Furniture/fittings	260.00				260.00	
Motor vans	2800.00				2800.00	
Rates account	320.00		320.00			
Insurance account	142.00		142.00			
Loss on sale (motor van)	50.00		50.00			
Commissions rec'd		40.00		40.00		

The loss (and expense) on the sale of the old van has been taken direct from the motor vans (ledger) account to the debit of profit and loss account. After the closure of all the nominal (expenses and gains) accounts by transfer of their balances to the debit or to the credit of the revenue accounts, the only accounts left with 'open' balances are the asset, capital and liability accounts. These open accounts are carried forward to the next trading period, and are shown on the skeleton balance sheet opposite.

Note that at this stage the whole of the profits and gains, losses and expenses of the business have been absorbed into the revenue accounts, ending with the net profit or loss on trading to be transferred to the proprietor's capital account.

Balance Sheet as at 30 June

Assets employed		
Fixed assets	£	£
Van account	2800.00	
Furniture/fittings	260.00	3060.00
Current assets		
Stock	—	
Trade debtors	16.00	
Bank and cash	—	—
Financed by		
Capital at 1 June		
Add net profit	———	
Less drawings		—
Current liabilities		
Trade creditors	96.20	
Expense creditors	—	—

Pause for thought

It is important to distinguish between a payment made (or a liability incurred) for a permanent fixed type of asset, and a revenue expense payment (or expense liability incurred). Later, in Chapter 20, this is explained in further detail.

Sometimes students are confused because *both assets and expenses have debit balances*. The main thing to bear in mind is that there is a credit entry, either in the cash book or on a creditor's account for *both asset and expense transactions*, but the ultimate destinations are quite different, as illustrated in this chapter.

Classify the following under the headings of real, personal and nominal:

(*a*) machinery   (*b*) wages
(*c*) bank overdraft   (*d*) insurance (paid)
(*e*) capital   (*f*) rates in advance
(*g*) new lease   (*h*) Delia Harlow (supplier)
(*i*) Judi Bray (customer)

Which of these ledger accounts would have credit balances?

Assignments

Key Points

1 Do not credit money received from the sales of old assets to cash sales.

   The correct procedure is to credit the old asset account with the sum realised, ascertain the *loss on sale*, and debit this to profit and loss account.

   If there is a small profit, this would be credited to P&L A/c, and the asset account debited. Since the asset has been sold, it must be taken out of the books.

2 Again, note that in assignment 17.2 you are operating a contra account with your wholesaler.

3 A personal ledger account contains a financial summary of the business transactions with a certain person or firm during some part of the accounting period.

4 Both asset and expense accounts have debit balances or totals. Their destinations, though, are quite different. The asset is taken to the balance sheet, whereas the *expense is absorbed* in working out the net trading profit or loss.

5 It may help to think of the expense incurred as paid to a *named* expense account such as the Midland Electricity Board.

6 Where sums of money (or goods) are withdrawn by the proprietor, think of his *personal* drawings account as receiving or benefiting, with the business relinquishing cash or goods.

17.1   List the following under account headings of real, personal or nominal:

Cash sales £54; van repairs £16; rates £200; commission earned £28; insurance paid £35; garage extension £850; new desk bought £80; bought new duplicator £180; sale of old duplicator £25; cheque from V. J. Pauli £45 in payment of goods bought three months ago.

17.2   Post up the account of Howard Tarver, a wholesaler, from these details:

July
1   You owe Tarver £122.44 for goods bought in June
3   Further purchases £60 less T.D. of 25%
5   Returns to Tarver £16 gross
    Paid his June account
    Bought further goods £72
    less 25%
11   Sales to Tarver £25.50 less 20% T.D.
15   Tarver returned £5 gross goods
24   Further supplies from Tarver £36 less 25%. He also made an allowance of £2.60 for packing case returned
31   Balanced the account.

17.3   Post up the account of Trevor Tongue in the books of Miller Bros and bring down the balance at 30 June:

June
1   Tongue owes Miller Bros £46.20 for supplies in May
3   Tongue buys further goods from Miller Bros to value of £80 less T.D. of 20%
5   He returns £10 gross to supplier, and settles May account
12   Further sales to Tongue £35.50 less usual discount
22   Cheque sent by Tongue for £50 'on account'. Allowance of £3.50 made for containers returned
25   Tongue's cheque returned by Bank to Miller Bros with remarks 'refer to drawer'
26   Tongue called on his creditor, handed in £40 in cash, tore up his cheque and promised balance early in July.

17.4   What kind of ledger accounts would be found in the accounting department of a large wholesale warehouse, specialising in household groceries and covering the Midlands and West Country?

Revision Exercise 2

1 David Shaw commenced business on 1 July with a capital of £3000 made up as follows:

	£		£
Cash in hand	30	Bank balance	2345
Fixtures/fittings	175	Van valued at	700

An amount of £250 was owing at 1 July to Roy Fenton for the van, recently acquired by the business.

After posting the above details to the cash book and the general ledger and the personal ledger account of Roy Fenton, you are required to record the transactions listed below for the month of July.

On completion of the postings, balance up all personal and nominal ledger accounts and take out a trial balance at 31 July.

July		£	
1	Bought some shelving	100.00	
	and a second-hand cupboard	20.00	
	Stamps and stationery	4.00	
3	Supplies bought for stock from Bryan Benson, subject to a trade discount of 20%	120.00	gross
5	Cash sales	45.30	
	Sold goods to Esther Allen (allowing her T.D. of £10)	70.00	gross
9	Cash sales	86.60	
	Paid cash into bank	80.00	
	Paid insurance (fire and theft)	12.50	
	Drew cheque for self	30.00	
12	Paid various advertising expenses	15.50	
	Bought further goods from Benson, being allowed 20%	150.00	gross

	14	Returned goods to Benson	15.00	gross
		Cash sales	74.40	
		Sale at special price to Dinah Symonds	104.00	
		Made urgent delivery to Owen Moore	38.80	
	18	Cash purchases	12.00	
		Drawings for self (cheque)	60.00	
		Cash sales	158.80	
		Sold goods to Judith Palmer		
		(making special allowance of £22.50)	130.00	gross
	23	Paid amount due on van to Roy Fenton	250.00	
	26	Received payment of Miss Allen's account	60.00	
	30	Paid wages for month in cash	240.00	
	31	Paid rent for July	36.00	
		Paid all surplus cash over £30 into bank		

2   Copies of two of David Shaw's personal ledger accounts are shown below:

Bryan Benson

July				£	July				£
14	PRB	13		12 00	3	PDB	28		96 00
31	Balance c/d			204 00	12	PDB	35		120 00
				216 00					216 00
					Aug.				
					1	Balance b/d			204 00

Esther Allen

July					July				
5	SDB	24		60 00	26	Cheque	CB		60 00

(a)   Which, of the two accounts shown, is that of the debtor? What was the position with regard to both accounts on 10 July and again on 13 July?

(b)   Is the trade discount allowed by the creditor greater than the trade discount allowed to the debtor? What would be the discount percentage allowed to David Shaw in the accounting records of Bryan Benson?

18

Final Accounts of a Sole Trader

This chapter may appear to be the ultimate target for many students, and indeed, with the ability to comprehend and classify the various accounts of a small trader and assemble them in final account form, it may be said that perseverance and concentration has been worthwhile, even though we are still at the elementary stage.

A sole trader's final accounts are now depicted with rather more detail than that we have already seen, followed by explanatory notes.

Trading and Profit and Loss Account
for the year ended 30 June

	£	£		£	£
Stock 1 July		2 000	Sales	18 500	
Purchases for year	8 000				
Less returns outwards	200	7 800	*Less* returns inwards	300	18 200
Carriage inwards		120			
		9 920			
Less Stock 30 June		2 500			
		7 420			
Warehouse wages & NIC		3 380			
Cost of Sales		10 800			
Gross profit c/d		7 400			
		18 200			18 200
Salaries & NIC		2 800	Gross profit b/d		7 400
Rates		360	Commission received		680
Advertising		410			
Carriage outwards		130			
General expenses		180			
Net trading profit, taken					
to capital account		4 200			
		£8 080			£8 080

**Balance Sheet of A. Trader
as at 30 June**

Assets employed				Figures for previous year
Fixed assets		£	£	
Premises at cost		10000		
Machinery at cost		3000		
Fixtures/fittings at cost		350		
Motor van at cost		2650	16000	
Current assets	£			
Stock 30 June	2500			
Trade debtors	1800			
Bank	670			
Cash	30	5000		
Current liabilities				
Trade creditors	1280			
Expense creditors	20	1300		
Working capital			3700	
Net assets			£19700	
Financed by				
Proprietor's capital				
Balance 1 July		19000		
Net trading profit		4200		
		23200		
Less drawings		3500	19700	
			£19700	

The trading and profit and loss account

Purchases are shown less *returns outwards* to give the net figure of £7800. *Carriage inwards* (on purchases) increases the cost of the goods bought and in consequence is a trading account expense.

Closing stock at 30 June is deducted from the total costs of materials bought to give the *cost of merchandise used or consumed*, i.e. £7420. To this figure is added warehousing wages (in preparing the goods for sale). This gives us the cost of the goods which have been sold to show the *cost of sales* figure of £10800.

On the credit side of the trading account is the net turnover of cash and credit sales, a total of £18200. The difference between the actual net sales (£18200) and the cost of those sales (£10800) is the gross trading profit of £7400.

Most of the profit and loss debits have originated from the cash book or from an expense voucher to be settled later by a cash payment. *Carriage outwards* is an expense of selling and distribution, debited to this lower account to distinguish it from *carriage inwards* (on purchases). *Both are expenses and debits.*

Salaries generally refer to payments made to the monthly paid staff, comprising office and administrative personnel, normally a more static figure than the wages paid on the production and warehousing side. The wages paid to office cleaners, however, should be charged to the profit and loss account.

The few items found on the credit of profit and loss account are usually recognised by the word 'received' and generally refer to small gains or miscellaneous receipts such as 'rents received', 'commissions received' and 'discounts received'.

It is important to remember that neither assets nor drawings appear in the revenue accounts, the only exception being the opening and closing stocks, needed to adjust the net debit for purchases to find the actual cost of the materials consumed during the trading period.

The balance sheet

The *fixed assets* have been listed and totalled first, in order of permanency, usually the case with merchanting and trading firms.

Premises would be regarded as more permanent and likely to be kept for a longer term than any of the other fixed assets.

Note that the valuation of all fixed assets is at cost, presumably their original cost. This is not likely to be their true worth, as wasting assets such as vehicles and machinery are subject to heavy wear and tear. Their reduction in value (called depreciation) is dealt with in Chapter 23.

The *current or circulating assets* are generally listed in the order shown. These assets change their form in the course of trading, stock sometimes being re-styled before the sale of the merchandise, sold to cash and credit customers (the unpaid accounts of the latter being recorded in the books as trade debtors). As the money comes in, further goods are bought for cash or on credit (thus creating trade creditors) and so the trading cycle goes on.

Bank and cash are called 'liquid assets' and petty cash is normally absorbed into the main cash or paid into the bank at the balance sheet date.

Working capital

A commercial enterprise conducts its daily activities and trading operations through the deployment of its working capital. These routine activities will include the buying, conversion and sale of merchandise, the collection of credit customers' accounts, the payment of regularly occurring expenses such as wages and salaries, postal expenses, advertising, telephone and electricity bills etc.

Working capital is not merely the cash available for use. It is the excess of current assets over current liabilities, as shown in the illustration on the balance sheet earlier in the chapter. In this instance the total of the current liabilities of £1300 is deducted from the total of the current assets (£5000) to give the working capital of this business as £3700.

Capital owned and capital employed

The capital owned by a sole trader is the final balance of his capital account. On this last balance sheet this would be £19 700. This is also the owner's equity and the net worth of the business according to the book values of the net assets.

There are a number of interpretations of *capital employed*, the two most common being:

(a)   the total of the fixed and current assets available for the full use and purpose of the business (£21 000 in this instance);
(b)   the same figure as in (a) but excluding debtors who have the use and benefit of the firm's money (£19 200 on this reckoning).

Proprietor's capital

The capital account of the sole trader is *his personal account* in the eyes of the business. Increased sales revenue, allowing for normal profit percentages, should increase his capital account, but money and goods withdrawn from the business for the proprietor's private use will reduce his holding of net assets and decrease his capital.

Care must be taken, in drafting the balance sheet, not to include ordinary trade creditors in the capital section, as the personal account of the proprietor shows the internal debt due by the business to him.

The capital account of A. Trader shown on his balance sheet is simply a vertical copy of his personal account kept in the private ledger, thus:

Dr. **Capital Account** Cr.

			£				£
June 30	Drawings for year		3500	July 1	Balance b/f from last year		19000
30	Balance c/d		19700	June 30	Net trading profit from P&L a/c		4200
			23200				23200
				July 1	Balance b/d		19700

It will be seen that A. Trader has increased his capital (and the net assets) by £700 during the past trading year. This amount is the difference between the profit made and the sum total of his drawings.

Current liabilities

The current liabilities are the trade accounts (amounts owing to suppliers) at the date of the balance sheet, and also any business expenses not yet paid (amounts owing for printing, heating and lighting, or perhaps for wages and salaries accrued at the balance sheet date). An overdraft at the bank is also a current liability.

The adjustments necessary with regard to expense creditors are explained in Chapter 25.

Pause for thought

Make up a small trading and profit and loss account, inserting your own figures, to include:

Sales, purchases, returns inwards and outwards, stocks at the beginning and at the end of the period, warehouse wages, carriage inwards and outwards, rents received, transport expenses, rates paid, salaries, postages, insurances, heating and lighting. Show the cost of sales in the trading account.

Following the drafting of the revenue account on the above lines, continue with a vertical-style balance sheet showing the layout similar to the illustration at the beginning of this chapter. Show the working capital and the net assets in completion of the assignment.

Assignments

Key Points

1 The one main and useful equation in accounting is simple enough to remember:

$C + L = A$

where C is the proprietary capital;
L the external liabilities of the business; and
A the sum total of the assets and property of the business.

When working out problems of capital, net worth and equity, given any two of these basic business elements, the third can easily be calculated.

2 In all these elementary exercises, the proprietor's capital account on the balance sheet should be presented clearly. In no circumstances should either trade or expenses creditors be jammed into the capital section.

18.1 Refer back to Revision Exercise 2 and make up the trading and profit and loss account for the month and a balance sheet as at 31 July from the trial balance already extracted, taking the valuation of Mr Shaw's closing stock at 31 July to be £45.

18.2 Make up the trial balance and a complete set of accounts, as at 30 June, from the following balances extracted from the financial books of Lucian Lane, a small retail merchant whose business is mainly cash with a small credit connection.
Show clearly on his balance sheet:

(*a*) separate headings for fixed and current assets, the capital, and current liabilities.

(*b*) In a vertical-style balance sheet show Mr Lane's working capital and his net assets at 30 June.

	£
Capital account 31 May	2000
Carriage inwards	42
Cash balance 30 June	67
Bank balance 30 June	1850
Carriage outwards	56
Warehouse expenses	235
Petrol and oil	86
Fittings and fixtures	340
General expenses	28
Returns inwards	66
Returns outwards	44
Van repairs	52
Stock 31 May	320
Purchases	3682
Sales	8760
Insurance	34
Advertising	44
Rent and rates	420
Stationery	32
Trade creditors	220
Drawings	800
Salaries	1600
Trade debtors	430
Van at book value	840

Mr Lane valued his closing stock at £480

19

Comprehension and Interpretation

The trading account determines the gross profit (or loss) over a defined period of trading, providing useful information to management, in particular when comparisons are made with the trading accounts of other periods, or with those of competitors.

To arrive at some of the bases of comparison, namely the cost of sales, gross profit percentages and the rate of stock turnover, a simple style of trading account is first shown:

Trading Account
for the month of January

		£			£	£
Stock 1 Jan.		800	Cash sales		450	
Purchases	£5000		Credit sales	£5800		
Less returns	300	4700	*Less* returns	250	5550	6000
		5500				
Less stock 31 Jan.		1000				
Cost of sales		4500				
Gross profit		1500				
		6000				6000

Cost of sales

The cost of sales (or the cost of the goods sold) is found by simple arithmetic on the debit side of the trading account by adding the opening stock to net purchases and deducting the figure for closing stock. This cost of sales figure is not the same as the goods bought or purchases, but the valuation of closing stock probably includes much of the merchandise recently bought.

The cost of sales figure is also increased by other trading account debits such as wages, carriage inwards and warehousing expenses, omitted here for simplicity.

Gross profit percentages

The trading results of one period may be compared with those of another period (or of a competitor) by expressing their gross profits as percentages of their relative sales turnovers. In the trading account illustrated the percentage is arrived at thus:

$$\frac{\text{Gross profit}}{\text{Net sales}} \times 100, \quad \text{that is} \quad \frac{1500}{6000} \times 100 = 25\%$$

This might be regarded as a fair gross profit percentage, but to a large extent it would depend upon the nature of the business.

If there were a wide variation between the gross profit margins of one period and the next (and it is not a seasonal business) management would investigate the reason for the discrepancy.

Rate of stock turnover

The number of times the stock in trade is turned over in the course of a month or a year has a direct bearing upon the gross profit of a business. Generally, profit increases if the rate of stock turnover can be improved and the cost of sales remains fairly proportionate to the turnover.

The rate of stock turnover is calculated by dividing the *cost of sales* by the *average stock*.

The average stock in the illustration is: $\quad \dfrac{£800 + £1000}{2} = £900$

The rate of stock turnover is then:

$$\frac{\text{Cost of sales}}{\text{Average stock}} \qquad \text{that is} \qquad \frac{4500}{900} = 5 \text{ times in the month.}$$

Comparison of stock turnover

Study these figures for two separate businesses in the same trade. Which do you think is the more successful of the two?

	Average stock £1000	Stockturn	Mark-up on cost
Business A	£1000	6 times a year	30%
Business B	£1000	10 times a year	20%

Business A has a much higher mark-up percentage than Business B, yet the trading results of the latter are the better of the two, as not only is the turnover of B increased on its lower profit margin, but the gross profit of B is also greater than that of A, as now shown:

Business A   Stock turnover $£1000 \times 6 = £6000$

Gross profit $6000 \times \dfrac{30}{100} = £1800$

Business B   Stock turnover $£1000 \times 10 = £10\,000$

Gross profit $10\,000 \times \dfrac{20}{100} = £2000$

Comparison of business profits

From the information tabled below you are asked to give your opinion, supported by percentages, as to which business (operating in the same trade) seems to be the more progressive of the two.

	Capital employed £	Turnover £	Gross profit £	Net profit £
Business A	7500	6000	3000	1500
Business B	10000	8000	3600	1800

At first glance, the second business may appear to be the more progressive, until it is noticed that the greater gross and net profit of Business B are based upon its greater (by one-third) capital and turnover than Business A, leading then to the natural assumption that the gross and net profits of Business B should be even larger than those shown.

A comparison by percentages will show the issue in a better perspective:

(*a*)   *Percentage of gross profit to turnover:*

Business A $\dfrac{£3000}{6000} \times 100 = 50\%$

Business B $\dfrac{£3600}{8000} \times 100 = 45\%$

(*b*)   *Percentage of net profit to turnover:*

Business A $\dfrac{£1500}{6000} \times 100 = 25\%$

Business B $\dfrac{£1800}{8000} \times 100 = 22.5\%$

(*c*)   *Percentage of net profit to capital employed:*

Business A $\dfrac{£1500}{7500} \times 100 = 20\%$

Business B $\dfrac{£1800}{10\,000} \times 100 = 18\%$

This comparison by percentages reveals that Business A, though operating on a smaller capital, is the more progressive business, providing, of course, that the figures given for both businesses are truly representative for their trade, with abnormalities excluded.

Claims for loss of stock

Sometimes insurance claims for loss or damage to stock (perhaps through fire or flood) have to be based upon past records and whatever figures are available. The following is a typical elementary examination problem.

Peter West's warehouse stock was destroyed by fire on 30 June, except for a salvaged amount valued at £350. The date of the fire was exactly half way through his accounting period, and these figures were extracted from his account books and papers, kept in a fire-proof safe:

	£
Stock at 1 Jan.	1500
Purchases (Jan.–June)	6300
Wages for six months	3200
Sales (Jan.–June)	12400

A trading account was prepared from this information and a figure approximated for gross profit based upon 25% of Mr West's turnover for the current year, as this percentage had been fairly constant in recent years and was confirmed to be the average within the same trade.

Make up the insurance claim for Mr West.

Answer

**Trading Account
for period 1 January to 30 June**

	£		£
Stock 1 Jan.	1500	Sales (Jan.–June)	12400
Purchases	6300	Estimated stock	
Wages	3200	at date of fire	
	———	(£14100 − £12400)	1700
	11000		
Gross profit			
(25% of £12400)	3100		
	———		———
	14100		14100

The insurance claim would be:

Estimated stock at 30 June	£1700
Less value of stock salvaged	350
	———
	£1350

Pause for thought

How would you obtain the following information from the financial records of a sole trader?

(*a*) the total money owing to suppliers

(*b*) total money owing by customers

(*c*) net turnover for the month	(*d*) month end bank balance
(*e*) total staff salaries for month	(*f*) NIC deductions from staff
(*g*) publicity expense for past year	(*h*) local rates paid last year.

Invoices of some dealers need to be perused carefully by the auditor. For instance, an antique dealer might buy two 19th century tables, priced at £250 each. One is delivered to the shop, and the other to his home. What would be the correct accounting entries?

Assignments

Key Points

1   In problems concerning cost of sales or stockturn, always make up a modern style trading account showing the deduction of closing stock on the debit side of the trading account.

2   A critical appraisal of trading account figures might invoke these questions:

   (*a*)   Are the figures as good as expected?
   (*b*)   Are the figures as good or better than those of the previous year?
   (*c*)   Are certain lines more profitable than others?
   (*d*)   Should economies be made in some departments?
   (*e*)   Is money or stock being embezzled and what precautions should be taken?

3   Students manage quite well, usually, with the kind of problem exemplified by assignment 19.3, finding little difficulty with the trading account. Sometimes, though, they show their final answer as the approximated closing stock, instead of *deducting the value of stock salvaged* to give the correct *net claim* against the insurance company.

19.1 The balances below were extracted from the books of Norman Deal on 31 January. Find his gross and net profit percentages on turnover; also his rate of stock turnover.

	£		£
Stock 1 Jan.	600	Net purchases	2300
Stock 31 Jan.	900	Net sales	6250
Warehouse expenses	205	Salaries	430
Carriage inwards	45	Advertising	80
Carriage outwards	50	Wages	1500
Rent and rates	400	General exes.	40
Heating/lighting	160	Comm. rec'd	535

19.2 Say which, in your opinion, is the more profitable of the two businesses, from the figures given below. Give your reasons.

	Average stock	Stock turn	Mark-up on cost
	£		
Business RS	2000	6.5 times	40%
Business KC	2000	8.5 times	32%

19.3 Jasmina Ling has built up a small but profitable business in household utilities. She makes up her annual accounts to 31 December.

A fire broke out in the early hours of 1 April and destroyed her entire stock except for the amount salvaged of £120.

Her accountant made contact with her insurance company, arranging to send them a trading account for the three months for the period 1 January–31 March, from figures which were available:

	£
Stock 1 Jan.	820
Purchases (three months)	3160
Carriage inwards	30
Warehouse wages	1890
Cash and credit sales for these three months	8000

Miss Ling's average percentage of gross profit to turnover for the past five years had been 40%. Prepare the claim on the insurance company for the loss destroyed by fire.

Revision Exercise 3

Gregory Bartel's balance sheet at 30 June was made up on these lines:

Assets employed			
Fixed assets at cost	£	£	£
Premises	5000		
Fittings	300		
Motor van	1800		7100
Current assets			
Stock	900		
Trade debtors	696		
Bank	1250		
Cash	54	2900	
Less: Current liabilities			
Trade creditors	825		
Rates owing	175	1000	1900
			9000
Financed by		£	£
Proprietor's capital		6000	
Loan from Mrs G. Bartel		3000	9000
			9000

Your assignment is to open a new set of account books from the information given above, and then post up Gregory Bartel's trading transactions for the month of July, as listed below from the original entry stage.

The trade creditors comprised two suppliers' accounts, viz. Hugo Jones £550 and Mohammed Ali £275, totalling £825 on the above balance sheet.

The trade debtors' total of £696 comprised four accounts, namely:

Hilary Fane	£180	Delia Harlow	£162
Petula Hill	£144	Richard Mead	£210

Balance up all accounts and take out a trial balance on 31 July. Make up the trading and profit and loss account for Gregory Bartel for the month of July, and a balance sheet as at 31 July, accepting his own valuation of closing stock at £860.

Transactions for July:

July
1   Bought £160 of goods from Hugo Jones, being allowed 25% trade discount
    Cash sales £84
2   Paid creditors for rates £175
    Cash sales £141. Paid £100 into bank.
6   Drew cash from bank and paid wages £150
    Miss Fane sent cheque for £180 in settlement of her June account
    Paid £300 'on account' to Hugo Jones
    Bought £80 desk for office; paid by cheque.
9   Cash sales £165. Paid £100 into bank.
    Paid advertising account £20, and garage account £25.
12 Daily takings amounted to £137
    Paid £150 wages out of cash
    Repaid Mrs Bartel £500, reducing loan account to £2500
14 Received cheque for £162 from Delia Harlow. She bought another £60 of goods. Allowed her 20% trade rate.
15 Cash sales £159; cash purchases £18
18 Paid wages £160
    Sold £80 of merchandise to Petula Hill less 10% trade rate:
    She paid £100 off her outstanding account.
23 Bought £240 of goods from Hugo Jones, being allowed the usual discount. Also paid £15 delivery charges in cash.
    Bought £120 of goods from Mohammed Ali who would only allow £10 trade rate. Gave him a cheque for £275 in settlement of his June account.
25 Returned £40 (gross) merchandise bought from Hugo Jones on 23 July.
    Cash sales £136. Paid £160 wages out of cash.
28 Sold £75 of goods to Dinah Mortimer allowing her 20% trade discount. Paid £6 carriage on various deliveries made during the month of July.
30 Cash sales £128
    Withdrew £100 cash for private and family use.
31 Paid £80 cheque to a part-time typist working from her home address.
    Retained £25 cash for office and paid surplus cash into bank.

20

Capital and Revenue Expenditure

The term 'capital' so far has been used to indicate the net worth or equity of various small businesses, and in particular the personal capital accounts of sole traders.

Sometimes, though, the term is used to describe *capital assets* acquired for the permanent use of the business, and the expenditure used to purchase or extend those assets is then known as *capital expenditure*, and would include land and buildings, plant and machinery, furniture and fixtures, motor vehicles and office equipment.

On the other hand, 'revenue expenditure' refers to the cost and expense of maintaining and operating these capital assets, including all renewals and repairs; in addition, revenue expense embraces all costs of maintaining sales revenue and relates to all normal trading and business activities involving the payment of wages and salaries, materials bought for re-sale or conversion, advertising, insurance, electric power, heating and lighting, repairs, renewals and transport of all description, in fact all those debits and charges to be found on the trading and profit and loss account.

Capital expenditure

A new business starting from scratch might have only a sum of money in the bank as its sole asset. In the course of trading, various fixed and permanent assets would be acquired, probably some fixtures and fittings, some machinery and perhaps a motor van. The payment for these capital assets would be made either from the original money capital, or from profit surpluses retained by the business. This is capital expenditure.

Again, these (or similar) assets could be acquired in the purchase price when a business is bought as a 'going concern', and any further payments made on improving or extending these assets would be debited to these same accounts and increase their 'book value' as now illustrated:

Dr.	**Machinery Account**							Cr.
			£					
Jan. 1	Balance b/f		4500					
May 5	Cheque (new machine)	CB	1200					

Dr.	**Furniture and Fixtures**							Cr.
			£					
Jan. 1	Balance b/f		720					
Oct. 15	Cheque (filing cabinet)	CB	40					

	Vans Account							
			£					
Jan. 1	Balance b/f (second-hand van taken over)		1800					

At the end of the financial year, the balances of these asset accounts would be shown on the balance sheet under the heading of *fixed assets*, thus:

Assets Employed

Fixed assets	£	£
Machinery at cost	5700	
Fittings at cost	760	
Vans at cost	1800	8260

Revenue expenditure

Revenue expense is charged and written off to the trading account or the profit and loss account at the end of the financial year, as now shown:

Dr.	**Warehouse Expenses**							Cr.
			£				£	
Mch. 4	Cheque for re-decorating, etc.	CB	420 00	Dec. 31	Transfer to trading account		498 00	
May 12	Cleaning	CB	24 00					
Aug. 6	Cleaning	CB	24 00					
Nov. 22	Cleaning	CB	30 00					

Advertising

			£				£
Jan. 6	Cheque	CB	15 50	Dec. 31	Transfer to		
Apl. 3	Cheque	CB	28 20		P&L a/c		68 70
Oct. 15	Cheque	CB	25 00				

Van Repairs and Renewals

			£				£
Mar. 25	Red Garage (service			Dec. 31	Transfer to		
	& new exhaust)	CB	68 50		P&L a/c		120 90
Sept. 2	Service, etc.	CB	52 40				

**Trading and Profit and Loss Account
for period ended 31 December**

	£		
Warehouse expenses	498 00		
Gross profit b/d	—		
Advertising	68 70	Gross profit c/d	—
Van repairs/renewals	120 90		

Money received from the sale of capital assets is debited to the cash book and *credited to the related asset account*. Receipts of this nature are not regarded as revenue income like sales and cash takings. Remember that an old asset has been sold and its book value must now be erased from the accounting records. This means that the balance remaining on the account (normally a small debit balance) must be written off to profit and loss account, as it is a loss and expense suffered by the business. In more advanced accounting there is an adjustment in connection with its depreciated book value if the asset has been subject to a depreciation charge.

The distinction between capital and revenue expenditure is important, as the charging of heavy capital outlay against profits reduces (often substantially) the net profit and the tax liability of the business.

Revenue Expense	**Capital Expense**
is debited and charged to profit and loss account, thereby decreasing the net trading profit with the consequent reduction of the income tax assessment.	is debited to the asset account and taken to the balance sheet under the heading of fixed assets. Capital expenditure must not be charged against profits.

Assignments

Key Points

1 The term 'revenue' refers to *either income or expense* having a direct connection or influence on the trading returns or profits of the business.

   Revenue expense is charged and debited against profits, whereas revenue income implies additional profit or gain.

2 Money spent on repair work and renewals (including redecoration) is *revenue expense* and is debited to profit and loss account.

   Money spent on improvements or extensions to existing capital assets is *capital expenditure* and must be debited to the asset account.

3 In examination problems on capital and revenue expenditure, ask yourself: Has the money been used up in the ordinary course of trading (like rent, stationery, wages, etc.), or will its use and benefit extend perhaps over a number of years (as in the case of a new van, office equipment or a building extension)?

   Another point about a building extension or the erection of machinery is that the *wages paid to the firm's own workmen engaged on the erection work is also capital expenditure* to be debited to the cost of the asset.

20.1   Re-draft this trading and profit and loss account of Miranda Moss, incorrectly drawn up by her younger brother:

Trading and Profit and Loss Account
as at 31 August

	£		£
Stock 31 July	680	Sales	7200
Purchases	3440	Rets. inwards	60
Rets. outwards	26		
Carriage outwards	18	Stock 1 July	550
Wages	520		
Salaries	1240		
Gross profit c/d	1886		
	7810		7810
Stationery	15	Gross profit b/d	1886
Drawings	360	Loss on sale of van	130
Van repairs	45	Sundry receipts	68
Rents received	84	Carriage inwards	42
Second-hand van	830	Net loss on trading	54
Sundry expenses	26		
Advertising	24		
Typewriter	96		
Showroom extension	580		
Decorating office	120		
	2180		2180

20.2   A firm bought some new machinery for £5000 on 1 January. The first year normal running costs were £150, and wages of £350 were paid to an engineer for his time spent on checking and improving its output. Discuss charges to capital/revenue at the year-end.

Pause for thought

Allocate the following debits between capital and revenue:

(*a*) repairs to van
(*b*) set of new tyres for van
(*c*) rates and taxes
(*d*) purchase of a second-hand filing cabinet
(*e*) fire insurance
(*f*) purchase of five-year old typewriter
(*g*) petrol and oil account
(*h*) donation to charity

In what circumstances would a motor vehicle be regarded as a current asset?

21

Cash Discount and the Three-column Cash Book

Trade discount was introduced in Chapter 13 as a rebate or allowance from the catalogue price of an article, an arrangement of long custom generally applicable between producers, wholesalers and retailers operating within the same or ancillary trades. This allowance is fairly substantial, often in the range of 20–30%, and is deducted from the gross amount of the invoice before the transaction is taken to the main sales or purchases column of the day book.

Cash discount, on the other hand, is generally a far smaller allowance, offered as an inducement to the prompt payment of the accounts of credit customers. There is no reason, though, why cash discount should not be offered in the form of a *spot* or *net price* to cash customers, but in this instance the discount would not be recorded as part of the cash sale, which would simply be shown at its reduced price.

Cash discount is entered in the discount column of the cash book on the left of the payment to which it relates, and the combined total of the *money paid plus the cash discount* allowed or received is posted to the personal account of the credit customer or the supplier of the merchandise.

The procedure for dealing with the monthly totals of the discount columns is similar to the posting of the day book totals, and is best explained by illustration, shown overleaf, but at this stage it should help to remember that:

(a) Discounts allowed (on the debit of the cash book) are small losses incurred in getting debtors' money in more quickly.

(*b*)   Discounts received are small compensatory gains, shown on the credit of the cash book, and offered by creditors for the prompt payment of *their* outstanding accounts.

Dr.   **THREE-COLUMN CASH BOOK**   Cr.

May			Disc. £	Cash £	Bank £	May			Disc. £	Cash £	Bank £
1	Brought forward			30 00	450 00	3	H. Hanson & Co.		3 00		57 00
8	Cash sales			28 20		16	Contra	c		50 00	
12	J. M. Hughes		2 00		38 00	20	Postages			6 00	
16	Cash sales			46 70		22	Drawings				20 00
	Contra	c			50 00	24	L. Lowe & Son		1 00	19 00	
25	G. Dawson		0 40	7 60		28	M.E.B.				25 00
						31	Balances c/d			37 50	436 00
			2 40						4 00		
				112 50	538 00					112 50	538 00
June											
1	Balances b/d			37 50	436 00						

NOMINAL LEDGER

Dr.   **Discounts Allowed**   Cr.   Dr.   **Discounts Received**   Cr.

May			£					May			£
31	Transfer from	CB	2 40					31	Transfer from	CB	4 00

SALES LEDGER   **BOUGHT LEDGER**

J. M. Hughes   **H. Hanson & Co.**

Apl.			£	May		£		May			£	Apl.			£
30	b/f		40 00	12	Cheque & discount	38 00 2 00		3	Cheque & discount		57 00 3 00	30	b/f		60 00

G. Dawson   **L. Lowe & Son**

May			£	May		£		May			£	May			£
2	SDB		8 00	25	Cash & discount	7 60 0 40		24	Cash & discount		19 00 1 00	5	PDB		20 00

Posting of cash discount

Cash discount is recorded in the discount column of the three-column cash book, now brought into use. The discount is entered in this column, for convenience, at the side of the payment to which it relates.

In the illustration, Hughes and Dawson are debtors owing £40 and £8 respectively. When they pay their accounts, they are allowed 5% cash discount, and so actually pay £38 and £7.60 in *full settlement*.

The discount debits of £2 and £0.40 are shown at the side of their related payments of £38 and £7.60, and the combined totals of cash and discount (£38 + £2) and (£7.60 + £0.40) are taken to the *credit and in full settlement* of the debtors' sales ledger accounts. This means that these discount debits must be accounted for as losses and expenses of the business. Consequently, at the end of the month, the total of the debit discount column is taken (transferred) to the *debit of discounts allowed account* in the nominal ledger.

Similarly with *discounts received*, on the credit side of the cash book. Hanson & Co. and Lowe & Son are creditors with amounts owing to them of £60 and £20 respectively. Again, advantage is taken of the 5% cash discount offered by these two firms for prompt settlement of their outstanding accounts, and net payments are sent by the buying firm to their suppliers of £57 and £19 respectively in *full settlement*. Since these amounts have been accepted in full settlement, the combined amounts of (£57 + £3) and (£19 + £1) are posted to the *debit of the creditors' bought ledger accounts*. In this instance small gains have been made by the purchasing firm through the prompt payment of these two accounts, and the total of the discounts received column will be *transferred*, at the end of the month, to the *credit of discounts received account* in the nominal ledger.

Final destination for cash discounts

The total of discounts allowed account is debited to profit and loss account, at the end of the trading period, as a loss and expense to the business. The *discounts received account* total, as a profit and gain to the business, is taken to the credit of profit and loss account.

Pause for thought

Discuss the difference between trade and cash discount. Why is the former not recorded in the books at all, and why is the debit discount column a loss to the business, and the credit discount column a small profit or gain?

Assignments

Key Points
1 Note that discount columns are not balanced. They are merely totalled, normally on a slightly raised horizontal above the cash and bank totals.

   In a way similar to day book procedure, the debit and/or credit discount totals, at the end of the month, are *transferred* to the discounts allowed and discounts received accounts in the nominal ledger.
2 The debit discount total in the cash book *remains a debit* because the double entry has already been dealt with by the posting of *both the net payment and the discount to the credit of* the debtor's ledger account.
3 Similarly with the credit discount total. It *remains a credit* because the double entry has already been completed by the *joint posting of the discount and the net payment to the debit* of the creditor's account.

21.1 Post up the transactions listed below in the books of Deborah Kay for the month of September. Bank all incoming cheques on the day of receipt and balance up her three-column cash book on 30 September.

Sept.		£
1	Bank balance brought forward	320.30
	Cash balance	42.40
3	Cash sales	76.20
	Paid Julian Lamb's August account of £60 less 5% cash discount.	
8	Cash sales	35.15
	Paid wages in cash	66.60
	Bought stationery	8.35
12	Cash sales	86.84
	Paid £100 cash into bank	
	Received cheque for £40 less 5% cash discount from Michele Sayle	
16	Janthea St. Just paid her August bill of £70 less 5%	
	Cash purchases	9.15
	Paid Jennifer Grey's account of £48 less 5% cash discount	
22	Emrys Jones called and paid £32 cash in settlement of his old account for £32.80. This was accepted.	
26	Cash sales	63.50
	Paid wages out of cash	66.60
30	Drew cheque for 'self'	60.00
	Paid all surplus cash into bank leaving a cash float of	20.00

21.2 Hayley Bayley is a credit customer of The Ashton Gate Company. She owed Ashton Gate £85.50 on 1 April. The following transactions took place during April:

April
4 Hayley Bayley bought further goods from Ashton Gate at the net price of £64.60. She paid her March account, being allowed a cash discount of £3.50.
6 Miss Bayley bought £120 further goods, subject to trade discount of 10%.
8 £10 gross goods returned by Miss Bayley.
10 £4 carriage charged by Ashton Gate.
25 Ashton Gate delivered £40.40 (gross) goods to Miss Bayley, same T.D. as before.

Assuming the two earlier invoices were settled on 9 April by Miss Bayley, write up her ledger account as it would appear in the books of The Ashton Gate Company.

22

The General Journal

We have already used journals (day books) in connection with the original entries for credit purchases and credit sales. Another subsidiary book, the *general journal*, is now brought into use as a memorandum record for transactions of a special or unusual nature which cannot conveniently be taken to another book of original entry.

In the UK, the general journal does not form part of the double entry system, but is used as an aid or a guide to help the ledger clerks with their postings. Examiners, though, sometimes introduce problems into their papers which are to be answered in journal form, even though the subject matter probably would not be journalised in practice. These problems, together with typical questions, would certainly embrace the recording of opening entries, adjustments between ledger accounts, year-end transfers, the correction of errors, and sometimes the journalising of the purchase and sale of fixed assets.

Opening entries

In some examination problems the proprietary capital at the start of the exercise is not disclosed. The student may be expected to find the commencing capital of the owner/proprietor from a list of assets and liabilities such as the following:

Fittings £250;   Machinery £1700;   Opening stock £1400;
Trade debtors: Jones £245   and   Brown £105
Trade creditors: Evans £65   and   Smith £210.

In addition to the assets and liabilities listed above, Frank Lawson, new owner of this business, after settlement of all commitments with the vendor, has the sum of £575 in the business bank account.

The first stage in this type of problem is to list the opening assets and liabilities in the journal in trial balance style, thus:

Opening Entries   1 July

		Debit £	Credit £	
Fittings		250		
Machinery		1700		
Stock on hand		1400		
Bank		575		
Debtors: Jones		245		
Brown		105		
Creditors: Evans			65	
Smith			210	
Capital F. Lawson			4000	◄— the difference or balancing figure
		4275	4275	

The commencing capital of Frank Lawson is worked out by addition and subtraction to give the balancing figure of £4000, also confirmed by the simple accounting equation of $A = C + L$, where A represents the assets, C the proprietor's capital, and L the external liabilities of the business.

If this problem formed part of an exercise, the asset balances would be posted to the debit of their respective accounts in the cash book, the sales ledger and the general ledger; the balances owing to the two creditors would be posted to the credit of their accounts in the bought ledger. In this manner Frank Lawson's new set of accounting books would be put on a proper double entry basis as from the beginning of the trading period commencing 1 July.

It is not usual to total journal entries except in the case of opening entries as shown in the illustration. From the examples below, it will be seen that these details are merely recorded in the journal so that the ledger clerks will understand the reason for the entries and be able to post the debits and credits to their correct locations.

Note the orthodox method of journalising by recording the debit entry first in the left-hand column, with the credit entry underneath in the right-hand column, the wording slightly indented to the right of its upper counterpart.

The brief explanation of the journal entry, typed or written before ruling off the entry, is called the 'narration'.

The General Journal

				£	£
March 5	**Special entries** Cash Fittings/Fixtures a/c Being sale of old cupboard	Dr.		25	25

June 30	Bad debts account
	  Alan Jones
	Irrecoverable balance written
	  off to Bad Debts a/c
		Dr.		14	14

July 9	**Correction of errors**
	T. N. Johnson
	  T. H. Johnstone
	Payment from T. H. Johnstone had
	  been incorrectly posted to the
	  credit of T. N. Johnson
		Dr.		8	8

Sept. 2	Machinery Repairs a/c
	  Machinery (asset) a/c
	Adjustment of item wrongly
	  charged to asset account
		Dr.		15	15

Dec. 31	**Year-end transfers**
	Trading Account
	  Stock at 1 Jan.
	  Purchases for year
	  Carriage inwards
	Transfer of year-end balances
		Dr.	9100		270
					8640
					190

Trial balance errors

The agreement of the trial balance totals should confirm the arithmetical accuracy of the books, but there may be certain undisclosed errors only brought to light through a good system of internal check, a rigid method of control, and in some instances simply the passage of time or a subsequent audit of the books. Five kinds of these errors are now listed.

1 *Error of omission*   This occurs when goods are bought or sold on credit, but the original documents in connection with the purchase or the sale are forgotten or mislaid. In consequence, neither the debit nor the credit entries are posted in the books.

2 *Error of duplication* In this instance the original records become duplicated and the customer is charged double the amount that he actually owes. Normally, this is found and rectified fairly quickly once the monthly statement of the supplying firm has been sent out.

3 *Error of commission* This occurs when the amount, usually a payment, is debited or credited to the account of the wrong person. On the previous page, a payment of £8 was received from T. H. Johnstone but was incorrectly credited to the account of T. N. Johnson, and has now been adjusted through the journal.

4 *Compensating error* Mistakes in arithmetic of similar amounts, often round figures of £10 or £100 commonly occur in additions, subtractions or carry-forwards, in particular in the day book and when the accounting system is not mechanised. For example, the bought day book may have been over-cast by £100 in a carry-forward, and an error also made of £100 on one of the big debtors' accounts with the balance at £100 less than it should be. This would be corrected through the journal by a debit of £100 to the debtor's account and a credit of £100 to Purchases Account.

5 *Error of principle* An amount may have been posted to an expense account instead of to an asset account, or vice versa. Again, see previous page, where the machinery repairs account is being debited, through the journal, with £15 which in the first instance has been wrongly charged to the asset account. This is an important aspect of capital and revenue expenditure.

Pause for thought

Describe the function of the general journal and the purpose in this country for which it is used, more as an aid to the book-keeper/ cashier than as an integral part of the double entry system. In what way does the general journal differ from the bought and sales journals?

Of the five kinds of trial balance errors which might, for a while, remain undetected, say in which category you would place the following:

(*a*) A £100 error in the carry-forward of the bought journal, offset by £100 error in the addition of the cash sales total;

(*b*) Wages of £400 paid to own workmen in erecting their new welding machine, the expense payment being debited to trading account;

(*c*) George Green has been invoiced £15 for goods ordered and sent to Miss Georgina Green.

Assignments

Key Points

1 The necessary requisites of a journal entry are:

   (*a*) the date entered in the journal.

   (*b*) the account to be debited is first shown, with the amount in the first column.

   (*c*) the account to be credited is shown underneath, indented slightly to the right, with the amount in the second (credit) column.

   (*d*) a brief explanation of the purpose of the entry, called the narration, is given before ruling off. With the exception of opening entries, totals are not necessary.

2 In examination problems, where errors are to be corrected through the journal, you are told that *something is wrong*, that a *mistake has been made*, and you are asked to put it right.

   All that is necessary is to *reverse the whole or part* of the incorrect posting already made. As long as you can comprehend what is wrong, it will be simple enough to put it right.

3 Some answers only need a single-sided correction. For example, the sales day book has been over-added by £100 to show an excess of £100 on the sales account. Instead of altering the ledger account, a single-sided journal entry is made on the debit of the journal. This is picked up by the sales ledger clerk and posted to the debit of sales account, to give the correct balance on this account.

22.1 Write up the opening journal entries of Wensley Dale's business from the information given below, and ascertain his commencing capital at 1 January.

	£		£
Premises	6000	Mortgage loan of	5000
Fittings	550	(secured on premises)	
Stock	1010	Machinery at cost	2500
Bank	865	Van valued at	1750
Cash	35	Rates owing	290

Trade debtors:			Trade creditors:
Leo Fraser £425	:		£320 Lesley Mansel
Abe Fisher £160	:		£185 Petra Nutkins

22.2 Journalise the following:

March
2 Bought new electric typewriter and paid by cheque £175
5 Cash purchases £138
12 £52 of goods sold to Anthony Fircone
15 Bought £130 of goods from Horace Heap
20 Sold old typewriter for £45 cash
22 Paid £5 for stationery
27 Drew £50 cheque for 'self'
31 Transferred opening stock of £950 to trading account at month end.

22.3 Make the necessary corrections, through the general journal, of the following:

July
1 A new duplicator bought for £250 has been debited to purchases account.
3 Sales of £38 on credit to Sue Palliser have been wrongly charged to her sister Sarah.
6 A cheque for £20 from A. J. Smith has been credited to the account of his cousin J. A. Smith.
12 Drawings of £25 were found debited to salaries account.
15 Repairs to machinery £75 have been debited to machinery (asset) account.
18 The purchase of a filing cabinet (£80) has been charged to stationery account.
28 The total of the purchases day book for June was found to have been posted to purchases account as £986 instead of the true figure of £968.
30 Bank interest received at end June £8.50 was debited to bank charges account.

Revision Exercise 4

Perdita Gale has a small trading business. Her assets and liabilities are listed at 1 March:

	£		£
Warehouse premises at cost	8000	Stock at 1 March	920
Fittings/fixtures at cost	350	Bank balance	475
Loan from bank (secured on premises)	4000	Cash in hand	55

At this date her trade debtors comprised three accounts:

Maud Foster £48   Judi Birch £60   Melanie West £42

Money was owing on three suppliers' accounts, namely:

Giles Stevens £80   Keith Owen £30   Rupert Kent £140

You are required to open a new set of books and post up Miss Gale's assets and liabilities, including her opening capital. Then you are to post up all the listed transactions shown opposite for the month of March, make up her trading and profit and loss account for the month, and draw up a vertical style balance sheet as at 31 March.

Miss Gale valued her closing stock at 31 March at £850.

The balance sheet of Miss Gale should show clearly her working capital and net assets. Also calculate her gross profit percentage on turnover and the net profit return on her commencing capital at 1 March.

March
2   Cash sales £78
    Sold goods £35 to Judi Birch less 20% trade discount.
    She paid her February account less 5% cash discount.
4   Cash sales £86. Paid £50 into bank.
    Miss Birch returned £5 gross purchases of March 2.
6   Paid part-time typist wages £50 in cash and applied to Inland
    Revenue for her PAYE tax code number, and also made contact with
    Ministry of Social Security with regard to weekly contributions.
    Paid stationery £4 and stamps £2 in cash.
9   Bought £60 of goods from Rupert Kent less 25% T.D. Paid £5
    carriage on purchases. Settled Kent's February account less 5% cash.
11 Returned £12 (gross) merchandise to Rupert Kent.
    Bought £85 filing cabinet. Paid by cheque.
14 Sold £72 of goods to Maud Foster. She paid her old account. Also
    sold £38 of goods to Melody Robson and opened up new credit
    account.
15 Cash sales £126. Cash purchases £6. Paid delivery charges on routine
    credit sales £3 cash. Paid wages £50.
19 Bought £80 of merchandise from Giles Stevens and settled his
    February account less 5% for cash. (*Note:* 'for cash' often implies 'by
    cheque'.)
22 Received credit note for £12 from Giles Stevens for trade discount on
    the purchases of 19 March.
25 Cash sales £140. Paid £50 wages.
    Miss Gale withdrew £100 cash for private use.
30 Paid local secretarial agency £60 for typing services.
31 All surplus cash above £20 paid into bank.

23

Depreciation of Fixed Assets

If you buy a car for £3000 on 1 January, would you expect to be able to sell it for £3000 on 31 December, twelve months later? You would probably consider yourself fortunate to be offered £2200 for a 'trade-in' price or perhaps £1950 from a cash buyer. Machinery and vehicles lose value through wear and tear and the passage of time, and in business the loss in value is regarded as an expense in the same way as any other routine expense of the business. Money has been paid out which will never be recovered, and to assess the true or approximately true trading profit of the business this loss in value of a fixed asset, which is called *depreciation*, must be taken into account.

Most fixed assets (the big exceptions being land and buildings) are subject to permanent shrinkage in value due to wear and tear (vehicles), the passage of time (leases), obsolescence (changes in method, style or fashion), or simply through general wastage and being used up or worked out in the case of coal and lead mines.

Elementary depreciation methods

In elementary book-keeping, it is customary to show the value of each fixed asset on the balance sheet at its commencing book balance as at the beginning of the financial year *less* the deduction for depreciation as charged against profits, the final amount and up-to-date value of the asset on the balance sheet corresponding with the adjusted ledger balance of the asset.

The accounting entries are thus:

(*a*)   a *debit* to profit and loss account of the depreciation amount, reducing the trading profit, and

(*b*)   a *credit* to the particular asset ledger account, with the consequent reduction of its book value.

Apart from the annual and periodic re-valuation of a fixed asset (like loose tools) with the difference in value being adjusted against profits, the two main depreciation methods encountered at first-year level are known as the *fixed instalment method* and the *reducing instalment method*, best explained by illustration:

Ten-year Lease – fixed instalments of £1000 a year

Year 1 Jan. 1	Cheque (original cost)		£ 10000	Dec. 31 Dec. 31	Depreciation P&L a/c Balance c/d		£ 1000 9000
Year 2 Jan. 1	Balance b/d		9000	Dec. 31 Dec. 31	Deprec. P&L a/c Balance c/d		1000 8000
Year 3 Jan. 1	Balance b/d		8000				

Van Account – 25% on the reducing balance

Year 1 Jan. 1	Cheque (original cost)		£ 3200	Dec. 31 Dec. 31	Deprec. P&L a/c Balance c/d		£ 800 2400
Year 2 Jan. 1	Balance b/d		2400	Dec. 31 Dec. 31	Deprec. P&L a/c Balance c/d		600 1800
Year 3 Jan. 1	Balance b/d		1800				

Note the difference between the two methods of elementary depreciation illustrated. The ten-year lease is depreciated by equal instalments of £1000 a year, whereas the van is depreciated by 25% on the *reducing balance of the account*, the depreciation instalments charged against profits also reducing each year.

The sections of the profit and loss accounts and the balance sheets applicable to the depreciation charges and the fixed asset account details will be shown thus:

Profit and Loss Account

Year 1		£	£			
	Deprec. of lease	1000				
	Deprec. of van	800	1800			
Year 2						
	Deprec. of lease	1000				
	Deprec. of van	600	1600			

Balance Sheet

Year 1	Fixed assets	£	£	£
	Lease	10000		
	Less depreciation	1000	9000	
	Van	3200		
	Less depreciation	800	2400	11400
Year 2	Fixed assets			
	Lease	9000		
	Less depreciation	1000	8000	
	Van	2400		
	Less depreciation	600	1800	9800

Scrap value

In instances where fixed instalment depreciation is adopted for machinery or vehicles, the working life of the asset is first estimated, and its likely scrap value on sale or disposal. The scrap value is then deducted from the original cost of the asset, and the residual amount divided by its estimated number of working years, to give the annual charge against profits for *fixed instalment* depreciation.

Say a machine's original cost is £4000, and its working life estimated at 12 years, with a possible scrap value of £400 on its replacement. The fixed annual charge for depreciation would be (£4000 − £400)/12 = £300 a year.

Provision for depreciation account

Aspects of depreciation with a view to replacement costs in today's inflationary world vary a good deal and belong to more advanced accounting. A legal requirement of the Companies Acts, however, in so far as joint-stock limited companies are concerned, is that fixed assets must be shown on the balance sheet at their cost price, the revenue account being debited in the normal way with the annual charge for depreciation with the corresponding credit being taken to a Provision for Depreciation Account, instead of taking it to the credit of the asset account.

This method is more informative to all those interested in the true finances and net worth of a company. The aggregate and cumulative depreciation is built up in the Provision for Depreciation Account, and deducted in total each year, from the original cost of the asset, shown on the balance sheet, in this way:

Machinery Account
(Depreciation by fixed instalments
of £500 a year via provision account)

Year 1 Jan. 1	Cheque for new machine	CB	£ 5000				

Provision for Depreciation Account

Year 1 Dec. 31	Balance c/d		£ 500	Year 1 Dec. 31	Profit & loss a/c		£ 500
Year 2 Dec. 31	Balance c/d		1000	Year 2 Jan. 1 Dec. 31	Balance b/d Profit & loss a/c		500 500
				Year 3 Jan. 1	Balance b/d		1000

The profit and loss account will be debited with the fixed amount of £500 a year, and the asset will be shown on the balance sheet at its *original cost less aggregate depreciation*, thus:

Year 1	*Fixed assets* Machinery at cost *Less* aggregate deprec.		£ 5000 500	£ 4500
Year 2	*Fixed assets* Machinery at cost *Less* aggregate deprec.		5000 1000	4000

Depreciation fund and investment account

The adoption of the provision for depreciation account is simply a change in the book entries and balance sheet presentation. It does not provide for the replacement of the asset at the end of its working life. This further aspect of accounting, where an investment account is opened to provide a replacement fund for the purchase of a new machine (or perhaps a new lease) is beyond the scope of this elementary textbook, and reference to it must be brief, similarly with the next paragraph on the Statements of Standard Accounting Practice.

Statements of Standard Accounting Practice

In more advanced accounting, authorities lay down certain fundamental concepts and rules of procedure in a document briefly referred to as SSAP 2. These accounting authorities insist that revenue accounts and balance sheets will not show 'a true and fair view' of the presentation of the figures unless certain key concepts are followed.

These key concepts would naturally be explained to students on the more advanced courses, and certainly where the final accounts of limited companies are involved. Briefly, these accounting concepts are known as:

(*a*) the *prudence concept*, concerning the actual revenue profit received (not anticipated in advance);

(*b*) the *going-concern concept*, where the belief is that normal trading will continue as before;

(*c*) the *accruals concept*, which lays down that all revenue earned and expense incurred, whether paid or not, shall be brought to account;

(*d*) the *consistency concept*, where the same or similar methods of treatment or valuation are applied each year, and any variation is disclosed.

Pause for thought

Explain what a wasting asset is: give one or two examples, and say how the depreciation should be dealt with in the accounting records.

What is the purpose of writing off depreciation? Is the value of the asset increased by these entries in the accounting records?

Apart from normal wear and tear, give two further instances where merchandise could lose value over a period of time.

Why does the depreciation account provide a more accurate picture of an asset's value on the balance sheet?

In addition to dealing with the paper entries involving depreciation, what safeguard should be taken to ensure that a certain machine can be replaced at the end of its working life?

Assignments

> **Key Points**
> 1 The loss in value of fixed assets is a business expense and chargeable against revenue. If not accounted for, the balance sheet does not present a true picture of the net worth of the assets.
> 2 The writing off of depreciation as a business expense does not in any way affect the cash position of the business. It is purely a book entry or paper adjustment at this stage. In advanced stages of accounting old and obsolete assets are often replaced at the end of their useful life, and various investment safeguards and funds are explained to students.
> 3 When a fixed asset such as a machine or a vehicle is sold, the sum realised on sale is debited to cash and *credited to the asset account.*
>
>   The depreciation charges that have been written off in the past are calculated to the date of the sale, and a profit or loss figure ascertained, as the asset must now be *eliminated from the books.*
>
>   The balance or difference left on the asset account is finally transferred to profit and loss account.

23.1 A machine is anticipated to have a working life of 15 years with a scrap value of one-tenth of its original cost at the end of that period. The original cost was £3000. What kind of depreciation charge should be written off each year if the fixed instalment method is adopted?

23.2   A lease costs £8000 for the term of ten years. Show the asset account for the first two years under what you might consider an appropriate depreciation method.

   £4000 of special machinery is bought on 1 January. Show the machinery account for the first two years, calculating depreciation on the fixed basis of 15% on the reducing balance of the asset.

23.3   Rory Macadam asks you to prepare, from this abbreviated form of trial balance, his final accounts as at 31 December, taking note of the adjustments for depreciation shown underneath.

	£	£
Capital a/c 1 Jan.		8000
Gross profit on trading		9300
Drawings for year	4500	
Debtors/creditors	1250	880
Carriage on sales	45	
Sundry expenses	85	
Machinery 1 Jan.	5400	
Additions during year	600	
Van account 1 Jan.	1200	
Fittings/equipt. 1 Jan.	520	
Discounts	50	60
Wages owing 31 Dec.		300
Salaries for year	4200	
Stock 31 Dec.	2200	
Bank overdraft 31 Dec.		1510
	20050	20050

Allow for depreciation as follows:
(*a*)   10% on the original cost of the machinery which was £9000. Ignore additions, as these were bought in December.
(*b*)   20% on the ledger balance of the van account.
(*c*)   5% on fittings/equipment account.

24

Bad Debts and Provision for Bad Debts

The balances of those debtors who cannot or who persistently refuse to pay their accounts, may, after a period of correspondence, be eventually 'written off' to bad debts account, although proceedings for the recovery of the money owing may continue for some time. Debts which are regarded as irrecoverable, like other business losses and expenses, are transferred at the end of the trading period, via bad debts account, to the debit of profit and loss account.

Later, should the debt or part of it be recovered, the sum received will be debited to the cash book and credited to a bad debts recovered account. Alternatively, the amount recovered from an old debtor may simply be taken to the credit of the current bad debts account, thereby reducing the *net* debit for the year.

Note, however, that amounts recovered from past defaulters are *not credited to their old personal accounts* in the sales ledger as these accounts will have been closed.

Provision for bad debts

Some debts are doubtful, not necessarily bad, though in time a proportion may prove to be irrecoverable. A *specific provision* for bad debts, covering those debts regarded as doubtful, is sometimes made on the lines now to be described. Note that this *provision is additional* to any debts known to be bad that are being written off as deemed irrecoverable.

The provision is normally a small percentage (perhaps 2 or 3%) of the total debtors' balances (net balances after deducting actual bad debts already written off).

In the first instance, when creating the new provision, say 3% of net debtors of £2000, profit and loss account would be debited with £60, and a credit for the same amount (£60) taken to a new account headed provision for bad debts account. The credit balance on this account is shown as a deduction from the trade debtors' total under current assets in the balance sheet. It is important to bear in mind, though, that *this is a paper entry, simply a provision against a possible contingency only*, as every trader and businessman would like to see his doubtful accounts recovered in full.

Once created, the provision account remains a credit balance in the books, subject to annual adjustment, usually dependent upon the increases or decreases in the trade debtors' total at the end of the financial year. In the illustration now shown, note that after the first year (the creation of the provision) only the amount of the *provision increase is debited to revenue*; alternatively, any *provision decrease is credited back to revenue*.

	Debtors' listed totals at year-end	*Actual bad debts to be written off*	*Bad debt provision*
Year 1	£ 2100	£ 100	3% of net balances
Year 2	3150	150	3% of net balances
Year 3	2565	65	3% of net balances

The actual bad debts (in the centre section) will be transferred from the sales ledger accounts to the debit of bad debts account, and then written off to profit and loss account at the end of the trading year.

Dr.   **Provision for Bad Debts Account**   Cr.

			£				£
Year 1	Balance c/d		60	Year 1	P&L a/c (3% of £2000)		60
			=				=
Year 2	Increased prov. carried down at end of second year c/d		90	Year 2	Balance b/d P&L a/c (provision increase to 3% of £3000)		60 30
			=				=
Year 3	Decreased prov. to 3% of £2500 P&L a/c Balance c/d		15 75	Year 3	Balance b/d		90
			=				=
				Year 4	Balance b/d		75

Profit and Loss Account

			£				
Year 1	Bad Debts a/c Prov. for B/Ds a/c		100 60				
Year 2	Bad Debts a/c Prov. for B/Ds a/c		150 30				
Year 3	Bad Debts a/c		65	Year 3	Prov. decrease written back		15

Balance Sheet

		£	£
Year 1	Current assets Trade debtors Less provision	2000 60	1940
Year 2	Current assets Trade debtors Less provision	3000 90	2910
Year 3	Current assets Trade debtors Less provision	2500 75	2425

Note that the actual bad debts each year are first deducted from the sales ledger balances *before* the operation of the provision. When first created, the new provision amount (£60) is debited to profit and loss account and credited to the new provision account. The trading profit is reduced by this £60, and on the balance sheet the trade debtors are reduced by the same amount.

In the second year, the net debtors' total has increased to £3000. Again, maintaining the same provision percentage, the provision is now to be increased to £90 (3% of £3000). But there is already a credit of £60 on the provision account, so that it is only necessary to debit an additional sum of £30 to profit and loss account in this second year. The corresponding credit is taken to the provision account, thereby increasing the provision to £90 at the end of this second year.

In the third year, the total of the trade debtors has been reduced to £2500, so that a provision of £75 (3% of £2500) only is required for this year. But since we already have a credit of £90 on provision account, £15 of this credit balance will now be recouped by the reverse process of crediting profit and loss account with the £15 written back, and debiting provision account with £15. This now leaves the balance of £75 as the adjusted and correct new provision as at the end of the third year.

Note that it is always the final adjusted figure on the provision account which is to be deducted from the trade debtors' total shown under current assets on the balance sheet.

Pause for thought

What is the difference between writing off as a bad debt the account of a defaulting customer, and the creation of a specific provision for bad debts?

Explain the difference between insolvency, being financially embarrassed temporarily, and being made a bankrupt.

Assignments

> **Key Points**
> 1 Sometimes the provision account is combined with the bad debts account, the balance of the joint account being taken to the profit and loss account at the year end.
> 2 The main difference between the two accounts, though, is that the bad debts account is a record of actual loss and expense suffered by the firm, whereas the provision account may be looked upon as more in the nature of a form of insurance against possible loss, and to show the trade debtors on the balance sheet at a conservative figure.
> 3 Amounts recovered from past defaulters are credited to the current bad debts account, or sometimes to a bad debts recovered account. In either case, they serve to reduce the actual bad debts at the end of the trading session.
> 4 After the creation of a new provision for bad debts, only the *difference between the old and the new provisions* is transferred to the profit and loss account, to the debit if an increase and to the credit if the provision is reduced.
> 5 The net total of the trade debtors (with actual bad debts already deducted) is shown under current assets on the balance sheet, *less the last credit balance* shown on the recently made up provision for bad debts account.

24.1 Luellen Blake has built up a small but profitable retail business, mainly on credit trade. Three years ago her accountant introduced an annual provision of 5% as a safeguard against bad and doubtful debts.

Her trade debtors' balances for last year totalled £4300 and for the current year £5800. The actual bad debts written off debtors' accounts and transferred to bad debts account amounted to £32 this year, and a payment of £24 had been received on account of an old debt written off two years ago.

Make up Miss Blake's bad debts and her provision for bad debts account for the year just ended at 31 December.

24.2 On 30 June a year ago, the provision for bad debts in Matthew Cole's books showed a credit balance of £440. During the year he had written off actual bad debts of £72, and an amount of £18 was recovered from an old customer who had returned from Melbourne; his ledger account had been written off two years ago. Trade debtors' balances for the current year totalled £7400.

You are required to maintain the provision at 5%, make up the main accounts affected, and show how the profit and loss account of Mr Cole is adjusted.

24.3 On 31 December, the following sales ledger balances were extracted from the books of Cavendish Smith:

	£		£
Angela Ward	280	Godfrey Bean	63
Trisha Benton	98	Rebecca Lawson	158
Pamela Potter	86	Oliver Fairfax	165

During the trading year ended 31 December two small accounts totalling £36 had been written off to bad debts account. The trustee in bankruptcy of one of these debtors on 20 December paid a dividend of 25% on Cavendish Smith's claim for £24.

The bad debt provision on the previous balance sheet was £48. It was decided to reduce this to 4% on the total debtors' balances for this year.

Make up the bad debts and provision for bad debts account, and show how the provision account will appear on this year's balance sheet.

25

Year-end Adjustments

The costs and expenses *incurred* during an accounting period are not necessarily those which are paid during that same period. The *real income*, too, earned during that period, may also be quite different from the actual payments received from customers and income from other sources.

Certain adjustments and amendments with regard to the trading profit of a business have been explained in the last two chapters. Further adjustments are often necessary to arrive at the true expenditure and the correct trading profit.

Prepayments or payments in advance

A payment made in advance indicates that money has been paid before the last date of the accounting period for a *benefit still to be received* (in the next accounting period). This often applies to local rates, where advance payment is always demanded, and to various insurances paid on certain dates throughout the business year, normally providing cover for the full calendar year.

The adjustment is made on the nominal account, the amount not yet used up being credited to the account and brought down as a debit balance, and shown on the balance sheet under the heading of current assets. The revenue debit is reduced by this advance payment, thus increasing the trading profit by the same amount.

In the example now shown, the annual premiums are paid to the insurance company on 31 March and 30 June providing cover for the full twelve months. Assuming the financial year ends on 31 December, a proportionate adjustment must be made charging only £21 against the profits in this year, and £11 is carried forward for unexpired insurance, and shown as a current asset on the balance sheet.

Dr. **Insurance Account** Cr.

Mar. 31	Cheque	CB	£ 20	Dec. 31	P&L a/c ¾ of £20 = 15		£
June 30	Cheque	CB	12		½ of £12 = 6		21
				31	Prepayment c/d		11
			32				32
Jan. 1	Balance b/d		11				

Accrued or outstanding expenses

Certain expenses may be owing at the date of the balance sheet. Among these typical expenses are wages and salaries due to the firm's own employees, and accounts probably invoiced but unpaid for advertising, gas, electricity and printing.

Again, a two-way adjustment is involved, this time *increasing the debit to revenue*, and bringing down, on the actual expense account, the *amount owing as a credit balance*, to be shown under current liabilities on the balance sheet.

Weekly wages are normally paid on a Thursday or a Friday, made up to the preceding day or sometimes two days beforehand.

In the wages account shown below, the sum of £9040 has actually been paid out up to 28 June, but since the firm's financial year ends on 30 June, two days' pay (say £80) is owing to the daily paid employees at the balance sheet date.

The wages account is adjusted in this way:

Wages Account

June 30	Total wages actually paid (CB summary)	£ 9040	June 30	Trading account (Wages paid plus wages due)	£ 9120
30	Wages owing c/d	80			
		9120			9120
			July 1	Creditors for wages b/d	80

The credit balance on wages account will be shown on the balance sheet at 30 June, following trade creditors, under current liabilities.

Adjustments in final accounts: Illustration

Robert Morris owns a small machine shop and retail business. The following balances were extracted from his books on 31 December, the end of his financial year:

Trial Balance   31 December

	£	£
Capital account: R. Morris 1 Jan.		30 000
Drawings for year	3 500	
Freehold premises at cost	25 000	
Machinery/equipment a/c bal. 1 Jan.	3 000	
Fittings, book balance 1 Jan.	400	
Van, book balance 1 Jan.	600	
Trade debtors/creditors	1 800	1 400
Bank overdraft		730
Cash in hand	25	
Bad debts provision account		120
Purchases and sales	8 500	23 250
Returns inwards/outwards	110	75
Carriage on purchases	145	
Carriage on sales	185	
Lighting/heating	330	
General expenses	665	
Discounts allowed/received	95	270
Commissions received		2 135
Advertising	400	
Bad debts written off	25	
Wages (storehouse and shop)	8 000	
Office salaries	4 000	
Stock on 1 January	1 200	
	57 980	57 980

In making up the final accounts of Robert Morris as at 31 December, the following adjustments and amendments are to be taken into account:

(a) Stock at 31 December valued at £1450.

(b) Rates pre-paid £400 (in general expenses account).

(c) Wages owing on 31 December £600; salaries owing £150.

(d) The bad debts provision account stands at £120 in the books. The provision for the current year is to be reduced to 5% of the debtors' total at 31 December.

(e) During the year Mrs Morris, wife of the proprietor, had taken goods for family use amounting to £245 at cost.

(f) Fittings are to be depreciated by 10% of their book value; vans by 20%, and machinery and equipment also by 20% of their book value at 1 January.

150   *Basic Accounting*

(g)   Carry forward 50% of the advertising debit, as this was recently incurred, and the benefit expected in the New Year.

(h)   The lighting/heating debit for £330 is to be split evenly between the trading account and the profit and loss account.

The model answer to this exercise should prove useful to the student for reference.

**Trading and Profit and Loss Account
for the year ended 31 December**

	£	£		£	£
Stock 1 Jan.		1 200	Sales	23 250	
Purchases	8 500		*Less* returns inwards	110	23 140
Add carriage inwards	145		Stock 31 Dec.	——	1 450
	——		N.B. Closing stock is		
	8 645		credited to trading account		
Less returns outwards £75			simply to emphasise a few of		
& goods for own use 245	320	8 325	the additional debits		
	——		in this instance.		
Wages	£8 000				
Wages owing	600	8 600			
	——				
Lighting/heating (50%)		165			
Gross profit c/d		6 300			
		24 590			24 590
Salaries	£4 000		Gross profit b/d		6 300
Add salaries owing	150	4 150	Discounts received		270
Carriage outwards	——	185	Commissions received		2 135
Lighting/heating (50%)		165	Decrease in bad debt		
Discounts allowed		95	provision (£120 less new		
Bad debts written off		25	provision of £90)		30
Advertising	£400				
Less carry forward	200	200			
	——				
General expenses	£665				
Less rates in advance	400	265			
	——				
Depreciation:					
Machinery/equipt.	£600				
Van	120				
Fittings	40	760			
Net trading profit	——				
transferred to Capital a/c		2 890			
		8 735			8 735

In many small retail businesses, some of the available stock for sale (in particular foodstuffs) is taken for the use and consumption of the proprietor and his family. The correct adjustment is to *debit the owner's drawings account and credit purchases account* at the cost price of the merchandise. In this instance the cost of the goods withdrawn by Mrs Morris (£245) is deducted from purchases on the debit of trading account, and added to her husband's drawings in the capital account section of the balance sheet.

An ordinary bank overdraft is a current liability, but a long-term loan made to the business (or a mortgage) is shown as a *fixed liability* under its own heading, positioned between the capital account and the current liabilities.

The new provision for bad debts is £90 (5% of the debtors' listed total). This new provision supersedes the old provision of £120 shown on the trial balance. This means that the £30 excess is no longer required and may now be *written back* (credited) to profit and loss account. Remember, too, that it is always the *last provision* to be deducted from trade debtors on the balance sheet.

The reason for the carry-forward of £200 advertising has been explained in the list of adjustments. The nominal account for advertising will have been adjusted to show this £200 as a *debit balance*, but remember that the expense has already been paid, and consequently this item is a *fictitious asset as it is not realisable*. Do not confuse with rates in advance, a benefit still to be used up, and if premises became unoccupied a claim for repayment could be made.

The working capital of this business is found simply by deducting current liabilities from current assets (ignoring the advertising expenditure carried forward) thus:

	£
Current or circulating assets	3585
Less current liabilities	2880
To give the working capital of	705

Balance sheet in vertical or report form

Most of the balance sheets drawn up in large-scale industry, and certainly all those of public limited companies, are presented in vertical narrative style to allow interested parties (company members, debenture holders, bankers and the creditors) to see at a glance the true state of the company's finances, its varied type of assets, its commitments to members and the full extent of its outside liabilities.

The balance sheet of Robert Morris as at 31 December drawn up below shows the net assets and the working capital of the business: comparison with last year's figures would be shown in brief in the right margin. Bear in mind, though, that a limited company balance sheet would show more detail of the *aggregate depreciation* of the fixed assets, and the capital section would be entirely different, showing the various classes of shares, reserves and undistributed revenue profits etc.

Balance Sheet of Robert Morris
as at 31 December

Assets employed				Last year's figures
		£	£	£
Fixed assets				
Freehold premises at cost		25 000		
Fittings less depreciation		360		
Machinery/equipment less depreciation		2 400		
Motor van, less depreciation		480	28 240	
Current assets	£			
Stock　31 Dec.		1 450		
Trade debtors	£1 800			
Less provision	90	1 710		
Rates in advance		400		
Cash in hand		25	3 585	
Current liabilities				
Trade creditors		1 400		
Bank overdraft		730		
Expense creditors		750	2 880	
Working capital			705	
Net assets			28 945	
Advertising expenditure carried forward			200	
			29 145	
Financed by				
Proprietary capital		£		
Capital account: Robert Morris 1 Jan.		30 000		
Add net trading profit for year		2 890		
		32 890		
Less drawings (£3500 + £245)		3 745		
			29 145	

Assignments

> **Key Points**
> 1 A prepayment (or payment in advance) refers to a benefit still to be used up. The amount paid in advance is deducted from its related debit on the profit and loss account, thereby increasing the trading profit.
>
>   The debit balance brought down on the expense account is listed on the balance sheet after trade debtors.
> 2 Year-end adjustments are dealt with between the trial balance and final account stage. It will be found useful to mark the items affected by these adjustments with the pencilled amount of the adjustment to be made.
> 3 An accrual or outstanding expense (wages/salaries owing and various expense bills unpaid) increases the debit to trading or profit and loss account and reduces the net profit. The credit balance brought down on the nominal expense account will be shown after trade creditors on the balance sheet.
>
>   In so far as *expense* creditors are concerned, think of the debt or money owing as being owed to a firm or organisation which has already supplied your own firm with gas, water, electricity etc.

25.1 This is the insurance account of a small trader at 31 December, the end of his trading year:

Insurance Account

			£			
Mar. 31	Fire insurance	CB	36			
Jul. 1	Motor insurance	CB	84			
Oct. 31	Employers' liability	CB	18			

All payments relate to full premiums paid. Complete this account to show the correct debit to revenue at the year end, and also show the balance sheet details.

25.2   Geoffrey Webb works a five-day week. Wages owing to his employees on 30 June amounted to £662. His wages sheets made up to the last pay day in the current year totalled £18 444. Show the net debit to revenue and how the item 'Wages owing' will appear on the balance sheet.

25.3   Valerie Seal balances her books on 31 December. Among other items on her trial balance are these two debits:

Electricity £180   :   Rates paid £260

The invoice for last quarter's electricity £38 was received early in the New Year. The amount of £180 refers to payments for the three previous quarters.

A cheque for £130 for the second instalment of the full year's rates had been paid on 8 October.

Miss Seal has been in business for one year. Complete her nominal ledger accounts to show the net debits to revenue, and also show how the adjusted items will appear on her balance sheet at 31 December.

Examination Exercise

Sole Trader's Accounts   **First-year paper**

ALL QUESTIONS TO BE ANSWERED TWO HOURS ALLOWED

Key Points

1 In book-keeping examinations, accuracy and neatness are mark-earning features, and the ability to *work at speed* is equally important, as marks cannot be awarded for questions not attempted.

2 Establish your confidence by tackling the smaller and easier questions first, ensuring that they have in fact been answered to the best of your ability, and that you will not be penalised through running out of time in the rush work of the last half-hour.

3 Accept the fact that few examinees manage to get *their accounts* to balance. A good deal of time is lost by candidates looking for mistakes made in balancing, time which could be put to better purpose. It is likely to be far more rewarding to aim at good average marks on the examination paper as a whole, rather than spend too much time on a large question, even though this question will carry maximum marks. Work as fast as you can on the larger problems, but when difficulties occur in balancing, and after a rapid re-check there is still a difference, *proceed to the next question* with all speed. If there is still time left before the papers are handed in, you can renew your re-checking after the completion of the remainder of the paper.

1   When checking and preparing information for the final accounts of Keith Warren for his financial year ended 31 December, you make a note of the following listed items.

   (*a*)   Repairs to van £68 had been charged to Van (asset) Account.

   (*b*)   A payment of £25 from Marilyn Ross, sub-tenant of Keith Warren, has been debited to the business Rates Account.

   (*c*)   The trustee in bankruptcy of Sara Booth has recently sent a cheque for £36, being the first and final dividend of 40p in the pound of a sum written off her account two years ago. The firm's cashier has posted the payment to the credit of the debtor's old account.

   (*d*)   Included in purchases is an amount of £820, and in wages an amount of £350, both payments made in connection with the construction of a new showroom for the business.

   (*e*)   The sales ledger account of Hilton Mills has been credited with a cheque payment of £40 received from Milton Hills.

   Make the necessary amendment or correction through the Journal.

2   The warehouse stock of Sharon Lane was destroyed by fire in the early hours of 1 July, except for a small salvaged amount valued at £240. Miss Lane's accounting period was the normal calendar year. Her accountant provides you with this information:

	£
Stock valuation 31 December (six months previous)	2 200
Purchases (1 January to 30 June)	6 366
Net sales (1 January to 30 June)	14 880
Warehouse wages for six months	5 600

   Prepare a draft trading account from this information, taking as the approximate figure for the gross profit a three-yearly average of 30% based upon the turnover of Miss Lane's business for the six months ended 30 June. State the amount of the claim for the destroyed stock to be made against the insurance company.

3   Titian Molloy owns a small dress-making business. The account balances listed below were extracted from her books at 30 June, the close of her financial accounting year.

   For information only, the loan to Miss Molloy's friend Dinah Marsden is only of a temporary nature, to be repaid early in July. Interest has been waived.

Trial Balance   30 June

	£	£
Capital account 1 July		12 000
Drawings for year	4 800	
Fittings/fixtures 1 July	1 420	
Additions during year	280	
Machinery/equipment 1 July	2 800	
Stock 1 July	1 450	
Purchases and returns	6 600	240
Sales and returns	280	18 680
Carriage inwards	88	
Carriage outwards	135	
Trade debtors/creditors	2 400	1 310
Expense creditors		75
Bad debts provision		160
Bad debts to be written off	120	
Wages of machinists	5 340	
Office salaries	3 800	
Discounts allowed/received	66	235
Commissions received		2 540
Advertising	1 350	
Lighting, heating and power	1 250	
Rent and rates	900	
Postages/stationery	36	
General expenses	72	
Cash at bank	1 023	
Cash in hand	30	
Loan to Dinah Marsden	1 000	
	35 240	35 240

In making up the final accounts for Miss Molloy, you are to take into account the following year-end adjustments:

(*a*)   Closing stock at 30 June was valued at £2850.

(*b*)   Insurance pre-paid £25 (debited to general expenses).

(*c*)   Lighting, heating and power expense is to be apportioned between the trading account and the profit and loss account three-fifths and two-fifths.

(*d*)   The advertising debit comprises a special campaign launched in May, and £500 is to be carried forward into the next financial year.

(*e*)   The bad debt provision is to be maintained at 5% of the total trade debtors' figure.

(*f*)   When questioned about goods withdrawn, Miss Molloy confirmed that she had taken material for her own use at the cost price of £180.

(*g*)   Fixtures and fittings are to be depreciated by 20% on the book balance of the asset, including the additions.

(*h*)   Machinery and equipment is to be depreciated by 20% on the book value at the beginning of the year.

4   (*a*)   There is a credit balance of £120.56 in the bank column of your cash book. This has been brought down from the debit on 31 December. Would you show this on your balance sheet as a
(i) fixed asset   (ii) current asset   (iii) current liability?

(*b*)   If your bad debt provision is decreased, would this mean
(i) a smaller gross profit   (ii) a larger net profit
(iii) an increase in trade debtors on the balance sheet?

5   Post up the Office Equipment Account of Anita d'Alvis from the information now given:

		£
1 January	Balance of account brought forward from last year	280
22 March	New filing cabinet bought	95
17 April	Old cabinet sold for	22
	(originally cost £35; shown in books at cost)	
28 July	Bought new table and chairs	240
	Also timber for shelving	56
	Paid carpenter for work done	24
12 August	Sold old table and chairs	20
	(at original cost of £48 in books)	
5 December	Paid for repairs to old cupboard and desk	38

6   These are entries in the rent account of RHJ Textiles Ltd:

		£			£
Jan. 5	Cheque – quarter's rent on 15 Main Street	200	Jan. 6	Cheque – quarter's rent on 20 Main Street	200

Two young sisters, Sara and Simone, came to Preston from Avignon ten years ago and took up employment at the local textile mill. They rented a house in Main Street and one sister still lives there. Sara married a wealthy widower five years back, bought another house in Main Street, and when her husband died went to live in Blackpool. The Company now pays the rent on Sara's house for one of the managers. At what address does Simone live, number 15 or number 20?

26

Incomplete Records and Single Entry

Single entry

The term 'single entry' implies the absence of a complete system of double entry. Where records are incomplete, the accountant must make use of all the available information he can find, estimating some of his figures by simple reasoning processes. The trading profit is found in this way by approximation.

Generally a rough form of cash book has been kept, and bank accounts are now in common use, even by small businesses. Year-end accounts must be made up for submission to the Inland Revenue, otherwise the trader will probably receive a grossly inflated assessment on assumed profits.

Where few records are kept

If accounts have not been prepared before, and there are neither records of business property nor of revenue income or expenditure, the visible existing assets should be verified, listed and valued. Then, checking backwards through a process of questioning and elimination, it should be possible to arrive at an approximate figure of the asset/liability position one year back.

To a large extent, the accountant has to rely upon his client's memory. Often the biggest complication is to agree with the proprietor the amount of his personal drawings. Even if a rough cash book has been kept, rarely will the physical cash on hand, or in the till, agree with the 'book' balance according to the cash book. The large discrepancy is assumed to be 'drawings'.

Profit statement

The calculation of the profit or loss by the increased (or decreased) net worth method simply entails the listing and comparison of the known or approximated value of the assets and liabilities between the two periods, say of one year ago and today. The accounting equation $A = C + L$ is then brought into use, where A = assets, C = capital and L = liabilities.

Calculation

(a)	List the known assets and liabilities at the year-end to establish the *closing capital* of	£4800
(b)	Similarly, as far as possible, list the known and approximated assets and liabilities of one year ago to establish the *commencing capital* of	3500
(c)	*Add back* the approximated figure for proprietor's drawings	2200
(d)	*Deduct* any additional capital brought into the business	800

Statement of Profit

		£
Increase of net assets (£4800 − 3500)		1300
Add back drawings		2200
		3500
Deduct additional capital brought in		800
	Trading profit	£2700

The closing capital account, shown in its conventional form on the balance sheet, is a check on the arithmetic of this estimated profit:

Capital account	£	£
Balance 1 January (one year ago)	3500	
Additions during year	800	
Ascertained trading profit	2700	
	7000	
Less drawings for year	2200	4800

The existence of a bank account makes working on incomplete records much easier. A double entry basis can be built up from a break-down summary of the recorded items on the bank statements, together with up to date information of the fixed assets, stock valuation and lists of trade debtors and creditors.

Examination question

A typical examination question is now illustrated. A statement of affairs (balance sheet) of Adam Smith has been established as at the beginning of the trading period, one year ago. This is followed by a cash summary in total form, and there are a number of year-end adjustments to be taken into account when making up the final accounts for the year.

Cash and bank have been lumped together, quite usual in this style of question.

Statement of Affairs
as at 1 January

	£		£
Capital account: Adam Smith		Premises at cost	4000
Balance 1 Jan.	6000	Fittings/equipment	850
Trade creditors	775	Stock	930
Expense creditors	25	Trade debtors	770
		Cash/bank	250
	6800		6800

Cash summary for the year

		£			£
Cash/bank balances b/f		250	Office salaries & NIC		1800
			Wages & NIC		2460
Cash sales total for year		6980	Cash purchases		326
			New counter		440
Cash/cheques from credit			Payments to suppliers		4350
customers		5150	Proprietor's drawings		1800
			Insurance		95
			Rates		120
			General expenses		89
			Balance c/d		900
		12380			12380
Balance b/d		900			

Adam Smith's current assets and liabilities at the year-end were:
Stock £1130 : trade debtors £810 : trade creditors £660
The year-end adjustments to be taken into account are:

(*a*) Wages due to sales assistants £42
(*b*) Rates pre-paid at 31 December £30
(*c*) Included in general expenses is a payment of £25 for an electricity bill shown as owing on the statement of affairs a year ago.
(*d*) Another bill for £32 is now due for electricity.
(*e*) Depreciate fittings and equipment by 10% on closing balance.

Solution

First of all, the figures for credit purchases and credit sales are established on these lines by making up *total accounts* for both debtors and creditors:

Total Debtors

		£			£
Jan. 1	Balance b/f	770	Dec. 31	CB receipts	5150
Dec. 31	CREDIT SALES	5190	Dec. 31	Balance c/d	810
		5960			5960
Jan. 1	Balance b/d	810			

Total Creditors

		£			£
Dec. 31	CB payments	4350	Jan. 1	Balances b/f	775
Dec. 31	Balances c/d	660	Dec. 31	CREDIT PURCHASES	4235
		5010			5010
			Jan. 1	Balance b/d	660

Note that there are four basic elements to this type of problem: commencing balances, purchases or sales for the period, payments made, and the closing balances. Given any three of these elements, the fourth can quickly be found.

Trading and Profit and Loss Account
for the year ended 31 December

		£		£
Stock 1 Jan.		930	Credit sales	5190
Credit purchases		4235	Cash sales	6980
Cash purchases		326	Stock 31 Dec.	1130
Wages	2460			
Wages owing	42	2502		
Gross profit c/d		5307		
		13300		13300
Salaries		1800	Gross profit b/d	5307
Insurance		95		
Rates	120			
In advance	30	90		
General expenses				
(£89 − 25 + 32)		96		
Depreciation of fittings		129		
Net trading profit		3097		
		5307		5307

Balance Sheet of Adam Smith
as at 31 December

		£	
Fixed assets			
Premises at cost		4000	
Fittings/equipt.	£850		
additions	440		
	1290		
less deprec.	129	1161	
		5161	
Current assets			
Stock 31 Dec.	£1130		
Debtors	810		
Rates in advance	30		
Cash/bank	900	2870	
		8031	
Capital and liabilities		£	
Capital balance 1 Jan.	£6000		
add net trading profit	3097		
	9097		
less drawings	1800	7297	
Current liabilities			
Trade creditors	£660		
Creditors for wages	42		
Expense creditors	32	734	
		8031	

Remember that all year-end adjustments are two-sided. Both debit and credit entries are involved. Revenue gains and losses are adjusted on the profit and loss account.

Pause for thought

There is a similarity between some incomplete record type of questions and the accounts of non-trading concerns (see the following chapter). In both instances it is often necessary to establish the final cash/bank balance for the balance sheet; often, too, forms of total accounts are needed to work out the purchases/sales in one case, and the correct subscriptions for the season in the other case.

In first-level Accounting examinations, the likelihood of getting one of these problems, as illustrated in Chapters 26 and 27, is fairly high.

Assignments

26.1   Zoë Chapati's accountant lists his client's assets and liabilities at the beginning and at the end of her second trading year as follows:

		1 January £	31 December £
Stock		850	920
Trade debtors		440	550
Trade creditors		310	380
Expense creditors		—	25
Fittings and fixtures		660	1375
Loan from sister		1000	800
Bank balance		230	150

Zoë had withdrawn a regular £30 a week for her personal use, and had taken provisions from the business for family use averaging £6 a week. She had sold her private car for £600 and bought £500 of new fittings and equipment for the business out of the car proceeds. Towards the end of the year, she withdrew £1000 from the business to put down as a deposit for a new private car.

Calculate Miss Chapati's profit for the year and show her balance sheet as at 31 December.

26.2 Saffron St Cloud is a milliner. She has a high class business in the centre of Hereford. Her statement of affairs at 31 December is now shown:

	£	£		£	£
Capital 31 Dec.		6000	*Fixed assets*		
Current liabilities			Machinery	4400	
Trade creditors	£635		Van	600	5000
Bank overdraft	290				
Wages owing	75	1000	*Current assets*		
			Stock	1025	
			Debtors	960	
			Cash	15	2000
		7000			7000

Her transactions for the following month of January are summarised in total form and listed below:

		£
1	Cash sales (cost price of goods £175)	280
2	Paid into bank	100
3	Cash purchases	20
4	Paid cheque for second-hand van	800
5	Received cheque for old van	550
6	Additional stock bought on credit	420
7	Sales to credit customers (cost price £640)	880
8	Sent cheques to suppliers	330
9	Cheques received from trade debtors	590
10	Paid expense creditors (wages owing—see BS)	75
11	Paid various expenses in cash	35
12	Proprietor's withdrawals in cash	40

You are required to draft a new balance sheet for Miss St Cloud as at 31 January, taking into account all the above transactions and finding her net trading profit for the month of January.

26.3 Ralph Edwards' statement of affairs, drawn up on 1 January, a year ago, is shown in brief detail:

	£		£
Capital (the balancing figure)	16500	Premises at cost	10000
Trade creditors	1500	Fittings/equipment	2100
		Stock 1 Jan.	3300
		Trade debtors	2400
		Bank/cash	200
	18000		18000

His accountant estimated his drawings for the year at £8300, after making up a cash summary of totals extracted from a rough cash book and the bank statements of Mr Edwards:

	£		£
Balance b/f	200	Cash purchases	1800
Cash takings	18130	Wages and NIC	6600
Payments from		New counter & shelving	4400
credit customers	9270	Rates and insurance	450
		Payments to suppliers	5500
		General expenses	120
		Drawings	8300
		Balance in hand	430
	27600		27600

On 31 December, the end of his financial year, the current assets and liabilities were:

Stock £4500   Debtors £3200   Creditors £1800

You are required to make up a revenue account and a balance sheet at 31 December for Mr Edwards, taking three adjustments into the accounts:

Rates in advance £80   Wages owing £140
Fittings and equipment to be revalued at £6000.

27

Non-trading Concerns and Club Accounts

Most clubs, societies and associations are non-trading organisations. They derive their main source of income from subscriptions and donations, and, as a general rule, allocate their surplus funds to the purpose or the project for which they have been formed; alternatively their surplus revenue is used to improve or develop their activities and amenities for their members.

Receipts and payments account

Small clubs and societies have few assets other than a local bank account and probably some printed stationery. The book-keeping records of this kind of organisation (where expenditure on furniture and/or games equipment is unnecessary) are simple and uncomplicated. The form of account produced by the treasurer at the end of the year or the season is easily understood by members. It is necessary only to draw up a receipts and payments account, which is simply a cash summary for the period covered by the account. This is an illustration of a receipts and payments account:

The Over-Sixty Social Club
Receipts and Payments Account for year ended 30 June

	£			£	
Cash in hand 1 July	24	50	Postages/stationery	12	20
Subscriptions rec'd			Hire of local hall	150	00
(124 members at £2)	248	00	Lighting/heating	55	40
Donations	15	00	Refreshments bought	102	80
Gross proceeds from			Prizes purchased	250	00
whist drives and			Donation to Oxfam	25	00
socials	350	00	General expenses	16	70
			Balance of cash		
			in hand 30 June c/d	25	40
	637	50		637	50
Cash in hand 30 June	25	40			

The receipts and payments account, shown above, is a brief summary of money received and money paid out during the year. Every receipt, subscription and donation is included in the total summary, and every payment made is also included in total form. No distinction is made between capital and revenue expenditure; this of course would probably be unnecessary in the case of a small society as all incoming cash and payments would be regarded for revenue purposes only, with no attempt made to show financial gain or loss beyond the difference in the commencing and closing cash balances.

This statement is simply a summarised copy of the club's cash book, and cash and bank have simply been combined for the sake of ease in comprehension by members.

Income and expenditure account

The receipts and payments account is incomplete in so far as real financial information is concerned. Clubs and societies of any size acquire certain assets and property, and a cash summary would disclose very little about the true finances and net worth of the organisation.

These larger clubs, societies and associations, at their annual general meetings, present to their members an income and expenditure account together with a balance sheet on the lines we already know. The long-sounding term 'income and expenditure account' is only another name for the profit and loss account with which we are familiar.

Often an examination question presents the candidate with a receipts and payments account (or simply a summarised cash book, which is the same thing), and subject to a number of adjustments, requires an income and expenditure account to be made up together with a balance sheet.

An illustration of a typical examination problem is now given:

The Heathside Tennis Club
Receipts and Payments Account for the year ended 31 October

	£			£
Balance 1 Nov.	97 20	Postages/stationery		37 80
Subs. rec'd (including		Refreshments bought		124 40
£30 in advance)	920 00	Dance expenses		70 40
Dance proceeds (gross)	137 00	New nets		460 00
Donations	50 00	General expenses		25 20
Receipts from teas		Wages of groundsman		612 00
and socials	244 60	Heating/lighting, etc.		83 40
		Balance c/d		35 60
	1448 80			1448 80
Balance b/d	35 60			

In making up the annual accounts as at 31 October for presentation to club members, the following information is to be taken into account:

The club's assets and property on 1 November, one year ago:

Clubhouse at original cost	£3000.00
Nets/equipment at book value	260.00
Stock of tinned drinks, etc.	43.00
Cash on hand (see cash summary)	97.20

There were no arrears of subscriptions one year ago, and all expense creditors had been paid.

Certain adjustments are now to be taken into account in making up the income and expenditure account and the balance sheet:

(*a*) invoice for electricity £22.80 unpaid at 31 October;
(*b*) subscriptions in arrears at 31 October amounted to £50;
(*c*) subscriptions in advance £30 (shown in cash summary);
(*d*) wages owing to groundsman at 31 October £24;
(*e*) stock of refreshments at end of current season £49.60;
(*f*) nets/equipment account to be depreciated by £200.

The first stage of the answer to this problem is to find the commencing capital (sometimes called the accumulated fund), and then make up the subscriptions account to find the true income from members for the year.

		£	
	clubhouse	£3000.00	
Accumulated	nets/equipt.	260.00	
fund	stock 1 Nov.	43.00	
	cash balance 1 Nov.	97.20	£3400.20

Naturally, any liabilities at the beginning of the year would have been deducted from this amount of £3400.20, but in this instance there were no liabilities.

Dr.			Subscriptions Account		Cr.
		£			£
Oct. 31	Subs. paid in advance by members c/d	30 00	Oct. 31	Actual receipts as per cash summary	920 00
31	Transfer to Income & Expd. a/c	940 00	31	Subs. owing by members c/d	50 00
		970 00			970 00
Nov. 1	Debtors for subs. b/d	50 00	Nov. 1	Creditors for subs. b/d	30 00

Subscriptions taken to the income and expenditure account must show the actual income from members for the year.

The final accounts of the club can now be made up on these lines:

Income and Expenditure Statement – year ended 31 October

Income	£	£	£	Last year's figures
Subscriptions		940.00		
Donations		50.00		
Gross receipts from dances, teas, etc.	381.60			
Adjustment on stocks	6.60			
	388.20			
Less dance & catering expenses	194.80	193.40	1183.40	
Expenditure				
Postages/stationery		37.80		
Groundsman's wages	612.00			
Wages owing at 31 Oct.	24.00	636.00		
Heating/lighting	83.40			
Electricity owing	22.80	106.20		
General expenses		25.20		
		805.20		
Deprec. nets/equipt. a/c		200.00	1005.20	
Surplus to accumulated fund			£178.20	

**Balance Sheet of The Heathside Tennis Club
as at 31 October**

Fixed assets	£	£	£	*Last year's figures*
Clubhouse at cost		3000.00		
Nets/equipment	260.00			
Additions	460.00			
	720.00			
Less depreciation	200.00	520.00	3520.00	
Current assets				
Stock of refreshments		49.60		
Debtors for subscriptions		50.00		
Cash in hand		35.60	135.20	
			£3655.20	
Capital and liabilities		£		
Accumulated fund 1 Nov.		3400.20		
Add surplus income		178.20	3578.40	
Current liabilities				
Subscriptions in advance		30.00		
Creditors for wages		24.00		
Creditors for electricity		22.80	76.80	
			£3655.20	

Key Points

1 Note that the vertical style of revenue statement has been adopted in the text, although the older style is still widely used.

2 In all problems involving income and expenditure, first establish the *closing cash balance* needed for the final balance sheet. Also make up a subscriptions account, or work out the subscriptions by arithmetic.

3 Sometimes a club has a small bar and/or offers catering facilities to members. A short trading account is then made up in the ordinary way, and the profit or loss on trading is carried down to a general income and expenditure account.

4 Do not confuse subscriptions in advance with rates in advance. If club members have paid subscriptions in advance, they become creditors of the club; if their subscriptions are in arrears, they are debtors of the club.

Assignments

27.1 Make up a receipts and payments account from this information listed by the treasurer of a small local dramatic society at 31
December.

	£
Opening cash/bank balances (combined)	115.50
Subscriptions actually received from members during the year	150.00
Donations received	25.00
Net receipts from rehearsals/socials etc.	14.80
Ticket sales on productions	280.60
Rent of local hall	130.00
Stamps/stationery	6.20
Purchase of reading material and plays	84.50
Payment of royalties	62.00
Lighting/heating	28.70
Refreshments and drinks bought	92.40
Honorarium to treasurer 31 December	10.00

27.2 The cash book of the White Collar Workers' Association was
analysed in total as follows: subscriptions from members £860;
donations received £430; sundry receipts £175; rates paid £120;
furniture bought £270; salaries paid £600; fees to lecturers
£250; general expenses £210. Cash balance 1 January £30.

The Association owned its own premises shown at cost of
£4000. The old furniture had been given to the Red Cross and
written off the previous year. The position with regard to
outstandings at the year-end was as follows:

Subs. owing at 1 Jan. £46; and at 31 Dec. £66. Creditors for
stationery £76 at the beginning of the year, and £24 at the end.

Take the valuation of stationery unused at £54, and make up
an income and expenditure account and a balance sheet at 31
December. A payment of £130 for stationery by the association
was found by the auditors to be debited to general expenses.

28

Control Accounts

Self-balancing ledgers

A control account is a convenient device used as a check upon the arithmetical accuracy of postings to a particular ledger or section of ledgers. In the latter case the system is sometimes called 'sectional balancing'.

The term 'self-balancing' refers to the inclusion of a control account, kept normally at the front or at the back of a ledger, and used as a check by the ledger clerk on the total of his balances extracted from that ledger.

In addition to providing a check on the work of the book-keeper, self- or sectional balancing is also an aid to any internal audit system in force.

The bank cash book

The control accounts themselves are merely *summaries of totals taken from other books*, in the main from the books of original entry. The rulings in these books of prime entry are adapted to suit the needs of the particular business and the control system adopted.

The bank cash book is a feature of the control system. The bank and discount columns are still used, but the old cash columns are replaced by 'details' columns. *All receipts*, cash and cheques, are *banked daily*, and all payments shown in the main cash book are *made by cheque*, leaving the small routine cash disbursements to be paid by the petty cashier. The total wages paid each week will be met by a cheque cashed for that purpose, and the salaried employees will be paid monthly by credit transfer from their employer to their own bank accounts.

The debit and credit details columns are extended in analysis form to provide the information required by the ledger clerks for their control summaries. For example, the cumulative total of the payments from debtors provides control with the total amount credited to all the customers' accounts in the sales ledger. Similarly all payments to suppliers are listed in one particular column on the credit side of the cash book, to establish the total amount paid to trade creditors during the period.

In all the big organisations, the old style cash book has been replaced by the bank cash book, which has also been divided into separate books (or cash analysis records housed in steel filing cabinets) to distinguish easily and quickly between the receipts and the payments side of the business.

The general principles of control are best explained by simple illustration. In this example, we are concerned only with transactions on the sales side of the business, the credit sales to customers during one month, their payments on account of goods they have bought, discounts allowed to them and credits for goods returned. The purpose of the control account is to prove the arithmetical accuracy of the total of the debtors' balances extracted by the sales ledger clerk on 31 July.

Illustration

The ledger accounts of only four credit customers are given for the month of July.

Smith

July		£	July		£
1	Balance	100	8	Cash	95
10	SDB	120		disct.	5
			12	SRB	15

Jones

July		£	July		£
1	Balance	50	18	Cash	48
20	SDB	75		disct.	2
			22	SRB	5

Robinson

July		£	July		£
1	Balance	20	25	Cash	19
				disct.	1

Brown

July		£	July		£
22	SDB	10	24	Cash	10
31	SDB	3			

The bank cash book (debit or receipts side only) is shown in brief detail, followed by the other books of original entry on the sales side, the sales day book and the returns inwards book.

		Fol.	Disc.	Sales ledger	Cash sales	Sundries	Bank
			£	£	£	£	£
July 1	Balance b/f					400	400
8	Smith	SL	5	95			95
12	Cash sales	NL			80		80
18	Jones	SL	2	48			
	Cash sales	NL			30		78
24	Brown	SL		10			
25	Robinson	SL	1	19			29
31	Cash sales	NL			40		40
			—	—	—	—	—
			8	172	150	400	722

Sales Day Book **Sales Returns Book**

July			£
10	Smith	SL	120
20	Jones	SL	75
22	Brown	SL	10
31	Brown	SL	3
			208

July			£
12	Smith	SL	15
22	Jones	SL	5
			20

Again it is emphasised that this small illustration concerns only sales control, in connection with the items and transactions affecting the sales or debtors' ledger only.

At the month end, the sales ledger clerk will extract his credit customers' balances, listing them as follows:

	£
Smith	105
Jones	70
Brown	3
to give the total	£178 owing by debtors

The sales clerk then proves the accuracy of his postings to the sales ledger by making up his control account, either at the front or at the back of the sales ledger. This account contains the summaries and totals *made up by other employees* in the firm, the figures being extracted from the bank cash book, the sales day book and the returns inwards book. The control account made up by the sales ledger clerk is called the general ledger control account, made up on these lines:

General Ledger Control Account for July

July			£	July			£
31	Sales returns	SRB	20	1	Balance b/f		170
31	Total payments			31	Total sales for		
	received	CB	172		month of July	SDB	208
	& discount allowed	CB	8				
31	Balance c/d		178				
			378				378
				August			
				1	Balance b/d		178

The commencing *credit* balance of the above control account (£170) is the sum total of the debtors' balances at the beginning of the month, 1 July. Note that the totals shown within this control account are on the reverse side to the individual items that are already posted to this ledger. There is always a *credit* balance on the control account kept in the sales ledger, generally referred to as the general ledger control account (in effect a contra account to the sales ledger control account kept in the general ledger mentioned in the next paragraph).

In another section of the accounting department, the clerk responsible for the posting up of the general ledger also makes up *his* control account to prove his own postings on the general ledger and expense side. That part of his control relating to the sales side of the business is called the sales ledger control account. It starts with the commencing debit balance of £170 and finishes with the total for the sales ledger balances of £178, and is an additional check on both the postings to the sales ledger and to the general ledger.

The purchase ledger control follows a similar procedure to that briefly outlined on the sales side, except that again, of course, it will be in reverse of the sales procedure as already illustrated.

At one time these masses of figures seemed to be extremely repetitive, with the totals being repeated many times. Now, however, with mechanisation being generally adopted, and calculations speeded up to a fantastic rapidity by the computer, the time saved and the facility for making instant checks on accuracy by far outweigh the costs of the paperwork.

Pause for thought

'Errors in balancing were numerous some years ago. Self-balancing ledgers have helped the book-keeper and the auditor a great deal.' Explain this statement and consider how the complete control system of a business has developed from total accounts and the self-balancing and sectional ledgers which were first put to use.

Assignments

Key Points

1 The main difficulty experienced by students is knowing either the heading of the control account or the correct side for their sales and purchases debits and credits, etc.

   First make sure of the ledger in which the account is to be written up.

   If it is the sales ledger, all totals will be in reverse (on the control account) to the actual items shown on the individual debtors' accounts.

   If it is the purchases ledger, again reverse the items on the control account, to the various postings within the bought ledger.

2 Note any mention of bad debts refers to the sales ledger. Bad debts are always shown on the same side as debtors payments and discount allowed.

3 Note also that small debit balances in BL and small credit balances in SL at the end of month must be shown *above and below the totals* when making up control accounts.

4 Be careful with transfers between ledgers, increasing the debit in one ledger and decreasing the credit in another – and vice versa.

28.1   Prepare the purchases ledger control account (as drawn up by the general ledger clerk) for the month of January and carry down the balance:

Jan.		£
1	Credit balances	30 884
	Debit balances	122
31	Purchases for month	41 350
	Paid to suppliers (cheques)	26 440
	Discounts received	586
	Small credit balances paid out of petty cash	45
	Returns outward	958
	Contras settling small debits	82
	Debit balances at month end	40

28.2   From the balances below you are required to make up the purchase and the sales ledger control accounts as they would appear at the back of their respective ledgers:

June		£
1	Bought ledger balances	2 433
	Sales ledger balances	3 486
30	Purchases for month	9 295
	Sales for month	13 840
	Paid to suppliers	7 616
	Discounts received	190
	Returns inwards	168
	Received from customers	12 327
	Discounts allowed	255
	Returns outward	117
	Bad debts written off	36
	Bills receivable	585
	Bills payable	480
	Dishonoured cheque of customer	42
	Debit balances transferred from sales ledger to bought ledger	58

28.3   Draft your own ruling of a bank cash book for both receipts and payments. Make a number of entries useful for a control system in force, and take the totals of your columns to a control account made up for this purpose. Complete this same control account with the day book and returns book totals for the same period.

29

Partnership Accounts

The ordinary book-keeping records of a partnership are kept exactly on the same lines as those of a sole trader. The cash book, the day books, and the customers' and suppliers' ledgers are posted up in the same way as that already shown. The net profit of the business is ascertained in the same way as before, but, because there are now two or more owners of the business, the proportions of profit entitlement have to be worked out separately.

The appropriation account

Since the trading profit is to be divided, not necessarily equally, the profit and loss section of the main revenue account is extended by a third appendage called the *appropriation account*. The trading profit for the period is split in the appropriation account, and divided according to the terms laid down by the partnership agreement or contract. *In the absence of any written or typed agreement, or by implied custom of the past, partners are presumed to share profits and losses equally*, irrespective of the size of their capital accounts or their holding of partnership assets. This is laid down in the Partnership Act of 1890.

Separate capital accounts

Partners' capital accounts have no direct bearing on their profit-sharing ratios, unless there are specific terms laid down to the contrary. The senior partner may have a capital of £8000 and his junior a capital of £2000 and yet their written agreement or past custom may indicate that their profit sharing ratios are three-fifths and two-fifths.

Interest on capital

Interest is sometimes allowed as a form of compensation for those partners with larger financial holdings in the firm. This interest is a charge against the net trading profit before its division between the partners, the double entry being a debit to appropriation and a credit to the individual current accounts of the partners.

Current accounts

This is a new term applicable to the private accounts of partners within the firm, not to be confused with the ordinary bank current account. A partner's current account replaces the old drawings account of the sole trader. The total drawings of the individual partner is debited to his current account; his share of profit is credited, and also any interest on capital or any partnership salary to which he may be entitled.

It is customary to keep fixed capital accounts of all partners quite separate and distinct from the individual current accounts of each partner.

Illustration

Ned and Fred are in partnership with capitals of £4000 and £2000 respectively. Their partnership agreement states that the net trading profits will be shared in the proportions of three-quarters and one-quarter, but that Fred should be credited with a partnership salary of £1000 a year before the final allocation of net trading profit. In addition, interest on capital of 10% per annum is to be credited to the current account of each partner. The net trading profit for the year under review, ended 31 December, was £13 600.

The credit balances of the partners' current accounts brought forward were: Ned £120 and Fred £80; the partners' drawings for the year were: Ned £9350 and Fred £4220. At the balance sheet date Fred had not yet withdrawn any part of his salary for the current year.

Show the appropriation account of the firm, the partners' capital and current accounts (as they would appear in the private ledger), and draft the capital and liabilities side of the balance sheet as at 31 December.

Profit and Loss Appropriation Account

	£			£
Interest on capital		Net trading profit		
Ned	400	b/d		13 600
Fred	200			
Salary of Fred	1000			
Shares of profit				
Ned	9000			
Fred	3000			
	13 600			13 600

Dr.   **Capital Accounts** (fixed original balances)   Cr.

			Ned	Fred				Ned	Fred
					Jan. 1	b/f		£4000	£2000

Dr.   **Current Accounts**   Cr.

			Ned £	Fred £			Ned £	Fred £
Dec. 31	Drawings		9350	4220	Jan. 1	Balances b/f	120	80
31	Balances c/d		170	60	Dec. 31	Int. on capital	400	200
						Salary		1000
						Shares of profit	9000	3000
			9520	4280			9520	4280
					Jan. 1	Balances b/d	170	60

Balance Sheet of Ned and Fred as at 31 December

Capital and liabilities section		
Capital accounts	£	£
Ned	4000	
Fred	2000	6000
Current accounts		
Ned: Balance 1 Jan.	120	
Int. on capital	400	
Share of profit	9000	
	9520	
Less drawings	9350	170
Fred: Balance 1 Jan.	80	
Int. on capital	200	
Salary	1000	
Share of profit	3000	
	4280	
Less drawings	4220	60
Current liabilities	—	

Partners' salary

In the illustration just shown Fred has been credited with his full salary of £1000 (on his current account) *because it has not yet been paid.* He becomes a creditor of his own firm for the time being. When the salary is withdrawn, cash will be credited and his current account debited. If Fred had withdrawn part of his salary (on account) prior to the balance sheet date, the double entry would have been a credit to cash and a debit to partnership salaries account, with *no credit appearing on Fred's current account for that part of the salary already withdrawn.*

Amalgamation of sole traders

Occasionally, two or more sole traders decide to amalgamate their respective businesses and become partners. The book-keeping entries in connection with the presentation of the balance sheet of the new firm are simple enough providing the capital account of *each sole trader is adjusted,* according to the terms agreed upon by the prospective partners, *before any attempt is made to draft a final balance sheet for the new firm.*

Illustration

Ellen and Emily are cousins with small retail drapery shops, both rented, in the town centre of Hereford. They decide to become partners and save a considerable sum on competitive advertising and also on bulk buying. The date of their amalgamation is to be 1 April. Their last individual balance sheets are now shown at 31 March in the older 'T' style of presentation.

Ellen's Balance Sheet as at 31 March

	£		£
Capital	5800	Fittings/fixtures	1500
Creditors	450	Van at cost	1250
Bank overdraft	250	Stock of goods	2200
		Trade debtors	1550
	£ 6500		£ 6500

Emily's Balance Sheet as at 31 March

	£		£
Capital	6460	Furniture/fittings	750
Trade creditors	840	Tools/equipment	1320
		Stock	1840
		Trade debtors	2880
		Bank	510
	£ 7300		£ 7300

The partnership agreement of the new firm states that profits and losses are to be shared equally as from 1 April, and that certain amendments and adjustments are to be made to some of the asset values as shown on the two balance sheets dated 31 March, namely:

All furniture, fittings, etc., is to be reduced by 20% of its book value; the van is to be revalued at £800, and tools/equipment at £1000. Provisions are to be made against possible bad debts of 10% of the trade debtors' balances. Miss Ellen is to repay her bank overdraft privately, and the bank account of Miss Emily is to be taken over by the new firm. The stock on hand shown in each balance sheet is to be depreciated by 25%.

Answer
First of all re-draft the individual balance sheets of the sole traders at 31 March, subject to the partnership terms agreed upon:

	Ellen £	Emily £		Ellen £	Emily £
Capital accounts	4595	5242	Fittings/fixtures	1200	600
Trade creditors	450	840	Van	800	
			Tools/equipment		1000
			Stock	1650	1380
			Debtors *less* prov. for bad debts	1395	2592
			Bank		510
	5045	6082		5045	6082

The balance sheet for the new firm as at 1 April can now quickly be drafted by lumping together the figures shown above:

Balance Sheet of Ellen and Emily
as at 1 April

Assets employed			
Fixed assets		£	£
Fittings/fixtures		1800	
Tools/equipment		1000	
Van at valuation		800	3600
Current assets			
Stock on hand		3030	
Trade debtors	4430		
Less provision	443	3987	
Bank	——	510	7527
			11127
Financed by			
Capital accounts			
Ellen		4595	
Emily		5242	9837
Current liabilities			
Trade creditors			1290
			11127

Overdrawn current account

When a partner overdraws his current account, he becomes a debtor to his own firm. His current account shows, temporarily, a debit balance, and at the balance sheet date, must be switched over to the bottom of the listed assets. However, it would be ignored in calculating the working capital of the business.

Interest on drawings

Interest is sometimes charged on partners' drawings with a view to curbing heavy and frequent withdrawals on the firm's bank account. This interest on drawings is debited to the partners' individual current accounts in addition to the sums withdrawn, and is credited to the firm's appropriation account as a small gain to the business.

For example, if the senior partner of a professional firm, by agreement, withdraws £2000 at the end of each quarter, subject to an interest charge of 8% per annum, the individual debits to his current account for a year would be calculated in this manner:

			£
31 March	(interest 1 April–31 December) 9 months at 8%	=	120
30 June	(interest 1 July–31 Dec.) 6 months at 8%	=	80
30 Sept.	(interest 1 Oct.–31 Dec.) 3 months at 8%	=	40
31 Dec.	(last day of trading year – no charge)		—
			£240

This total of £240 would be credited to the firm's appropriation account at the end of the trading year, and the amount of £8240 (£8000 drawings plus £240 interest) would be debited to this particular partner's current account.

Goodwill in accounts

Goodwill has been defined as 'the likelihood that the old customers will continue to deal with the old firm' and as 'the benefit arising from connection and reputation'.

Occasionally there appears at the top of the fixed assets on a balance sheet the descriptive term 'Goodwill £___'. It looks impressive, particularly if it is a large amount, but actually it does not mean very much beyond the fact that a debit balance for this intangible asset is still being carried forward in the books. This debit balance is a paper entry from the past (probably created when the business last changed hands or when a new partner was admitted to the old firm). It is an intangible asset; you cannot see or touch it, and its value is indeterminable until the business is sold or there is a change in the ownership. Even on the sale of the business, the value of goodwill, as part of the purchase price asked by the vendor, is always problematical and subject to much discussion and deliberation before the final price is agreed upon by the new owner.

A new business has no goodwill. It has to be earned and developed. As the business expands, its connection and reputation increases, so that when it is sold or a change of ownership takes place, the valuation of the business 'as a going concern' is worth substantially more than the listed value of its net assets and property. *The difference in value between the net assets and the actual purchase price is the goodwill of the business.*

Illustration

Sam Brown has rented a corner shop in the suburbs for the past twenty years. He is now retiring, and his last balance sheet, dated 30 June, is shown below on the left. It has been checked over by George Smith, who agrees the vendor's price of £18000 for the business, advertised with 'all assets and property to be taken over at balance sheet figures, and the trade creditors to be settled by the new owner'.

Balance Sheet of Sam Brown, vendor, as at 30 June

Assets and property		
Fixed assets	£	£
Van at valuation	1950	
Fittings/equipt.	7800	9750
Current assets		
Stock at 30 June	2800	
Trade debtors	450	3250
		13000
Financed by		
Capital: S. Brown	£	
Balance　1 July	14000	
Net profit for year	5500	
	19500	
Less drawings	7500	12000
Current liabilities		
Trade creditors		1000
		£13000

Balance Sheet of George Smith, purchaser, as at 1 July

Assets and property		
Fixed assets	£	£
Goodwill at cost	6000	
Van at valuation	1950	
Fittings/equipt.	7800	15750
Current assets		
Stock at 1 July	2800	
Trade debtors	450	3250
		19000
Financed by		
Capital: G. Smith		£
Balance　1 July		18000
Current liabilities		
Trade creditors		1000
		£19000

Comparing the two balance sheets it will be seen that George Smith has acquired the whole of the assets and liabilities of Sam Brown at their valuation at 30 June, and, in the agreed purchase price of £18000 has, in effect, paid a premium of £6000 in acquiring these assets. The capital account of the new owner thus becomes £18000, the price he has paid for his new business. The excess amount paid over and above the valuation of net assets taken over (i.e. £6000) is debited to goodwill account, and on his first balance sheet dated 1 July, is taken to the top of the fixed assets. This intangible asset, though only a paper entry, is a debit balance in the accounting records of George Smith, and will continue to be shown at the top of his assets on future balance sheets, unless he decides to reduce or write off part of the debit through appropriations of good years of profit.

Sometimes, too, where a new partner is being admitted to an existing firm, the old partner(s) create a goodwill account, perhaps only temporarily, by debiting an agreed figure, say £10000, to a new asset account headed goodwill, crediting amounts to their capital (or current) accounts in the proportions they previously shared profits and losses, shown in this way by journal entry:

Dec. 31		£	£
	Goodwill account	10000	
	Capital accounts:		
	A		6000
	B		4000
	Goodwill account created on admission of C, credited to capital accounts of A and B in their old profit sharing ratios.		

The creation of a goodwill account provides some compensation for the past work and effort of the old partners. It often relieves the new incoming partner from finding a fairly substantial sum on admission to the firm, although generally he would still be expected to bring in a small introductory capital.

There is no hard and fast rule laid down for the valuation of goodwill. Some of the small retail traders might adopt a goodwill valuation of ten times the average gross weekly takings, with property, stock etc. at a separate valuation. Professional firms like accountants and solicitors sometimes require double their annual gross fees or perhaps three times their net fees (average net profits over recent years).

Since the goodwill debit is simply an arbitrary figure used as an adjustment on business valuation perhaps a long time ago, often bearing no relationship to the present-day true worth of the business, it is advisable to write down its book value out of profits as early as possible, in this way strengthening the reserves or perhaps substituting genuine fixed assets in lieu.

Assignments

Key Points

1 In the absence of written agreement or laid-down policy or custom, Section 24 of the *Partnership Act* of 1890 states that partnership profits and losses will be shared equally.

2 Appropriations and charges against trading profit such as interest on capital and partnership salaries are debited to the appropriation account before final distribution of profit.

3 When two or more sole traders amalgamate to become partners, revalue and adjust their capitals separately *before* making any attempt to lump together the joint assets/liabilities of the new firm.

4 Partnership salaries are debited *in full* against the firm's trading profit. If part of salary is not paid, it will be shown as a credit on individual partner's current account.

5 Adjustment of profit-sharing ratios.

A and B share profits 2:1. They admit their chief clerk to take one-fifth of profits; the old partners still to maintain their previous ratios.

The new profit-sharing ratios:

C, the new partner, will take one-fifth of the profit, leaving four-fifths between A and B.

A will take ⅔ of ⅘ths = 8/15ths

B will take ⅓ of ⅘ths = 4/15ths

Thus the ratios of the new firm will be: 8:4:3

29.1   Make up the appropriation account and the partners' current accounts from the information given below:

	Capitals £	Current a/cs £	Drawings £
Melon	4000	250 Cr.	6500
Lemon	2000	100 Dr.	6800

Lemon is to be credited half-yearly with a salary of £500. Each partner is to be credited with 8% per annum interest on capital. The net trading profit for six months ended 30 June was £14 500.

29.2

Cash Book

Jan. 1	Capital a/cs		£	June 30	½ yearly		£
	A		5000		salary of C		500
	B		4000	Dec. 31			
	C		3000		Drawings		
					A		4800
					B		3500
					C		2500

A, B and C share profits in the ratios of 3:2:1. Net trading for this year is £12 000 after charging C's salary in full. Interest on capital allowed at 10%. Make up the partners' current accounts on the balance sheet at 31 December.

29.3   Sue Pugh's assets and liabilities at 30 June are listed:
Fittings £8000; bank overdraft £550; Stock £1800; trade creditors £1750; Trade debtors £1200.

She takes her friend May Day into partnership as from 1 July. Miss Day pays the sum of £2000 into the firm's bank account, and also brings in her own car (valued at £1500 and some useful equipment valued at £200).

The partnership agreement provides for interest on capital at 6% per annum, and the profit sharing ratios of the new firm are to be:

Miss Pugh, two-thirds
Miss Day, one-third

You are required to make up the balance sheet of the partnership as at 1 July.

Revision Exercise 5

1 The Overlanders' Club was established ten years ago for social and recreational purposes, in particular travel abroad. The secretary of the club prepared the following summary of the cash book transactions for the year ended 31 March:

	£		£
Balance (cash and bank combined)	804	Furniture bought	120
Subscriptions received	915	Catering expenses	266
Donations received	28	Repairs/maintenance	15
Receipts from socials, raffles, etc.	384	Rent of rooms	180
		Wages of temporary staff	620
		Lighting/heating	88
		Books/magazines	76
		Printing and stationery	22

The club rents two large rooms overlooking the park at the economic annual rent of £240, paid quarterly, the landlord paying the rates. Fixtures and fittings on the last balance sheet stood at £680. The Committee decided to revalue this at £650, including the additions bought earlier in the year.

Books and magazines were regarded as expendable, to be treated purely as revenue.

The position with regard to members' subscriptions was:

1 April (beginning of year): subscriptions owing £44
subscriptions in advance £28
31 March (end of the year): subscriptions owing £56
subscriptions in advance £24

A catering account of £35 was owing on 31 March; £16 was due to the Midland Electricity Board and £12 owing for wages.

From the above information, you are required to make up the income and expenditure account of the club and a balance sheet as at 31 March.

2   Janetta Meade and Philippa Richmond are in partnership sharing profits and losses in the proportions two-thirds and one-third. Interest at 6% is allowed on capital and Miss Richmond is entitled to a partnership salary of £400 a year before the profits are apportioned. Draw up the final accounts of the partnership from the trial balance and adjustments below:

Trial Balance   31 December

	£	£
Capital accounts 1 Jan.		
J.M.		7000
P.R.		4500
Current accounts J.M.		120
P.R.	45	
Partners' drawings J.M.	2800	
P.R.	1700	
Partnership salaries	200	
Purchases/sales	5600	16750
Returns inwards/outwards	40	70
Wages & NIC	2200	
Carriage outward	120	
Provision for bad debts		105
Trade debtors/creditors	2400	1250
Machinery (less depreciation)	7650	
Depreciation for year	850	
Fittings and equipment at cost	460	
Lighting/heating	330	
Office salaries & NIC	1600	
Stock 1 Jan.	1550	
Warehousing expenses	230	
Advertising	400	
Rent, rates and insurance	960	
Bad debts	85	
Cash and bank balances	705	
Discounts allowed/received	325	455
	30250	30250

(a)   Stock on hand 31 December £1820
(b)   Rates paid in advance to 31 March £100
(c)   Provision for debtors to be maintained at 5%
(d)   Wages owing at 31 December £25
(e)   Carry forward £200 already paid on advertising account.

30

Accounting for Management

Figures belong to the 'counting house', the province of the accountant. Management is more interested in their significance, in the story they have to tell.

Simplicity of presentation is as important as accuracy. Revenue accounts should show not only the ultimate calculation of profit or loss, but also how the results have been achieved. Balance sheets should be presented so that the non-accountant can interpret the figures.

Most students at this stage adapt their trading account to show the cost of sales figure, thus:

	£			£
Stock 1 June	1000	Sales for month	£6500	
Purchases for month	£2200	*Less* returns	100	6400
Less returns	50 2150			
	3150			
Stock 30 June	850			
	2300			
Production wages	1800			
Warehousing expenses	120			
Cost of sales	4220			
Gross profit c/d	2180			
	6400			6400

By way of comparison, the smaller statement now shown is even more informative with less detail to absorb, and would be easier to understand by the non-accountant:

Net sales for the month of June		£6400
Cost of sales		
Materials consumed	£2300	
Production wages	1800	
Warehousing expenses	120	4220
	Gross profit	£2180

We could also group the various losses and expense items of the old-style profit and loss account in a manner which would mean something more to the casual observer, thus:

			£
Gross trading profit			2180
Distribution expenses	£		
Carriage (outwards)	25		
Van repairs	36		
Petrol and oil	23		
Depreciation of vans	65	149	
Selling expenses			
Advertising	52		
Postages (proportion)	14	66	
Office and administration			
Salaries	490		
Telephone	44		
Insurance	18		
Printing/stationery	33		
Postages (proportion)	28	613	
Financial			
Discounts	30		
Depreciation office equipment	20	50	
Total expenses			878
Net profit before tax			£1302

For comparative purposes, in the marginal space on the right, the figures for the previous year could be shown. Sometimes, too, each item of expense is calculated as a percentage of net sales.

To present final accounts in narrative form, the trial balance can be made up on these lines, *after all adjustments* have been dealt with and the cost of sales figures ascertained:

Trial Balance   30 June

	£	£
Fixed assets		
Premises at cost	6000	
Van (book balance)	300	
Current assets		
Stock 30 June	1230	
Trade debtors	1300	
Rates in advance	80	
Cash/bank	520	
Loan capital		
10% mortgage on premises		2000
Current liabilities		
Trade creditors		600
Expense creditors		40
Interest due on mortgage		200
Claims of proprietorship		
Capital owned		4000
Revenue income		
Net sales		12760
Revenue expenditure		
Cost of sales	6500	
Salaries & NIC	2200	
Office expenses	630	
Advertising	220	
Van expenses	50	
Rates and insurance	270	
Mortgage interest	200	
Depreciation of van	100	
	19600	19600

Note that the inclusion of the cost of sales figure on the trial balance means that stocks and purchases have already been adjusted to arrive at the total debit of £6500. In consequence, the stock figure of £1230 on the trial balance is that of the closing stock of 30 June. Note also that the van account shows the up-to-date balance, after the adjustment for depreciation, and that the mortgage interest, being due and not yet paid, is shown both as a debit (to be charged to revenue) and also as a credit (under current liabilities).

Revenue Account for the month of June

		£	*Previous year*
Net sales for the month		12760	
	£		
Cost of sales	6500		
Selling/distribution			
Advertising	£220		
Van expenses	50		
Depreciation of van	100	370	
Office/administration			
Salaries & NIC	£2200		
Office and general	630		
Rates and insurance	270	3100	
Financial expense			
Mortgage interest		200	10170
	Net trading profit for month	£2590	

The vertical narrative style of presentation, for both the revenue account and the balance sheet, has been adopted generally throughout the commercial world. In particular, this new format, with its many explanatory footnotes for greater ease in interpretation, lends itself to the final accounts of limited companies. It is shown in further detail in Chapter 33.

The balance sheet in this illustration is shown overleaf, but since it refers in this instance to the accounts of a sole trader, note that there is a certain paucity of detail, on the capital side, when compared with the balance sheet of a limited company.

Note that in this illustration the proprietor's capital account has been made up to date at 30 June, presumably after deduction of his drawings for the month, but before the addition of his net trading profit. The term 'retained profit' would not be suitable in this instance. The proprietor may have some good reason for not disclosing his withdrawals from the business, and, in any event, he is not subject to the strict procedure and regulations of the Companies Acts.

Balance Sheet as at 30 June

Assets employed	£	£	£
Fixed assets			
Premises at cost		6000	
Van, *less* depreciation		300	6300
Current assets	£		
Stock 30 June	1230		
Trade debtors	1300		
Payments in advance	80		
Cash/bank	520	3130	
Current liabilities			
Trade creditors	600		
Expense creditors	40		
Mortgage interest	200	840	
Working capital			2290
			8590
Financed by	£		£
Proprietary capital			
Balance 30 June	4000		
Net trading profit	2590		6590
Fixed liability			
10% Mortgage loan			
(secured on premises)			2000
			8590

Assignments

30.1 What is meant by the statement 'Figures belong to the "counting house"' and why is management likely to be more interested in the real story they have to tell?

30.2 Comparative figures are given of the average stock, the stock-turn, and the mark-up cost of two distinct businesses. Through the medium of gross profit percentages indicate which, in your opinion, is apparently the more successful business.

	Average stock £	Stock-turn	Mark-up on cost
Business A	3500	6 times in the year	35%
Business B	3500	10 times in the year	22½%

30.3 Edwina and Selina Black are equal partners in a gown shop, bought fifteen years ago, with financial help provided by Edwina's husband in the first instance, and he still has a priority claim upon the net assets of their retail venture. The last balance sheet of the firm is now shown:

Balance Sheet of E. and S. Black
as at 30 June

	£	£
Assets employed		
Fixed assets		
Goodwill	5 000	
Premises at cost	8 000	
Fixtures/fittings at cost	1 500	
Motor van at valuation	1 250	15 750
Current assets		
Stock	1 480	
Trade debtors	2 340	
Insurance in advance	65	
Cash in hand	15	3 900
Current account S. Black		350
		£20 000
Financed by		
Partners' capitals		
Edwina Black	2 000	
Selina Black	2 000	4 000
Current account E. Black		240
Mortgage loan Ian Black		10 000
(secured on premises)		
Current liabilities		
Bank overdraft	1 400	
Trade creditors	4 000	
Expense creditors	360	5 760
		£20 000

Discuss or give your views upon the following points with regard to this balance sheet.

(*a*) At first glance, does this appear to be a good business?

(*b*) Say last year's net profit was £15 000 divisible between the two sisters. Would this be a good return on the capital finance?

(*c*) What is the working capital of this business? Why is the current account of one partner on the assets side?

(*d*) If the bank and the trade creditors insisted upon early or immediate repayment of their debts, how could the business survive?

31

Costs of Production and Manufacturing Accounts

Measurement of working capital

Working capital is profitable only when fully employed. When a merchanting business regularly carries a huge bank balance, the bank probably makes far more money out of that current asset than the business owner.

Banks use money to create money. The trader or merchant, too, can make good use of surplus money in a variety of ways, such as buying reserve commodity stocks in economic markets, obtaining maximum discounts from suppliers, purchasing up-to-date machinery and equipment, and extending the market scope through wider publicity. In the inflationary markets of today, money wisely spent now is more profitable than money used in six months time.

Minimum cash cover must, of course, be available for both routine purposes and possible contingencies, so a certain degree of liquidity is important. This means that a close and constant watch must be kept on the amount of working capital and its most profitable allocation between current assets and current liabilities.

The regular and systematic measurement of working capital has become a general function of the accountant and the financial director. Certain arithmetical devices are used to measure liquidity, including various ratios such as stock to sales, debtors to sales, current assets to current liabilities, and quick assets to current liabilities, the latter commonly known as the 'acid test ratio'.

Prime cost and oncost

A manufacturer must buy his raw material and allow for all manner of huge labour and factory costs long before he sells his finished product, sometimes weeks, perhaps months afterwards. Meanwhile, he probably has to borrow money at a high rate of interest to maintain production.

Prime cost is the term used for the direct expenses of production – the materials, labour and the actual expenses that can be definitely allocated to certain production schedules. In addition, the manufacturer incurs many other expenses that cannot, as a rule, be allocated easily to a particular job or contract. These expenses include the rent and rates of the factory, lighting and heating, factory power, the wages of foremen, time-keepers and greasers, and the wear and tear (depreciation) of the factory plant. These necessary and essential expenses of maintaining the factory in a productive state have to be charged to each job or contract under the heading of **oncost** or **overhead expense**, generally on a percentage basis over the whole production.

Stocks and their turnover

Large stocks held in the warehouse do not earn their keep, yet minimum stocks must be maintained, based upon past experience.

The aim of management is to increase the rate of stock turnover, thereby increasing trading profit. Periodic checks are made by the cost accountant (in big industry) comparing the rate of stock turnover with that of earlier periods. An illustration of a small manufacturer's cost statement is now shown, providing useful information for both the cost and financial accountant.

Note how the cost of production fits into the trading account, as shown on the next page, taking the place of the ordinary purchases of a non-manufacturing concern. The comparison of the gross profit ratios between the two periods reflects the general price trend, always rising under inflationary conditions. To maintain existing prices means that many producers and manufacturers are pressurised out of business by their ever-increasing costs.

Cost of Production Statement

	£	£
Stock of raw materials 1 Jan.	8 500	
Purchases of raw material	72 350	
Carriage on raw material	150	
	81 000	
Less stock of raw materials 31 Dec.	10 000	
Raw materials consumed	71 000	
Production wages & NIC	110 000	
Direct expenses of production	2 200	
Prime cost		183 200
Factory overheads:		
Heating and lighting	1 700	
Rent and rates	3 500	
Power	2 400	
Supervision (foremen)	8 800	
Depreciation of machinery	2 000	
Overhead expense		18 400
Cost of production		£201 600

Trading Account for the year ended 31 December

	Current year £	£	Previous year £	£
Net sales for year		275 000		220 000
Cost of sales				
Stock of finished goods 1 Jan.	32 000		34 000	
Cost of production b/f	201 600		158 800	
	233 600		192 800	
Less stock of finished goods 31 Dec.	36 000		32 000	
	197 600		160 800	
Warehouse wages & NIC	4 400		4 200	
Cost of sales		202 000		165 000
Gross trading profit		£73 000		£55 000

Rate of stock turnover

Current year	*Previous year*
$\dfrac{202\,000}{34\,000} = 5.94$ times in the year (approx. every two months)	$\dfrac{165\,000}{33\,000} = 5$ times

The gross profit ratios in the above illustration are:

$$\frac{73\,000}{275\,000} \times 100 = 26.55\% \text{ for the current year}$$

$$\frac{55\,000}{220\,000} \times 100 = 25.00\% \text{ for the previous year.}$$

The increased ratio may be due to a variety of causes – increased prices, reduced level of overheads through greater production, or perhaps more effective control over publicity and administrative expenditure despite the inflationary conditions, etc.

Manufacturing accounts

The heavy costs and expenses at basic production level determine, to a large degree, the ultimate selling price of the finished product. These bulk costs normally occur long before the retail stage.

The manufacturer must obtain his raw material at world commodity prices, and provide both an efficient labour force and the machinery of production involving heavy capital finance, months ahead of the estimated demand for his marketable product.

The cost of production statement (see page 200) is also a manufacturing account, preceding and leading into the business trading account. Generally, it would comprise a greater list of debit items, all costs and expenses of production, the total being referred to as the *cost of production*. This cost of manufacture or production is brought down to the debit of the trading account we already know, taking the place of the purchases figure to which we have become accustomed. But now that we are about to make up a manufacturing account, remember that some finished goods may have been bought from outside suppliers at this stage. These are shown as an additional debit in the ordinary way.

Several classes of stock

In making up another more detailed manufacturing account, and processing it through to the final net trading profit stage, take note of the three different kinds of stock: raw material, partly finished goods (sometimes called 'work in progress'), and finished goods. The latter belongs only to the trading and selling section of the business, whereas the first two type of stocks are found only in the manufacturing or production account. The *closing balances*, however, of all three kinds of stock are eventually taken to join the current assets on the balance sheet.

The older orthodox style of manufacturing account has been drafted below to emphasise the various 'account' stages and sections, and to draw the student's attention to the sectional terms in use – materials consumed, prime cost, factory/works cost, and the cost of sales.

Manufacturing, Trading and Profit and Loss Account for the year ended 31 December

	£		£	£
Stock of raw materials 1 Jan.	2000	Work in progress		
Purchases of raw materials	36000	31 Dec.	£6000	
Carriage on raw materials	1000	*less* 1 Jan.	5500	500
	39000			
Less stock of raw materials 31 Dec.	5000	Cost of production c/d		75840
Materials consumed	34000			
Direct wages & NIC	30000			
Direct expenses	6740			
Prime cost	70740			
Overhead expense				
including deprec. of plant	5600			
Factory/works cost	76340			76340
Stock of finished goods 1 Jan.	30000	Net sales		130000
Cost of production brought down	75840			
Purchases of finished goods	1440			
Carriage on finished goods	60			
	107340			
Less stock of finished goods 31 Dec.	25000			
Cost of sales	82340			
Gross profit c/d	47660			
	130000			130000
Carriage outwards	700	Gross profit b/d		47660
Salaries & NIC	8800	Discounts received		300
Office expenses	4400			
Discounts allowed	440			
Advertising	3120			
Net trading profit	30500			
	47960			47960

Note on the market price of goods manufactured
This type of examination problem is quite straightforward, provid-

ing examples have been studied. Sometimes, though, examiners like to add a footnote about the retail value or price of the goods manufactured on the open market.

If, for instance, in addition to all the information above, the examiner had introduced the figure of £90 000 as the approximate market value of the manufactured goods (shown as the cost of production amounting to £75 840), to show an estimated 'profit on manufacture' of £14 160, the simple adjustments to the manufacturing account already illustrated would be as follows:

In place of the cost of production figure of £75 840 on the credit of manufacturing account insert the current market value of £90 000. Carry down and debit this £90 000 to the next section of this account (the trading account) in place of the figure £75 840 for the cost of production.

The estimated profit on manufacture £14 160 will be debited (as the balance of the manufacturing account) and *brought down to the credit of the third section of this combined account*, the profit and loss account.

This is simply a management accounting concept to measure performance and compare production costs with the prices of finished goods on the open market. There is no change in the ultimate and actual net profit.

Assignments

31.1 Draw up a comparative trading account from the information given below. Ascertain the cost of sales and calculate the rate of stock turnover for both periods.

	Current year £	Previous year £
Raw material consumed	60 000	53 000
Manufacturing wages	77 000	69 000
Warehousing wages	6 000	5 300
Direct expenses	5 000	4 900
Overheads	10 000	8 800
Net sales	240 000	200 000
Stocks of finished goods		
1 January	26 000	25 000
31 December	24 000	26 000

31.2 Prepare a manufacturing account from the following figures, to show clearly:

(i)   the raw materials consumed   (ii)   the prime cost
(iii)   factory overheads   (iv)   cost of production.

		Raw material £	Work in progress £
Stocks	1 July (one year ago)	2500	450
	30 June (at year end)	3000	520

	£		£
Manufacturing wages	14400	Fuel and power	1500
Indirect wages	4300	Direct expenses	430
Works manager's		Royalties on production	350
salary	3000	Deprec. of machinery	200
Raw material		General maintenance	150
purchases	18700	Insurance of factory	100
Factory rent and		Carriage on raw	
rates	2200	material	120

31.3 You are required to make up a combined manufacturing, trading and profit and loss account from the following information, and give details of:

(i)   materials consumed   (ii)   cost of production
(iii)   profit on manufacture   (iv)   cost of sales
(v)   net profit for the year.

		Raw material £	Finished goods £	Work in progress £
Stocks	Jan. 1	1000	2375	1900
	Dec. 31	625	2760	1750

	£		£
Salaries	3350	Carriage outwards	410
Office expenses	1190	Raw material purchases	7500
Factory expenses	3188	Carriage on material	125
Discounts received	350	Sales less returns	49000
Advertising	1800	Warehousing expenses	865
Discounts allowed	300	Purchases/finished goods	1175
Factory wages	12110		

Factory plant and machinery is to be depreciated by £2750. The market value of the actual cost of production at the balance sheet date is estimated at £30450. This is to be taken into account in drafting the manufacturing account.

32

Introduction to Company Accounts

The law relating to joint-stock companies, including the distinction between public and private limited companies, is a separate subject in itself. Since it can barely be touched upon in these two short chapters, the text is confined to the requirements of the typical first-level Accounting syllabus. A brief insight is given into the way a public company raises its main funds in the first instance, followed by the modern presentation of the final accounts of a public limited company.

Companies registered under the Companies Acts are legal entities with separate identity from their members (shareholders). When a shareholder has paid the full amount on his allotted shares, he has no further liability for the debts and obligations of the company. This is the meaning of 'limited liability'.

Two of the more important statutes governing the financial affairs of joint-stock companies are the Companies Acts of 1948 and 1967; additions and amendments to these acts, though, come up with the regularity of our annual Budget.

The paper work and the ordinary trading and accounting records of a limited company are similar to those of a private firm or a partnership, but there are certain distinctions, from the outset, in the creation and raising of capital finance, in particular through public subscription. The interests of both the shareholders and the creditors of a limited company are protected at law, and the final accounts must be presented in strict compliance with the regulations laid down by the Companies Acts.

Formation of a public limited company

The promoters (usually the first directors) of a new company advertise full details of the organisation and its anticipated trading prospects in the national press in a statement called 'The Prospectus'. The general public are invited to apply for membership in the new company by subscribing for shares according to the terms of the prospectus.

Registered and issued share capital

The nominal, authorised or registered share capital is that stated in the company's charter, the Memorandum of Association. That part of the authorised capital which is issued to the public is shown under the heading of issued capital on the balance sheet in this manner:

	£	£
Authorised and issued share capital		
Authorised capital		
100000 10% preference shares of £1 each	100000	
400000 ordinary shares of 50p each	200000	300000
Issued capital		
100000 10% preference shares of £1 each fully paid	100000	
300000 ordinary shares of 50p each fully paid	150000	250000

Note that it is only the issued share capital which forms part of the double entry system, and consequently the authorised capital is ruled off when it has not been fully issued.

There are various categories of capital. In the figures shown above, the nominal, registered or authorised capital is £300000. The issued capital is £250000, consisting of 100000 10% preference shares fully called and paid up, and 300000 ordinary shares of 50p called and paid up. The uncalled capital of 100000 ordinary shares of 50p has not yet been issued to the public.

There are also various classes of shares, the two main classes being preference and ordinary. The former carries a fixed rate of interest which is payable, dependent upon the company's available profits, *before* the payment of any dividend recommended by the directors to ordinary shareholders.

Share certificates are issued to the company members. The name of the shareholder is also entered on the members' register to show the registered numbers of his holding. From time to time, when shares are bought and sold through the medium of the stock exchange, the name of the old member is erased from company records and a new certificate issued under the seal of the company showing the holding of the new member.

Share issues

With most public share issues, it is customary for the payment of the shares taken up to be made by instalments, in this manner:

A new company is 'floated' with an authorised share capital of 200 000 ordinary shares of £1 each. Half of the registered capital is to be offered to the general public and to be paid in three distinct stages, thus:

> 20p on application by 30 April
> 30p on allotment on 1 June
> 50p first and final call on 1 July.

The build-up of the company's finances is now shown over these two months. No complications are assumed (refunds, unpaid calls, etc.). The money comes in direct to the company's bank account, and the ordinary share capital is built up in this way, via application, allotment and final call accounts:

CASH BOOK Bank receipts (debit) side

		30 April	1 June	1 July	Total
		£	£	£	£
Application a/c		20 000			20 000
Allotment a/c			30 000		50 000
Call a/c				50 000	100 000

Ordinary Share Capital (credit) side

		30 April	1 June	1 July	Total
		£	£	£	£
Application a/c		20 000			20 000
Allotment a/c			30 000		50 000
Call a/c				50 000	100 000

Assuming that no trading operations have yet taken place, the company balance sheet on 1 July appears thus:

Assets of the company	
Bank account	£100 000

Represented by		
Authorised share capital		
200 000 ordinary shares of £1 each	£200 000	
Issued share capital		
100 000 ordinary shares of £1 fully paid		£100 000

Application and allotment

This is a general guide to the double entry procedure:

		Debit	Credit
(*a*)	Completed forms for the purchase of shares and application money received from the general public.	Bank	Application account
(*b*)	Company confirms allotment to successful applicants	Applic. a/c	Share capital a/c
(*c*)	and aks for amounts due on allotment.	Allot. a/c	Share capital
(*d*)	Some money may be returned to unsuccessful applicants with letters of regret	Applic. a/c	Bank
(*e*)	Allotment money comes in.	Bank	Allotment account
(*f*)	If some money is unpaid (owing) on allotment.	Calls in arrear	Allotment a/c
(*g*)	The directors decide to make a call for further money.	Call account	Share capital
(*h*)	The call money comes in	Bank	Call account
(*i*)	If some calls are unpaid (owing).	Calls in arrear	Call account

Application and allotment accounts are generally combined.

Note that after the application stage, the share capital of the company is *credited before the money is actually received* on the allotment and call accounts.

Calls in arrear

The liability of a company member is limited to the amount he has contracted to pay for his shareholding. If he has not paid all the 'calls' made on him by the company, he becomes a debtor for the money that is due. Sums owing by a defaulting shareholder are referred to as 'calls in arrear'.

If, in the last illustration, John Brown failed to pay the final call of

50p on his allotted 500 shares, he would become a debtor of the company for £250 (50p on 500 £1 shares).

The share capital at 1 July would show the full credit balance of £100000, but cash would be short by £250.

In making up the company's balance sheet at 1 July, John Brown's debt would not be included in the ordinary trade debtors' total in the current assets, but would be deducted as 'calls in arrear' from the issued share capital in this manner:

Assets of the company			
Bank account			£99750
Represented by			
Authorised share capital			
200000 ordinary shares of £1 each		£200000	
Issued share capital			
100000 ordinary shares of £1		£100000	
	Less calls in arrear	250	£99750

The directors of the company will give John Brown notice that unless he pays his final call of £250 by a certain date, his shares will be forfeited and sold (probably to another member). No refund would be made of the amount he has already paid.

Premium on shares

A successful company, probably needing further capital for expansion, might put out an additional issue of shares at a premium, i.e. at an amount above the nominal or par value of the shares. If, for instance, the nominal value of the shares was £1 and they were issued at £1.20 per share, the premium would be 20%. An applicant for 100 shares would pay £120 for them.

The Companies Acts require amounts received as premiums on shares to be taken to a share premium account as a capital reserve. This kind of reserve can only be used for special purposes (such as off-setting capital losses) and is not available for transfer to the credit of the revenue account and to be used for payment as a dividend, as in the case of a general reserve.

Normally the premium is paid with the allotment money, the book entries, in the first instance, being the full debit to the allotment account, with the separate amounts being credited to share capital and the share premium account. Then, when the allotment money (and the premium) is received, the bank is debited and the allotment account credited with the full amount of the allotment money plus the premium.

The premium, as a credit balance in the books, is shown on the balance sheet under the separate heading of *capital reserve*, between the issued capital and the revenue reserves, thus:

Authorised and issued share capital		
200 000 ordinary shares of £1 fully paid		£200 000
Capital reserve		
Share premium account		10 000
Revenue reserves		
General reserve account	£25 000	
Profit and loss undistributed balance	8 000	33 000

Debentures

Debentures are certificates, made under the seal of the company, acknowledging loans to the company. Instead of making a share issue, money is borrowed from the general public in this way, a fixed appreciable rate of interest being paid to the debenture holder. Debentures are often secured on the company's property such as the freehold premises and called 'mortgage debentures'; if not secured, they are termed 'naked debentures'.

Debenture holders are creditors of the company. In event of the liquidation of the company, their claims are met prior to those of the shareholders. Their interest is a fixed charge, payable whether the company makes a profit or incurs a loss. This is quite different from the payment of a share dividend, which is an appropriation of profit and must be recommended by the company's directors.

A debenture issue is similar to a share issue, often by instalments, and it is referred to as *loan capital*. Generally, on the vertical style balance sheet, the total figure for debentures is deducted from the total of the *net assets* to give the net worth or equity of the company (see the end of the next chapter).

Assignments

32.1 The Colby Mail Order Company Limited was registered on 1 January with an authorised share capital of £200 000 in ordinary shares of £1. On 1 February, one-hundred thousand shares were offered for public subscription by instalments as follows:

On application	10p per share
On allotment	20p per share
On 25 March	30p on first call
On 20 June	40p second and final call

The issue was fully subscribed. All monies were received on the due dates with the exception of the second and final call of one member, a Mr Frank Evans, who had been allotted 1000 shares.

Journalise the accounting entries and make up the balance sheet of the company, in so far as these particulars are concerned, as at 20 June.

32.2 Jaybee Enterprises Ltd issued 200 000 Ordinary Shares of £1 at a premium of 10%, and also £60 000 12% debentures at par.

Applications were received for 212 000 shares. The money surplus to the company's requirements was sent back with 'letters of regret' to those applicants who had asked only for small batches of shares.

The shares were received in three instalments: 20p on application, 40p on allotment (including the premium), and 50p two months after allotment. All monies were received on the share issue except in the case of one shareholder of 400 shares who could not meet his final call. The Board decided to allow this member another month to pay the amount outstanding, otherwise his shares were to be forfeited.

The debenture issue was subscribed in full and all monies banked.

Write up the cash book of the company and all relevant ledger accounts, and show the balance sheet, incorporating these details, made up on 30 September, the day after the date set for the final call.

32.3 Is there any difference between these three terms: (*a*) registered capital, (*b*) authorised capital, (*c*) nominal capital?

33

The Final Accounts of a Limited Company

This final chapter, on company accounts, is still introductory and simply intended to cover the requirements of the first-level Accounting examination syllabuses.

The 'published section' of the profit and loss account

The manufacturing and trading accounts of a limited company are generally prepared on the same lines as those of large privately owned businesses and partnerships. No special form is needed for these accounts, prepared to suit the internal needs of each type of business.

The Companies Acts, however, require full public disclosure of certain items which, normally, are found either in the general profit and loss account or its appropriation appendage. A clear distinction must be made between expense charges and appropriations of profit, and full details must be given of directors' fees and salaries, loan and debenture interest, and the depreciation of fixed assets. In this part of the profit and loss account, known as 'the published section' information must also be given of the following 'appropriations' of profit:

amounts paid or reserved for taxation,
dividends paid or recommended,
amounts transferred to (or withdrawn from) reserves.

The turnover (net sales) figure for the accounting period is disclosed, but the balance of the net trading profit need only be brought down to the 'published section' of the profit and loss account. In this section, too, is shown any income from quoted or unquoted investments as separate credits, and any profits or losses of a non-recurring nature (perhaps the sale of fixed assets).

The purpose of these disclosures, and that in the balance sheet following, is for the benefit of the shareholders, creditors, debenture holders and the Inland Revenue.

Note the grouping of this essential information and the distinction between charges and appropriations of profit on the 'published' part of the profit and loss account shown below.

Published Profit and Loss Account
for the year ended 31 December

	£	£	Previous year's figures
Balance of profit from general profit and loss account		80000	
Directors' fees	£8000		
Other emoluments of directors	3500	11500	
Audit fee	1500		
Debenture interest	2400		
Depreciation of machinery	18000		
Depreciation of fixtures	900	22800	34300
Net trading profit		45700	
Less Corporation Tax		19194	
Profit after taxation		26506	
Transfer to general reserve	5000		
Proposed dividend	15000	20000	
Retained profit for current year		6506	
Add Profit and loss balance from last year		1994	
Credit balance taken to balance sheet		£8500	

The vertical narrative presentation, of both the published part of the revenue account and the related balance sheet, lends itself to explanatory marginal and comparative figures and footnotes, in anticipation of leading questions from company members at the annual general meeting.

Note that company members receive 'dividends', portions of profit according to the size of their shareholding, and as recommended by the directors and approved by members at the Annual General Meeting. Not all profit is paid in dividends. Generally some surplus profit is carried forward, and referred to as 'retained profit'. Part of the profit may also be transferred to a general reserve and used later for emergencies or to be transferred back to revenue to bolster up profits in a poor year.

Balance sheet disclosures

The detailed requirements of the Companies Acts need not be memorised at this level of study. The next few paragraphs are included by way of interest, emphasising the fair and common sense aspects of much of the recent legislation to ensure that the final accounts of the limited companies, financed to a large extent with the savings of many thousands of ordinary people, do, in fact, 'show a true and fair view' of the finances of each joint-stock company.

The authorised share capital, where it is a different amount to the issued share capital, is simply presented for information and ruled off as it does not form part of the double entry.

Capital and revenue reserves are to be shown under separate headings. The former cannot be paid away in dividend, whereas the latter can be written back to the credit of profit and loss appropriation account if recommended by directors and approved by members.

Long-term liabilities are to be shown under their own headings. Generally they are either shown after the capital reserves section or deducted from net assets.

Current liabilities will include any bank overdraft, loan and debenture interest owing, expense accruals, and *dividends proposed but not yet paid*. It is customary to itemise these separately and deduct in total from the current assets to give the figure for working capital.

Footnotes or marginal references are made to any arrears of dividend of certain types of shares (cumulative preference shares); also details of any contingent liabilities, and capital expenditure authorised by the directors.

A company's fixed assets are shown at *cost less aggregate depreciation written off*. The fixed assets are normally grouped in order of permanency (land, buildings, plant and machinery, fittings and fixtures, motor vehicles) and totalled separately from the current assets.

Current assets are generally shown in this order: stock on hand at the date of the balance sheet, trade debtors, pre-payments such as rates in advance, and the bank and cash balances.

Footnotes or marginal notes are to be made of acquisitions or disposals of fixed assets during the year, and a statement made of

The Company Balance Sheet at 31 December

Fixed assets	Cost	Aggregate depreciation	Book value		Comparative figures
	£	£	£	£	£
Buildings	55 000	–	55 000		
Machinery	140 000	92 000	48 000		
Fixtures	6 000	3 750	2 250		
	201 000	95 750	105 250	105 250	

Investments (quoted)				
20 000 10% Preference shares of £1 in XYZ Ltd				
(market value £6 600)			4 000	
Current assets				
Stock		7 850		
Trade debtors		14 500		
Prepayments		350		
Bank		35 744	58 444	
Current liabilities				
Trade creditors		6 250		
Expense creditors		1 750		
Corporation tax		19 194		
Proposed dividend		15 000	42 194	
Working capital				16 250
Net assets				125 500
Less 12% Debentures (secured on buildings)				20 000
Net worth or equity				£105 500

The assets of the company are represented by:
Authorised share capital

200 000 Ordinary Shares of 50p each		£100 000
Issued share capital		£
150 000 Ordinary Shares of 50p fully paid		75 000
Capital reserve		
Share Premium Account		15 000
Revenue reserves		
General reserve	£2 000	
Addition this year	5 000	
	7 000	
P&L credit balance brought forward	8 500	15 500
		£105 500

the method of arriving at the valuation of the stock of finished goods and the work in progress.

Investments held by the company should be shown under their own heading between the fixed assets and the current assets, and listed as 'trade', 'quoted' or 'unquoted'. The market value of those with a stock exchange quotation should be given. The directors should estimate the value of unquoted investments and mention this as a footnote.

Formation or preliminary expenses (debit balances not yet written off) appear at the bottom of the assets. They are ignored when calculating the working capital.

The vertical presentation of the balance sheet discloses the working capital, net assets and the equity of the company at a glance.

The auditor's report is usually attached to the balance sheet, generally confirming that it depicts a 'true and fair view' of the company's financial affairs and complies with the requirements of the Companies Acts. A qualified report is issued when the auditors are not quite satisfied about one or two matters, and feel that questions should be raised by members at the Annual General Meeting.

Auditors do not prepare the final accounts of the company and are not employed by the company. They belong to a completely separate and distinct firm of professional accountants.

In addition to the profit and loss account and the balance sheet disclosures, the 1981 Companies Act requires the publication of a statement showing the sources and applications of the company's funds (in total) during the financial year.

Pause for thought

Which of these items would you find included under current liabilities in the balance sheet of a limited company?

(a) debenture interest due
(b) profit and loss credit balance
(c) general reserve account
(d) capital reserve account
(e) bank overdraft
(f) mortgage loan on premises
(g) recommended payment of preference dividend

Assignments

33.1 Make up the profit and loss account, including a separate 'published section', of the Kaypee Trading Co. Ltd from the following information:

	£
Turnover (net sales) for the year ended 31 December	380 000
Gross trading profit for the year	168 900
Undistributed profit from previous year	4 500
Rent and rates	8 600
Bad debts written off	460
Insurance paid	380
Commissions received	7 400
Directors' fees	10 000
Salaries of directors	16 000
Office salaries and NIC	37 500
Depreciation of vehicles	3 250
Half year's preference dividend paid June 30	5 000
Advertising and publicity	3 520
Audit fee payable	2 000

Adjustments are to be made for the following:

Payments in advance: rates £1400; insurance £80
Commissions earned, not yet received £720
Provision for Corporation Tax £40 000
Increase of bad debts provision by £150 to £1000.

The directors recommend the payment of the second half of the preference dividend, and the transfer of £8000 to general reserve. They further recommend a dividend of 15% to ordinary shareholders amounting to £30 000, and ask for the approval of members for the writing off of one-third of the formation expenses debit, standing in the books at £4800.

33.2 The MM Company Limited was registered with an authorised capital of £50 000 in 100 000 ordinary shares of 50p each. All the capital had been issued and was fully paid.

You are required to draw up the balance sheet of the company from the information listed overleaf:

	£
Plant and machinery (cost £30000; depreciation to date £12500)	17500
Van (cost £3400; depreciation to date £1850)	1550
Freehold premises at cost	34000
Credit balance on profit and loss of undistributed profit	5660
General reserve account	4000
Trade debtors and creditors £6400:£4230	
Wages owing £440 Rates in advance £320	
Stock on hand at 30 June	16500
Bank overdraft at 30 June	300
Provision for bad debts	640
Provision for Corporation Tax	10000
Investments held by the Company (9% Treasury Stock, present market value £2800)	3000
Ordinary dividend recommended by directors at 8%	4000

A Typical Examination Paper

Key Points

1 Certain types of questions are favoured by examiners. Those of high frequency, carrying good marks, are: partnership problems from the trial balance stage, with the appropriation account, year-end adjustments and the balance sheet; the final accounts of limited companies, in particular the balance sheet; the correction of errors through the journal; incomplete records and income and expenditure accounts.

   Among the subsidiary questions will be found one or more of the following: manufacturing accounts; control accounts; problems on stock (loss by fire); year-end adjustments on nominal ledger accounts; occasionally a bank reconciliation; some general theory and explanation of accounting terms.

2 In the examination hall, neatness and accuracy are still important, but the main emphasis now is on speed and the completion of the paper in the time allowed.

   Valuable marks will be lost if one or more of the smaller questions remain unanswered due to the time element. Make sure that you pick up some of these essential marks by answering the *shorter questions first*. A kind examiner will often give you a couple of marks for part of a problem attempted, but he cannot give you a mark for a question never started! In these competitive examinations, more than 50% of the candidates are borderline cases, and a little commonsense combined with a fair basic knowledge sometimes outweighs the specialist knowledge of the more academic student.

3 Use a separate sheet of paper for each question; then you can come back, given the time, to try to complete an unfinished problem. Examiners prefer only one answer to a sheet of paper. It looks neater and makes marking easier.

The following examination paper is modelled on the Accounting/Principles of Accounts papers set at GCE 'O' level and BTEC National (first year).

1   The treasurer of the Glen Tennis Club extracted the following information from his cash book at 30 September, the end of the current season:

	£		£
Bank balance 1 Oct.	139.50	New nets bought	250.00
Entrance fees (new members)	30.00	Lighting/heating	78.30
Total subs. received	580.00	Stationery	33.40
Competition fees	25.50	Loan repayment	200.00
Donations received	50.00	Refreshments bought	180.70
Gross receipts from raffles,		Wages of groundsman	240.00
dances and socials	232.90	New crockery	35.50

The club was founded five years before when a loan of £2000 was obtained from the local bank, guaranteed by six members. A wooden clubhouse was erected at the cost of £1750, and paid for out of the loan account. £800 has now been repaid to the bank on account of the loan.

At the beginning of the current year the games equipment account showed a balance of £360, and crockery account stood at £22.50.

At the end of the year an electricity bill for £14 was outstanding, and £18 was owing to the part-time groundsman. The committee decided to write off 25% from the old balance on equipment account and re-value the crockery at £20 (including additions during the year).

The position with regard to members' subscriptions was as follows:

	1 Oct. (a year ago) £	30 Sept. (year-end) £
Subscriptions in advance	18	12
Subscriptions in arrear	44	28

You are required to make up the income and expenditure account of the Glen Tennis Club, and a balance sheet at 30 September.

2   Drake and Hake are in partnership, sharing profits two-thirds and one-third. Their trial balance at 31 December has been made up *after* the gross profit on trading has been established:

		£	£
Capital account 1 Jan.	Drake		30000
	Hake		17000
Current account 1 Jan.	Drake		240
	Hake	30	
Drawings for year	Drake	5250	
	Hake	3800	
Freehold premises at cost		25000	
Machinery (cost less depreciation)		15000	
Office equipment (cost less deprec.)		1500	
Gross profit on trading			39000
Bank overdraft			850
Investment 8% Treasury Stock		10000	
Dividend from investment			800
Carriage outwards		240	
Salaries and NIC		16600	
Creditors for wages 31 Dec.			150
Rates and insurance		1640	
Debtors/creditors		8800	5500
Discounts allowed/received		430	670
Commissions			330
Bad debts		120	
Provision for bad debts			200
Lighting/heating		1180	
Bank charges		60	
Stationery and postages		140	
Stock on hand 31 Dec.		4950	
		£94740	£94740

The partnership deed provided that:

(a)   Hake should be credited with a salary of £1000 a year before the final distribution of profit.
(b)   Interest on capital is to be allowed at 6% per annum.

You are required to make up the profit and loss account (with the appropriation section) and a balance sheet at 31 December, taking into account these adjustments:

(a)   Machinery is to be depreciated by 20% and office equipment by 10% on the book balances.
(b)   Expenses accrued: electricity £35, printing bill £20.
(c)   Insurance in advance £90; rates in advance £360.
(d)   Increase provision for bad debts to 3% of year-end debtors.
(e)   An amount of £5000 is to be set aside, before final distribution, for a new general reserve account.

3 Sam Crowther has a busy little shop in a Salford suburb, but seldom finds time for 'book work'. However, he does have a bank account and keeps a rough sort of cash book. This enables his accountant to make up his annual accounts to the satisfaction of the Inland Revenue.

There are a few credit customers, but Sam prefers cash business in the main. Suppliers' invoices are not posted up to any ledger accounts; they are kept in a box file and stamped 'Paid' when the creditors' statements are settled at the end of every month.

Mr Crowther's statement of affairs on 31 December, one year ago, is shown in brief detail. His capital account was the balancing figure as his personal drawings could only be estimated.

	£		£
Capital account	3250	Shop fittings	
Trade creditors	350	(at valuation)	2500
		Stock 31 Dec.	450
		Trade debtors	80
		Bank and cash	570
	3600		3600

An analysis of the proprietor's ready-made cash book, together with the checking of his bank statements, revealed, in total form, the following:

Total cash takings for the year	£8645
Cash and cheques received from credit customers	£95

An analysis of the cash payments and the cheques drawn provided this information:

	£		£
Cash purchases	230	Payments to suppliers	2980
New counter	350	Wages paid	3020
Rent and rates	480	General expenses	20

The proprietor's drawings were estimated at £1700 for the year, drawn mainly from the cash till, and he also confirmed that he had withdrawn supplies for the family totalling £140 for the year.

The current assets and liabilities at 31 December were:

Stock on hand £380: Owing by debtors £110: Owing to creditors £420.

There was no change in the nature of the fixed assets during the year apart from the purchase of the new counter, revalued on 31 December at £300. Adjustments are to be made for £48 wages owing to part-time assistant, and for £40 rates paid in advance.

You are required to make up Sam Crowther's revenue account and a balance sheet as at 31 December.

Section B
Answer only THREE *questions*

4 The following list of balances was extracted from the trial balance of a small manufacturer on 31 December:

	£		£
Production wages	7750	Sales for year	48000
Office salaries	6600	Warehouse wages	3200
Rent from sub-tenant	800	Advertising	1540
General expenses	1130	Director's salary (part time)	2000
Carriage on raw material	550	Factory rates	1600
Carriage on sales	360	Office/showroom rates	850
Purchases, raw material	10350	Discounts allowed	670
Factory heating/lighting	1420	Discounts received	780
Deprec. of machinery	2500	Selling expenses	1320
Office heating/lighting	880	Sales returns	440

The position with regard to stocks was as follows:

	Raw material £	Finished goods £	Work in progress £
1 January	3200	4810	1760
31 December	3600	5620	1650

The manufactured goods (to be transferred to trading account) have a current market value of £29 900.

From the above information, you are required to prepare a combined manufacturing, trading and profit and loss account to disclose:

(a) the cost of raw material consumed
(b) the cost of production
(c) profit on manufacture
(d) cost of sales
(e) gross profit on trading
(f) net profit on trading.

5 (*a*)   Explain briefly, in about eight to ten lines, the purpose and usefulness of self-balancing ledgers.

(*b*)   Extract sufficient information from the listed balances and totals below to make up your *sales ledger control account*. Make up this account as it would appear in the general ledger and carry down the balance.

		Bought ledger		*Sales ledger*	
1 January	Debit balances	£56	Debit balances	£5324
	Credit balances	£4259	Credit balances	£62

		£
31 December	Credit sales for year	28750
	Goods bought on credit	15480
	Payments by customers	26338
	Payments to suppliers	14825
	Discount allowed	245
	Discount received	183
	Bad debts written off	72
	Sales returns	127
	Purchase returns	98
31 December	Credit balances in sales ledger at year-end	54
	Debit balances in bought ledger at year-end	42
	Credits in bought ledger transferred to sales ledger	120

6   Record (or make the correction) by journal entry, of each of the following in the financial books of Jenna Sivel:

(*a*)   A page of the purchases day book has been over-cast by £100 and carried forward to the month end.

(*b*)   The provision for bad and doubtful debts (at present £250 in the books) is to be reduced to £200.

(*c*)   A payment of £45 for repairs to the firm's car has been debited to vehicles (asset) account.

(*d*)   A cheque received from Frances Owen has been correctly entered in the cash book as £56, but has been credited to her sales ledger account as £65.

(*e*)   An old machine (book value £120) has been taken in part exchange at £150 against the purchase of a new machine costing £750, the balance being paid by cheque. Journalise full details of this composite entry, including the profit or loss on taking the old machine out of the books.

(*f*) Tamsin Smith's account for £18 was written off to bad debts two years ago. A first and final dividend of 20% has now been received from her trustee in bankruptcy.

(*g*) Wages amounting to £2400 paid to the firm's own workmen building an extension to the showroom, have been debited to wages account.

(*h*) At the close of the financial year Miss Sivel agreed with her accountant that some of the firm's products, approximating to £10 a week, had been taken by members of her own family, and should be chargeable to her private drawings account.

7 On 28 June, two days before the close of the financial year, the accountant of The Patonga Press Limited (an old family business), extracted these balances from his books as a temporary check on his double entry records, which were not mechanised:

	£		£
Machinery	35000	Fixtures & fittings	2400
Premises	29500	12½% debentures	20000
Stock on hand	5230	Trade creditors	4800
Trade debtors	9650	Directors' salaries	10000
Bank	6520	Expense creditors	320
Undistributed profit		Debenture interest	
from last year	4500	paid	2500
Audit fee	500	Depreciation – fixed	
		assets	2400

The net turnover for the year was £92000. A rough trading account was drawn up for the current year before incorporating items to be shown in the published section. The net trading profit was £24280.

The authorised share capital of this company was 50000 Ordinary Shares of £1 each. The company was incorporated six years ago, but final calls had only been made on members recently. All monies had been received except for the final call of 20% on one member's 1000 shares.

The 12½% debentures are secured on the freehold premises, still shown at their cost of £29500. The debenture interest is paid up to date. The other fixed assets now stand at their book value less depreciation. Machinery had originally cost £45000 and had been depreciated at £2000 a year. Fixtures originally cost £4400 and has been depreciated by £400 each year. There are no additions to the fixed assets.

The transactions now listed took place over the last two days of the month and are to be incorporated into the final figures:

		£
(a)	Cash sales (cost of merchandise sold £120)	210
(b)	Sales to credit customers (cost £150)	260
(c)	Payments from customers (banked)	345
(d)	Cash purchases for stock	90
(e)	Goods bought on credit	330
(f)	Payments to suppliers	420
(g)	Payment of account for stationery (listed under expense creditors)	46

The directors decide to reserve £3000 for taxation and recommend the payment of a 10% dividend to members.

You are required to draft the 'published section' of the profit and loss account, and make up a balance sheet at 30 June, in compliance with the requirements of the Companies Acts.

Additional Exercises

Exercises on Chapter 2

1 Make up a simple form of cash account from this information:

July
1 Sold £100 of goods for cash
2 Bought £50 of goods for cash
4 Paid £10 in expenses
5 Received £30 from cash customers.

2 Enter the following cash transactions in your cash account for the first week of June:

June		£
1	Cash in hand	200.00
2	Bought goods for cash	66.50
	Cash sales	117.25
3	Paid for printing	10.25
4	Paid wages	50.00
	Receipts from cash customers	45.80
5	Withdrew cash for own use	60.00

3 Assuming you have £350 cash in hand on 1 October, make up a cash account from the following receipts and payments:

Oct.		£
4	Goods bought for cash	150.00
16	Further purchases	62.50

Money received from cash customers:
Oct. 5   £43.20   Oct. 12   £33.62
Oct. 21   70.48   Oct. 28   86.27
Wages paid . . . 8 October £60.00, 15 October £60.00, 23 October £65.00
Electricity bill for £18.30 paid on 24 October
Drawings in cash for own use 30 October £80.00

4 Roy Adams has a pensionable post. He has now reached the maximum salary of £4000 a year for his grade, and plans to buy a small business from his uncle when the latter retires in three years' time. The price asked for the business (goodwill, fittings, equipment etc.) is £8000. Adams has already saved £2400 towards his objective. Assuming that his family and personal expenses average £3000 a year, how much more money will he need to borrow on loan or mortgage, to complete the purchase price of the business in three years' time?

Exercises on Chapter 3
Enter the receipts and payments for each of the exercises below in a separate cash account, balance and rule off each account, bringing down the new balances at the end of each month.

1 Jan.

		£
1	Cash balance	100.00
	Bought goods	50.00
3	Paid for stationery	2.50
8	Cash takings	135.75
12	Bought further goods	25.00
13	Paid salary of new typist	60.00
	Cash sales receipts	112.25
22	Payment from Alfred Brown	8.15
	Paid salary	60.00
31	Withdrew cash for 'self'	120.00

2 March

1	Cash in hand	200.00
2	Paid rent for month	28.00
	Bought goods for sale	45.00
6	Cash sales	47.50
10	Paid salary	55.00
14	Paid insurance premium	16.80
17	Cash takings	139.30
20	Paid Albert Smith	18.80
23	Paid salary	55.00
26	Cash purchases	36.60
31	Drawings for own use	80.00

3 June

1	Cash balance	120.00
3	Cash sales	42.60
5	Paid rent for month	20.00
8	Cash purchases	38.50
14	Tom Jones paid his account	14.20
	Cash sales to date	33.30
19	Paid carriage on deliveries	2.40
22	Paid for repairs to desk	3.60
28	Paid Willie Robson's account	18.70
	Advertising account paid	10.00
30	Received month-end commission	25.00
	Refund from Jim Blake	10.00

Exercises on Chapter 4

1 Make up the cash account of Alan Ramsden from the information given below, balance the account, and post up the corresponding ledger accounts:

June		£	June		£
1	Cash in hand	120.00	16	Cash sales	102.70
5	Bought goods	33.40	20	Cash purchases	35.90
8	Paid salary	65.00	24	Paid salary	65.00
12	Cash sales	37.10	25	Drawings	85.00
14	Paid rates	25.80	30	Cash sales	144.60

2 Study this cash account and then answer questions (*a*) to (*d*) below:

Cash Account

Jan.			£	Jan.			£
1	Balance b/f		100 00	2	Purchases		40 00
5	Cash sales		37 20	8	Stamps		2 50
14	Cash sales		35 80	12	Salary		60 50
26	Cash sales		133 40	19	Drawings		25 00
				30	Salary		60 50

(*a*) Explain each item in date order.
(*b*) What is another name for *cash sales*?
(*c*) Both purchases and salaries refer to payments. Why is it necessary to make a distinction between them?
(*d*) Balance up this cash account, open up corresponding ledger accounts and post up the double entry.

3 What do you understand by the word *balance* as applied to the cash account? Would it be possible to finish with a closing balance brought down beneath the total on the credit side of the cash account?

4 There are several mistakes on the cash account now shown of Amanda Black. Amend them, re-draft and balance the account, and post up the corresponding double entry to the various ledger accounts:

Cash Account of Amanda Black

Jan.			£	Jan.			£
2	Sales		122 90	1	Balance b/f		200 00
10	Cash takings		46 00	5	Daily takings		12 20
16	Purchases		38 10		Salary		54 00
	Stamps, etc.		2 30	6	Drawings		125 00
22	Petrol account		14 40	9	Cash from Sam Pye		35 80
31	Cash sales		98 70	17	Van repairs		8 90
				22	Salary		54 50

5   Write up the cash account of Julian Hoyland from the information now listed:

Feb.		£	Feb.		£
1	Money in hand	142.38	2	Bought goods	25.43
8	Paid insurance	17.56	8	Paid salary	75.00
9	Cash sales	68.50	14	Cash sales	27.91
18	Cash purchases	14.78	24	Drawings	130.00
	Petrol/oil	3.58	26	Payment from	
27	Paid Henrietta Hawks	12.12		Jean Spring	123.22
	Cash sales	153.32	28	Bought goods	45.36
28	Paid salary	75.00	29	Credit sale to	
				Simon May	50.00

Exercises on Chapter 5

1   On 1 June you start in business with £200 cash. The next day you buy goods to be re-sold (at a profit) which cost you £50. On 4 June your cash sales amount to £85, and you pay £3 carriage on deliveries. At the end of the first week you pay £56 to your teenage assistant, and sell another £28 of goods to other cash customers.

Post up your cash book and the double entry to ledger accounts, balance all accounts and take out a trial balance on 6 June.

2   Follow the same instructions as in Exercise 1 in connection with these figures for the first fortnight of May:

May		£
1	Cash in hand	500.00
2	Paid for goods	140.50
	Bought stationery	10.00
4	Cash sales	84.65
5	Cash sales	22.33
8	Paid salary	63.50
	Cash purchases	88.82
11	Carriage on purchases	5.25
12	Cash sales	72.74
14	Withdrew for own use	25.00

3   Robin Adare started in business with £150 cash only as his capital on 1 January. He bought £45 of goods on 2 January and paid £3 transport costs. On 5 January cash customers paid him £48 and out of that amount he paid a printing bill of £6. Further cash sales the next day realised £44. On 6 January he paid his part-time assistant £42 and withdrew £50 for himself.

Write up Mr Adare's books, balance all accounts and take out a trial balance on 6 January.

4 Janet Mansfield has a small office supplies agency. She invested £250 in this new venture on 1 November, and details are now given of her trading receipts and payments for the first month:

Nov.		£
1	Cash at start (and capital)	250.00
3	Bought supplies	85.20
5	Cash sales	42.80
	Paid for stamps	3.50
8	Salary of part-time employee	30.00
12	Cash sales	24.90
	Cash purchases	68.75
16	Paid carriage on purchases	4.25
	Cash sales	94.00
20	Paid garage account	18.10
22	Paid salary	30.00
	Rates for half year	36.00
	Cash sales	52.55
27	Paid advertising account	8.80
30	Paid salary	30.00
	Drawings of Miss Mansfield	53.25

Write up the cash book for the month of November, post the double entry to the ledger accounts, and take out a trial balance on 30 November.

5 Assemble the information shown below in trial balance form in order to ascertain the business capital of the proprietor, Cecil Crosby, as at 30 September, the date of the extraction of these balances:

	£		£
Net sales	3880	Net purchases	1240
Salaries	1500	Cash in hand	800
Stationery	105	Sundry expenses	80
Insurance	15	Rent and rates	420
Advertising	120	Drawings	1000

6 Make up a trial balance from the following balances extracted from the books of The Trent Hardware Stores on 31 December:

		£
Jan. 1	Opening capital	1630
Dec. 31	Net sales for year	6220
	Net purchases for year	3445
	Advertising	250
	Rent and rates	560
	General expenses	75
	Wages/salaries	1860
	Drawings	1250
	Petrol/oil	385
	Transport charges	25

Exercises on Chapter 6

1 Why is the valuation of stock so important? What would be the effect on a business profit of £4500 if

(*a*) the closing stock was overvalued by £200
(*b*) the closing stock was undervalued by £300?

2 Calculate the gross profits of these three businesses and in each case show the cost of sales figure:

	Stock 1 Jan.	Purchases	Sales	Stock 31 Jan.
	£	£	£	£
Business A	500	2500	4800	650
Business B	100	1800	2500	300
Business C	750	6820	9330	540

3 Make up the trading account of Percy Symons from the following information, ascertain his final stock figure, and then work out his gross profit on trading:

> Symons had a stock of 500 articles on 1 June, bought at the average cost of £2 each. He bought 1500 similar articles during the month of June also at the average price of £2 each, and his total sales (of 1400 articles) realised £4500.

In this instance, in order to calculate the final stock figure, it is necessary to find by arithmetic the physical number of articles available for sale and those actually sold, in addition to their money value.

4 Ann Flitcroft started in business on 1 January with a stock of £220 value. During the month she bought £40 of new merchandise, paying transport costs of £4. Cash customers paid her a total of £62, though one customer returned the goods sold to him and he was refunded the £2 he had paid. The stock valuation on 31 January was £245.

   You are required to make up Miss Flitcroft's trading account from the above information.

5 At the end of October Thomas Duckworth's accountant extracts certain details from his books prior to drawing up a temporary trading account for the month. From these figures now shown, make up his trading account for October:

	£		£
Stock 1 Oct.	570	Stock 31 Oct.	430
Cash sales	2450	Purchases	880
Carriage inwards	30	Warehouse wages	440

At the same time the accountant verified the cash balance at 31 October to be £250, and Mr Duckworth's drawings for the month at £100.

6 Extract the necessary detail from the trial balance below to make up a trading account showing the gross profit made by Sean Dean's business for the month ended 31 March.

Trial Balance   31 March

	£	£
Capital: S. Dean 1 March		500
Drawings for month	200	
Net sales		1500
Net purchases	650	
Carriage on purchases	20	
Warehousing expenses	330	
Stock 1 March	375	
Cash balance	425	
	2000	2000

Mr Dean valued his closing stock at 31 March at £525.

Exercises on Chapter 7

1 Re-draft the following statement to show clearly the true gross and net profit figures for this business:

**Trading and Profit Account
of Evadne Price
at 30 June**

	£	£		£
Purchases	920		Sales	1800
Stock 30 June	450	1370	Stock 1 June	350
Office salaries	——	200		
Gross profit c/d		580		
		2150		2150
Stamps/stationery		10	Gross profit b/d	580
Travelling expenses		35		
Drawings		50		
Carriage inwards		15		
Rent and rates		40		
Net profit		430		
		580		580

2 A trader buys £300 of goods for sale. He pays £20 carriage and warehousing charges of £15. He sells two-thirds of the consignment for £420, incurring office and distribution costs of £56.

Work out this problem arithmetically to begin with, and then show his gross and net profits in the proper accounting manner.

3 From the information given below, ascertain the gross and net trading profits of Daisy Bell. She started in business on 1 May with a capital of £500. During the month of May she withdrew £50 for private purposes and her trading operations involved the following:

	£		£
Purchases for month	350	Sales for month	620
Carriage inwards	15	Petrol/oil	22
Rates	25	Stationery	3
Carriage outwards	10	Insurance	5

Miss Bell valued her closing stock at 31 May at £88.

4 Percy Pullet made up his books to 31 December, after six months' trading. The balances were extracted from his books and taken to a trial balance, as shown below.

He asks you to work out his gross and net profits in a proper accounting manner, taking his final stock to be £145, according to his own valuation.

Trial Balance   31 December

	£	£
Capital: P. Pullet 1 July		800
Van account	310	
Cash balance 31 Dec.	192	
Fittings	120	
Purchases/Sales	222	550
Stock 1 July	108	
Insurance	20	
Drawings	240	
Van repairs	32	
Miscellaneous expenses	14	
Salaries for temporary typists	60	
Advertising	9	
Heating of office at home	23	
	1350	1350

Exercises on Chapter 8

1 Norman Parker's transactions for the month of February are detailed below. At the beginning of the month his capital was represented by one asset – £200 cash on 1 February. Mr Parker uses a room at home for his office.

Feb.		£	Feb.		£
2	Bought goods for re-sale	124	6	Cash sales	106
8	Payment for temporary office work	18	9	Purchases	62
16	Paid insurance	6	14	Cash sales	84
17	Salary	18	20	Purchases	33
23	Paid carriage on purchases	2	25	Cash sales	98
	Office cleaning	12	28	Drawings	60
26	Lighting/heating proportion of use of room at home	5			

Open up a new set of books for Norman Parker, and post up his cash book and all ledger account. Take out a trial balance at the end of February and make up his final accounts, including a balance sheet. His closing stock valuation at 28 February was £125.

2 You are required to make up Angela Peel's final accounts, including a balance sheet, for the year ended 30 June. The trial balance shown below is a summary of her trading operations made up *after her gross profit on trading has been ascertained.*

Trial Balance   30 June

	£	£
Capital 1 July		3000
Cash balance 30 June	2790	
Gross profit on trading		2500
Drawings for year	2000	
Insurance	50	
Rates	162	
Advertising	48	
Stock June 30	450	
	5500	5500

3 Draw up a trial balance from the following details extracted from the cash book and the ledger accounts of Rupert de Winter on 31 March.

	£		£
Stock 1 March	1500	Advertising	350
Sales	6700	Warehousing expenses	
Salaries	480	& storemens' wages	150
Drawings	200	Cash balance 31 March	2055
Insurance	72	Carriage inwards	18
Office cleaning	30	Stamps/stationery	45
Purchases	3800		

Complete the full set of final accounts with the closing stock valuation at 31 March being £800.

4 If the capital of Sam Roberts on 1 January was £3000, and he makes a profit of £2250, withdrawing £1650 for his private and family use, what will be his capital on 31 December at the end of his trading year?
Can you also work out the percentage increase on his original capital?

5 Complete the following table.

Business	Capital 1 January	Profit for year	Drawings	Capital 31 December
	£	£	£	£
A	500			720
B	1500	770	500	
C	4800	1600		5200
D		850	900	1950

236   Basic Accounting

Exercises on Chapter 9

1 The transactions listed below are taken from the books of Sara Dawson. Post the details to the appropriate accounts, take out a trial balance, and then make up her trading account and a balance sheet as at 30 June. Miss Dawson's closing stock valuation at 30 June was £80.

June		£	June		£
1	Cash in hand	300	16	Cash sales	68
3	Bought office desk	50	18	Purchases	44
	Paid for goods	120	20	Carriage paid	2
5	Cash sales	81		Cash sales	75
10	Bought goods	40	25	Drawings	100
12	Cash sales	52	28	Cash sales	145
13	Paid wages	50	30	Paid wages	50

2 Fleur Lindsay lists her transactions for the month of July for you to make the postings to her cash book and ledger accounts, and, after that, to draft her final accounts preparatory to typing for management.

July		£	July		£
1	Cash on hand	500	2	Bought goods	150
	(her only asset at this		3	Cash sales	66
	date)		5	Paid wages	48
4	Paid joiner for fixing			Cash sales	154
	shelves	50	12	Insurance	15
10	Stationery	16	16	Cash sales	113
	Bought goods	72	20	Travelling exes.	4
18	Paid wages	48		Cash sales	176
28	Commission rec'd	80	26	Bought stamps	5
29	Paid wages	48	27	Bought filing cabinet	28
31	Paid office salaries for			Drawings	50
	month	178	30	Drawings	50

Miss Lindsay valued her closing stock at 31 July at £100.

3 The assets and liabilities listed below furnish the information required to find out the trading profit of Ruth Bilston during her first year's trading.

	1 January £	31 December £
Premises	4000	4000
Stock	600	850
Machinery	1000	1200
Fixtures/fittings	300	300

You are required to draw up Miss Bilston's balance sheet as at 31 December, allowing for her private drawings of £1000 during the year, and to show the trading profit made in her first year.

4 Make up the final accounts of Richard Marlowe for the month of August from the transactions listed below. Mr Marlowe started in business on 1 August, transferring £500 from his Post Office Account to the business account, and, on the same day, he bought £150 of merchandise to be re-sold to the general public at his marked-up prices.

Aug.		£
2	Paid rent for month	20
6	Bought stamps	2
	Cash sales	65
9	Bought shop counter	48
12	Cash sales	72
	Bought goods	34
15	Carriage paid on purchases	3
22	Paid for repairs	6
23	Cash sales	88
	Advertising	16
25	Travelling expenses	7
27	Cash sales	85
	Drawings	30
31	Paid salaries	60

Mr Marlowe's stock valuation on 31 August was £65.

Exercises on Chapter 10

1 Enter the following transactions in your cash book and balance up at the end of June.

June		£
1	Cash in office	20.00
	Money in the bank	300.00
3	Ron Lawson paid his account to the end of May by cheque	22.50
4	Cash sales	37.80
	Paid cash into bank	25.00
9	Paid rent by cheque	15.00
12	Cash purchases	8.50
15	Cashed cheque for own use	10.00
	Paid cash for stationery	2.75
26	Received cheque from Alan Brown	52.25
28	Sent cheque to Ted Edmondson	36.30
	Cash sales	94.90
30	Paid cash into bank	30.00
	Paid wages in cash	62.60

In this question you are told precisely whether the receipts and payments are made by cheque or in cash. In most examination problems the method of payment is generally left to the student's discretion. This practice (of leaving the student to decide for himself) will be followed from this stage onwards, but *read again the note on Cash or Cheque* on page 54 of the text.

238   *Basic Accounting*

2   Angelica Jane is a hairdresser. She asks you to post up her cash book for
    the month of August from the details given below, and balance the cash
    and bank columns on 31 August:

Aug.
  1   Bank balance £200
  2   £30 cheque drawn for office cash
  4   Bought £25 of equipment for shop and also £50 of hairdressing supplies
  8   Paid £3 postage on circulars
      Daily takings £85
  9   Paid Nan Soper's account for £32
 14   Received £5 cash from Laura Jamesson
 16   Withdrew £20 cash from till for own use
 18   Cash takings £68. Banked £60
 21   Cash purchases £15
 22   Paid £48 wages in cash
 24   Paid £25 rent for month
      Cash takings £112
 26   Paid £12 for cleaning
 28   Gloria Flashen paid £14 for appointments over the past two weeks
 30   Paid £8 insurance
 31   Paid all surplus cash over £10 into bank.

3   What effect would these transactions have upon the balance sheet of
    George Allen who started in business a month ago with a capital of £200
    in cash?

    (*a*)   Goods bought for re-sale £50
    (*b*)   Fittings bought for £45
    (*c*)   The sale of half of his stock for £35
    (*d*)   Personal drawings of £25.

    Draft his up-to-date balance sheet, giving effect to these adjustments.

4   How would the balance sheet of George Allen (in the previous ques-
    tion) be affected by these further transactions, as itemised:

    (*a*)   A filing cabinet bought for £30
    (*b*)   Cash sales of £40 (the cost price of the goods sold being £25)
    (*c*)   Expenses paid £12
    (*d*)   Further goods bought for re-sale £50

    Draw up another balance sheet, giving full effect to these additional
    adjustments.

Exercises on Chapter 11

1   Karen Mason's cash book at 30 June shows a debit balance of £216.64.
    Her bank statement, received the following morning, indicated that the
    customer was in credit to the extent of £282.78. On checking, it was
    found that cheques sent to suppliers in settlement of their June
    accounts, amounting to £134.58, had not yet been presented for pay-

ment; and cheques and cash received from two customers on 30 June, totalling £68.44, had been posted to the cash book on 30 June but was entered on the bank paying-in slip and paid into the bank the next morning.

Draw up a statement reconciling these two balances.

2 This extract is copied from the last page of Francina Drake's cash book (bank columns only):

Sept.			£	Sept.			£
1	Balance		336 20	2	Ninian Hall		33 20
3	Sue Fleming		55 80	8	Terry Fallon		10 50
	Cash banked		120 65	15	Wages (cheque)		150 00
12	Len Fraser		24 50	19	Stan Martin		8 36
28	Josh Morgan		28 75	24	Merle Newton		17 34
30	Wesley Dale		16 10	29	Abe Manson		15 80

On checking Miss Drake's bank statement for Sept., you find that the cheques of Morgan and Dale have not yet been cleared by the bank and credited to the business account; and that the cheque paid to Abe Manson on 29 September had not yet been presented for payment. Make up a reconciliation statement confirming the balance according to the records of the bank.

3 The bank columns of Donald Corlett's cash book for the month of May are shown below, followed by Corlett's bank statement, received by him on 1 June:

May			£	May			£
1	Balance b/f		268 00	2	Hilda Walker		52 90
6	Lesley Law		23 50	7	Kay Watson		16 84
13	Cash paid in		75 45	10	Jan Tempest		15 22
19	Ned Leader		8 68	16	Wages cheque		80 00
27	Tim Norton		12 63	26	Ben Saver		28 75
30	Max Kneale		22 92	28	Petty cash		20 00
31	Seb Norris		38 60	30	Roy Wiles		36 65

May			Debit £	Credit £	Balance £
1	Balance b/f				268.00
4	Walker		52.90		215.10
8	Law			23.50	238.60
9	Watson		16.84		221.76
13	Cash			75.45	297.21
14	Tempest		15.22		281.99
16	Wages		80.00		201.99
19	Leader			8.68	210.67
28	Petty cash		20.00		190.67
31	Bank charges		3.00		187.67

It is suggested that you bring the firm's cash book up to date as far as possible, and then reconcile the *amended cash book bank balance* with the bank balance according to the bank statement.

4 Jonathan Lane's cash book shows a bank balance of £182.55 on 31 December. On checking with the bank statement on 2 January he discovers these differences:

(a) Cash sales and cheques amounting to £115.35 paid into the bank on 31 December had not been credited to the firm's account.

(b) Cheques in settlement of two suppliers' accounts (Lawson & Son £28.90 and Fred Jackson £46.20) had not yet been presented for payment.

(c) Bank charges and commission totalling £5.50 had been charged and debited by the bank against the firm, but had not yet been posted in the firm's cash book.

Draw up a reconciliation statement and find the bank balance according to the bank statement.

5 You are asked to help a friend to balance his cash book for the month of March from the details given below:

Debit balances brought forward from February – Bank £335.50; Cash £16.60
Cash payments made during the month of March:

March		£
8	Stamps	2.20
15	Window cleaning	1.50
21	Stamps	2.00
30	Salaries	140.00

Three credit customers paid their outstanding accounts by cheque during March:

March		£
5	Arnold Gibson	21.20
12	Bertram Gordon	12.90
22	Penelope Potts	6.00

Cash takings as per till rolls		Cheques paid or cashed as per counterfoils		
March	£	March		£
3	33.50	3	Brown Bros.	35.10
8	68.20	9	Advertising	10.00
12	22.20	15	Rent	25.00
18	28.40	26	Garage account	14.60
24	44.80	30	Brown Bros.	42.50
26	62.40	31	Drawings	120.00
30	64.60			

Cash takings surplus to office requirements were banked on three occasions, as shown by the bank paying-in book:
March 10 £50   March 20 £45   March 31 £80

After completing the cash book posting with all detail, bring down the new commencing balances for the month of April.

Exercises on Chapter 12

1 What do you understand by the term *petty cash imprest*? If you were given the responsibility of keeping the petty cash account with a weekly imprest of £15, and the first week your total disbursements amounted to £11.78, what would be:

(a) the petty cash balance in hand at the end of the week, and
(b) the amount of imprest refund you could expect from the main cashier to bring your cash back to the amount of the original imprest?

2 Write up the petty cash book for Peter Hastings & Company, which is under the control of the chief cashier with a weekly imprest of £25.

July		£
1	Cash in the petty cash box	25.00
	Paid for stamps	2.00
	Travelling expenses	2.50
2	Office cleaning	5.00
3	Postage stamps	3.50
4	Bus fares for typist	0.42
	Milk and tea	0.86
	Subscription to Oxfam	0.50
5	Typewriter repairs	4.75
	Office sundries, brown paper and string	3.28

Use a petty cash book with four analysis columns, bring down the balance at the end of the week, and show the amount to be refunded to you to bring the imprest up to the original sum of £25.

3 Robin Wood is the petty cashier of Sherwood Foresters, operating a monthly 'float' of £40. His petty cash payments for the month of May are listed below. Show the manner in which he would write up his Petty Cash Book, and the amount of the imprest refund he would receive from the chief cashier at the beginning of June.

May		Voucher	Amount
2	Cleaning	1	£4.80
4	Bus fares	—	3.22
5	Stationery	2	2.85
8	Stamps	3	2.00
10	Travelling	—	0.75
14	Cleaning	4	4.80
18	Telegram	—	1.45
22	Tea and milk	5	0.62
25	Donation to Red Cross	6	3.00
27	Stamps	7	2.00
	Repairs to chair	8	3.10
30	Cleaning	9	4.80
31	Tea and milk	10	0.62

4 Your capital on 1 April comprised £480 in a bank account and £20 petty cash. Post up these various details in the main cash book, the petty cash book, and ledger accounts, and take out a trial balance to prove the accuracy of your postings on 6 April.

April
  2   Paid £20 rent by cheque
  3   Bought £50 of supplies and paid by cheque
      Cash sales £35; paid £30 into bank
  5   Paid £2 for postage stamps (PCB)
      Drawings £25 (cashed cheque)
      Bought £40 desk (second hand). Paid by cheque.
  6   Paid £3 bus fares out of petty cash
      Cash sales £65
      Paid all surplus cash into bank.

Exercises on Chapter 13

1 'Original records of entry are used as aids to simplify the posting of ledger accounts.' Explain this statement.

2 On 8 April, Martin Westdale, hardware merchant of Thornbrook Grove, Spalding, bought £60 of garden fencing from his wholesaler Jeremy Price & Co. of Main Street, Grantham. The creditor's invoice was sent by post the following day, an allowance of 25% trade discount being made.
   Make a copy of the supplier's invoice, and post the details of the transaction in the purchase day book of Martin Westdale in Spalding.

3 Enter up the purchases day book of Anne Michele, high class milliner of Knutsford, Cheshire from the information given below:

Nov.
  1   Bought 6 latest creations from Paris Fashions Ltd. for £50.50 less 20% trade discount.
  6   Received urgent delivery from Stardust Dream for the Countess of Delamere – a garden fête chapelette at £25.00 net.
  15 Monofleur sent 20 Riviere-type hats at £88 less 25% trade discount.
  26 Bought another 6 hats from Paris Fashions for £10 each less the usual discount.

4 Lilian Moss settles her outstanding account with Gertson & Dazey on 2 October. This was for September, totalling £4.56.
   The next day she received a credit note from the wholesalers of 50p for the return of containers.
   During the month of October the following invoices were received from Gertson & Dazey, all in connection with supplies delivered in accordance with her telephone instructions:
October 4 £2.73   October 16 £3.88   October 22 £5.25
Show the creditor's account in the books of the purchaser from 1 October to 31 October, bringing down the balance at the end of the month.

5 On 1 March Robert Parry commenced business, paying £200 into his account at the Central Bank Ltd.

His transactions for the month of March are listed below. Enter all details in the original records, make all postings to the ledger and extract a trial balance. Finally, taking Mr Parry's stock valuation at 31 March at £60, draft a full set of final accounts of his business, including a balance sheet as at 31 March.

March		£
2	Cashed cheque for the office	30.00
4	Bought goods from F. Holloway £50 (gross) subject to 20% trade discount.	
8	Cash sales	134.62
	Paid wages out of cash receipts	60.00
9	Paid rent for month	15.75
12	Bought goods from L. Landers (gross) £40.40 less trade discount of 25%	
	Cash sales	44.90
18	Paid Holloway's account	
22	Cash sales	138.14
	Paid wages	60.00
25	Paid general expenses in cash	5.50
28	Withdrew cash for self	130.00
31	Paid cash into bank	80.00

Exercises on Chapter 14

1 John Bancroft has built up a small credit connection. During the month of May he sent out these invoices to his customers:

May
3 Credit sale to A. Morris £20 less 20% trade discount
13 Urgent delivery of £6 of goods to James Platt
23 Daniel Twist called and bought £32 worth of merchandise; he was allowed trade rate of 25%
28 Further credit sale to A. Morris of £45 gross less 20%

Enter up Bancroft's Sales Day Book for May, post the debits to the personal ledger accounts and complete the Sales Account for the month.

2 Alan Neave buys most of his supplies from a wholesaler trading under the name of The Eastgate Trading Company. At the beginning of July Neave owed his creditor £24 for goods bought in June.

Details of their transactions are given below for the month of July:

July		£
5	Purchases by Neave	8.33
9	Purchases by Neave	13.50
17	Bought from E.T.C.	26.20
26	Bought from E.T.C.	6.57

On 30 July Neave settled his old account for June.

Make up the ledger account of the debtor in the books of the creditor, showing the balance brought down on 31 July.

3 Jonathan Turner commenced business on 1 October with a capital of £1000 represented by:

		£	
Bank		500	
Van valued at		350	
Stock		150	£1000

After opening the three asset accounts and the corresponding credit to Mr Turner's capital account, you are required to post up the detail shown in the day books and the cash book to the various accounts in the ledger, and then extract a trial balance on 31 October.

Purchases Day Book

Oct.		£
5	H. Vickers	30
10	M. Watton	65
20	D. Savage	48

Sales Day Book

Oct.		£
8	P. Winter	46
12	L. Yarrow	58
24	S. Stevens	72

Cash Book

Oct.			£	Oct.			£
1	Balance		500	2	Contra		20
2	Contra	20		5	General exes.	5	
4	Cash sales	28		10	H. Vickers		30
15	P. Winter		46	30	M. Watton		30
20	Cash sales	36			Wages	40	
25	L. Yarrow		58	31	Drawings		25

4 James Dunn has a small grocery business. He deals with one main wholesaler (Andrew Crowe) on credit, otherwise all transactions are for cash. On 1 June Dunn had £300 in the bank and £200 of goods for sale. He still owed £80 to his supplier on account of recent stock purchases.

Write up Mr Dunn's cash book and ledger accounts from the information given above and that tabled below:

(*a*) Total cash sales for June £325
(*b*) Cash paid into bank £220
(*c*) Cash payments: Salaries £25; advertising £15
                      fittings bought £28; own drawings £10.

Further supplies bought from Andrew Crowe during June totalled £120, and a cheque was sent in settlement of his creditor's outstanding account on 3 June.

After posting up all ledger accounts, take out a trial balance and make up James Dunn's final accounts for the period ended 30 June, the closing stock valuation being £105.

Exercises on Chapter 15

1 Explain the double entry procedure when (a) goods are returned by you to your supplier, and (b) goods are returned to you by your credit customer.

2 Explain, in date order, the entries on these two accounts:

Duncan Sharp

Jan.			£	Jan.			£
8	Returns	PRB	5 50	5	Purchases	PDB	25 50
15	Cheque	CB	10 00				

Evonne Evans

Mar.			£	Mar.			£
2	Sales	SDB	16 25	10	Returns	SRB	4 60
9	Sales	SDB	24 60	31	Cheque	CB	36 25

3 Enter up these transactions between Robert Burnett and yourself in your sales ledger and bring down the balance on 28 February:

Feb.
1 Burnett owes you £22.50
4 He buys £18 further goods from you
6 He returns £2 of goods bought on February 4
18 You receive payment of his January account
24 Further sales to Burnett of £10.80
28 Balanced up account.

4 Write up Sally Baldwin's account in the appropriate ledger from these details for the month of June:

June
1 Miss Baldwin owes you £25.25
4 She pays her May account and buys £16 more goods
6 She returns £4 of recent purchases
10 Further sales to Miss Baldwin £36.60
20 Received £20 payment on account
30 Balanced up account.

5 You owe Peter Barrett £12 on 1 May. Record the following transactions in his ledger account and balance up on 31 May.

May
2 Paid old account
3 Bought £24 further goods from Barrett
5 Returned £2 goods bought on 3 May
16 Further purchases of £56 value
   Returned £6 of these as unsuitable
20 Paid £30 on account
31 Balanced the account.

6 The financial year of Rebecca Reed ends on 30 June.
   On 1 June her purchases and sales accounts recorded this information:

Purchases

June 1	Total purchases to date Cash purchases to date	PDB CB	£ 4360 822	June 1	Returns to date	PRB	£ 84

Sales

June 1	Returns to date	SRB	£ 165	June 1	Total sales to date Cash sales to date	SDB CB	£ 9690 1540

During the month these transactions took place:

June
  3 Credit sale to David Marks £36
  5 Cash sales £24
 12 Bought £52 of goods from Dennis Walton
 14 Returned £12 of goods to Walton
 20 Cash sales £18
     Cash purchases £15
 26 Credit sale to Alfred Frost £66
 28 Frost returned £6 goods as 'damaged'
 30 Cash sales £35.

You are required to enter up the original records (day books), post up the personal ledger accounts, complete the purchases and sales accounts already shown, and bring down all balances at 30 June.

Exercises on Chapter 17

1 What kind of sales ledger accounts are likely to be found in the accounting department of a large wholesale warehouse covering the needs of the Midlands and the North of England, and specialising in household groceries of all description?

2 Balance up the ledger account of Herbert Danby in the books of Hoyland & Barnsley Ltd from these details illustrated:

Feb.			£	Feb.			£
1	Balance b/f		16 20	4	Cheque	CB	16 20
5	Sales	SDB	24 50	6	Returns	SRB	2 50
9	Sales	SDB	32 00	15	Cheque	CB	22 00
16	Sales	SDB	14 80				

(a) Explain each entry on the above account
(b) In what ledger will the account be found?
(c) Is this an account of debtor or creditor?
(d) Where would you find the opposite entry of each item?

3   Post the following details to the account of Arthur Cross and bring down the balance at 31 July:

July		£
1	You owed Cross	27.40
2	Bought from Cross goods priced at	28.00
4	Returned to him goods as charged	5.60
8	Paid June account	27.40
15	Further purchases from Cross	24.00
20	Returned packing case and allowed	2.50
24	Sold goods to Cross	18.80
28	Charged him carriage on delivery	1.50

4   John Finch's assets and liabilities on 31 January were as follows:

	£		£
Van valued at	400	Bank account	500
Fittings at cost	350	Cash in hand	50

Stock at 31 Jan. £200
Trade debtors: H. Norman £220; P. Nixon £58
Creditors (trade): S. Webb £102; J. Milsom £216

First of all ascertain Mr Finch's opening capital from the figures above, and then open ledger accounts for all assets and liabilities as at 31 January. Next post up transactions for the month of February, detailed below in the books of original entry. Balance up the cash book and all ledger accounts and extract a trial balance on 28 February.

Credit Purchases

Feb.			£
3	S. Webb		55
8	L. Wilson		80
16	J. Milsom		24

Credit Sales

Feb.			£
4	H. Norman		30
18	F. West		76
26	P. Nixon		124

Returns Outwards

Feb.			£
5	S. Webb		5

Returns Inwards

Feb.			£
20	F. West		6

Cash Book Details

Feb.		£	£	Feb.		£	£
1	Balance b/f	50	500	2	S. Webb		102
4	Cash sales	36		5	Stationery	3	
8	Cash sales	163		10	Contra	100	
10	Contra		100	20	Drawings		25
	H. Norman		220	27	Wages	130	
28	F. West		70	28	L. Wilson		80

Exercises on Chapter 18

1   Explain the terms:

   (*a*)   fixed assets   (*b*)   current assets
   (*c*)   current liabilities   (*d*)   working capital
   (*e*)   capital owned   (*f*)   capital employed.

2   Make up the capital account of Leslie Owen from the figures given below, and then show how it would appear, in vertical form, on his balance sheet at 31 December:

		£
1 Jan.	Commencing capital	5500
31 Dec.	Drawings for year	1850
	Net trading profit	2350
	Additional capital paid in during year	1000

3   State which side of the trading or profit and loss account each of the undermentioned items would be debited or credited:

   (*a*)   returns inwards   (*b*)   warehousing wages
   (*c*)   insurance   (*d*)   carriage inwards
   (*e*)   carriage outwards   (*f*)   commission received.

4   Amend the draft of Alistair Swift's trading and profit and loss account below:

Monthly trade account
as at 30 June

	£		£
Purchases	1240	Stock 30 June	580
Stock 1 June	460	Sales	1620
Sales returns	30	Carriage outwards	25
Gross profit c/d	495		
	2225		2225
General expenses	75	Gross profit b/d	495
Carriage inwards	15	Loan from Mrs Swift	550
Advertising	40		
Drawings	100		
Filing cabinet	50		
Rents received	80		
Net trading profit	685		
	1045		1045

5   Make up the balance sheet of Jacob Foster from the information given below. Show detail clearly, with separate sections for the proprietor's capital, current liabilities, fixed assets and current assets.

	£		£
Van at book value	880	Fittings and equipment at cost	420
Stock 30 June	500	Net trading profit for year	1880
Money in bank	760	Drawings for year	1500
Cash in hand	15	Trade debtors	820
Trade creditors	640	Creditors for expenses	125

Give the working capital of this business.

6 Prepare the trading and profit and loss account of Douglas Page's business, and also a balance sheet as at 31 December, from the detail given on the trial balance below:

Trial Balance 31 December

	£	£
Capital: D. Page 1 Dec.		9860
Drawings of Mr Page	1400	
Premises at cost	6500	
Fittings at cost	440	
Bank	420	
Cash	55	
Trade debtors/creditors	1320	1250
Stock 1 Dec.	1080	
Wages	2220	
Salaries	1780	
Purchases and returns	3430	70
Sales and returns	120	7860
Rates for month	250	
Advertising	180	
Lighting/heating	110	
Carriage inwards	80	
Carriage outwards	50	
Rents received		480
General expenses	85	
	19520	19520

The closing stock of Mr Page was valued at £1200.

Show clearly all four sections of the balance sheet under their respective headings and state the working capital of the business at 31 December.

Exercises on Chapter 19

1 Your closing stock at the end of the trading year includes 500 articles bought at £2 each which you still hope to sell at 25% profit on cost in the new trading year. The present market price of these articles is £2.40. What valuation would you place on your stock?

2 Georgina Lawson started in business on 1 June with £500 of stock and £1500 in the bank. On 4 June she bought £200 worth of the same stock. On 15 June she sold half of the original stock for £800. What was her gross profit position at that stage?

3   Find the cost of sales figure from the details below:

	£		£
Stock 1 June	400	Stock 30 June	600
Purchases	3650	Sales	6660
Returns inwards	60	Returns outwards	50
Wages	260	Carriage inwards	40

4   From the trading account of Rosella Peach, you are required to calculate her (*a*) average stock, (*b*) cost of sales, (*c*) gross profit percentage on sales, and (*d*) gross profit percentage on the cost of sales:

Trading Account for the year ended 31 December

	£		£
Stock 1 Jan.	2200	Net sales	13200
Net purchases	8400	Stock 31 Dec.	1800
Gross profit	4400		
	15000		15000

5   Make up the trading and profit and loss account of Gloria Haigh from the information below:

	£		£
Stock 1 July	800	Stock 1 June	1200
Purchases	3200	Sales	8800
Wages	1600	Salaries	2400
General expenses	200	Carriage outwards	100

Calculate:
(*a*)   the average stock and cost of sales,
(*b*)   the rate of stock turnover,
(*c*)   the percentage of gross profit to turnover,
(*d*)   the percentage of net profit to turnover.

6   Martina Wedge's stock of merchandise was destroyed by fire in the early dawn of 30 June. It was a total loss apart from a small salvaged amount at £200.

   Her accounting records were recovered from a fireproof safe, making these figures available:

	£
Stock 1 Jan.	1600
Purchases (1 Jan.–30 June)	5400
Warehousing wages	3200
Net sales (1 Jan.–30 June)	12500

   You are required to prepare a statement to forward to Miss Wedge's insurance company as a claim for the value of the stock destroyed. During the past three years her average percentage of gross profit to turnover has been 30%.

7 The capital and trading details of two businesses are shown below. You are asked to decide which, on the basis of these figures, is the more likely progressive business of the two.

	Capital employed £	Turnover £	Gross profit £	Net profit £
Business X	6000	8500	3400	1500
Business Y	9000	14400	4800	2000

Make your comparisons by calculating these percentages:

(a) gross profit to turnover, (b) net profit to turnover, and (c) net profit to capital employed.

Exercises on Chapter 20
1 Allocate the following debits between capital and revenue:

(a) repairs to van
(b) set of new tyres
(c) purchase of new van
(d) loss on sale of old van
(e) local rates
(f) charity donation
(g) second-hand safe for office
(h) fire insurance premium
(i) drawings
(j) wages to workmen in erecting new machine
(k) purchase of second-hand filing cabinet.

2 Re-draft this revenue account in its correct form:

	£		£
Stock 1 Jan.	800	Sales	14800
Carriage outwards	60	Returns inwards	40
Purchases	3500	Carriage inwards	20
Returns outwards	30	Stock 31 Dec.	1400
Salaries	1200		
Gross profit c/d	10670		
	16260		16260
Rates	480	Gross profit b/d	10670
Sundry expenses	50	Loss on sale of	
Second-hand van	2800	old van	200
Wages	5000	Rents received	120
Stationery	35		
Drawings	880		
Van repairs	75		
Garage extension	240		
Embezzlement loss	25		
Donations	10		
Commission received	220		
Heating/lighting	115		
Net trading profit	1060		
	10990		10990

3 A firm bought some new machinery for £5000 on 1 January. During the year extensions and additions cost £2000, and wages paid to own workmen on erection totalled £350. Repairs and renewals amounted to £150.

Make up the machinery (asset) account for the year, and show the debit to revenue at the year-end.

4 Write up the van (asset) account of Belinda Bossam from these details:

		£
Jan. 1	Cost of new van	2800
June 30	Sale of van	2200
July 1	Purchase of new van	3000
31	Radio equipment fitted	150
Dec. 31	New tyres for van	75
	and general servicing	60

5 The trial balance below has been extracted *after* the net trading profit for the year has been ascertained.

	£	£
Net trading profit		3600
Premises at cost	8500	
Machinery at cost	1500	
Fittings at cost	420	
Trade debtors/creditors	1450	1280
Capital account 1 July		6700
Drawings for year	2000	
Stock 30 June	1820	
Bank overdraft		840
Expense creditors		
(wages & loan interest)		300
Cash in hand	30	
8% loan from H. Smith		3000
	15720	15720

You are required to prepare a balance sheet showing clearly the fixed and current assets, proprietor's capital and current liabilities, and, in this particular instance, a separate section for the fixed liability (loan from H. Smith). Calculate the working capital of the business at 30 June.

Exercises on Chapter 21

1 Explain the difference between trade discount and cash discount.

2 Enter up a three-column cash book from the following information and balance the account at 31 March. Assume transactions are by cheque where there is any doubt.

March
1 Bank balance £450; cash balance £50
5 Cash sales £35.80
8 Paid Lew Ayres his February account of £60, being allowed 5% cash
   discount
   Cash purchases £22.20
10 Minnie Martin called and paid her outstanding account of £40. Allowed
    her 5%
15 Received £18.80 in cash, being full settlement of Roberta Allen's account
    for £19.50
20 Allowed Bart Plowright 5% off his £25 ledger account invoiced back in
    January
25 Paid £30 cash into bank
28 Paid Kate Berwick's old account of £66.60 deducting 5% as agreed

3 Make up a three-column cash book from the details below:

June		£
1	Bank balance	300.00
	Cash balance	25.00
4	Paid Alan Gibson's account for £80, deducting 5% as	
	arranged	76.00
8	Received cash from Roland Jay in settlement of his May	
	account less C.D. of £1.50	28.50
15	Cash sales	24.20
	Cash purchases	16.10
22	Lois Pearson paid her May account of £44 less 2½% for early	
	settlement	42.90
25	Paid cash into bank	50.00
28	Sent Jasmina Jones a cheque in settlement of an old account	
	of £36, less 2½%	35.10
30	Cash sales	32.40

4 Write up these two ledger accounts in the books of ABC & Sons Ltd
   from the details given, bringing down the balances on both accounts:

   (*a*) X, a debtor, owes £28 on 1 July. He buys £35 further goods on 8
         July and settles his June account less 5% cash discount. He returns
         £2 of the goods bought as faulty, being given credit and an
         allowance is made by his supplier on 12 July.
   (*b*) A balance of £68.00 is due to creditor Y on 1 July. Further goods
         are bought from him, invoiced thus:

         July 5   £40.00   July 12   £35.50   July 18   £60.60

         All purchases are subject to trade discount of 20%, the above bills
         being invoiced gross. Carriage on purchases £3.00 charged on 20
         July. Cheque for £66.30 in settlement of Y's June account sent on
         25 July, the deduction being agreed discount.

5 Arthur Nash owes Joe Roe £54 on 31 October. Write up his ledger account in the books of Joe Roe from these transactions:

Nov.
- 4   Nash paid his October account less £4 cash discount
- 8   Nash bought £40 more goods less 20% trade discount
- 10   He returned £10 (gross) goods to Roe
- 18   Further goods bought by Nash £60 less 20% T.D.
- 20   Roe charged Nash £2 on deliveries
- 30   Nash sent Roe cheque for £25 on account.

6 Flotsam is a small manufacturer. His transactions with Jetsam during the month of July were as follows:

July
- 1   Balance owing by Flotsam £80
- 2   Further goods bought by Flotsam £100 less 25% trade discount
- 5   Flotsam paid his June account less 5% cash discount
- 20   Jetsam delivered another £60 of goods allowing the customary trade rates
- 25   Flotsam returned £12 (gross) goods bought on 20 July as 'not up to standard'.

You are required to write up the account of Jetsam as it would appear in the books of Flotsam.

Exercises on Chapter 22
1 Describe the functions of the general journal. In what way does it differ from the purchases and sales journals?

2 Journalise the following:

- (*a*)   Cash sales of £18.20
- (*b*)   Wages paid £80
- (*c*)   Goods invoiced to you from George Brown at £25.80
- (*d*)   A £65 cheque for an office table bought
- (*e*)   The sale of goods on credit £8.40 to Frances Owen
- (*f*)   £20 commission received in cash.

3 Record by journal entry these transactions:

- (*a*)   Payment of £15 for advertising, by cheque
- (*b*)   Receipt of £25 cash for rent from a sub-tenant
- (*c*)   Transfer of opening stock £1500 to the trading account
- (*d*)   The bringing of £1850 closing stock into the books
- (*e*)   Payment of £24 cheque for annual fire insurance premium
- (*f*)   A sale of some old fittings for £40 cash
- (*g*)   Goods priced at £60 bought on credit from Gary Hampson
- (*h*)   The erection of a new showroom extension at the cost of £8000, against a deposit of £1000 paid to Builders Ltd
- (*i*)   The payment of £1200 in wages to own workmen engaged on the decoration of the showroom extension.

4 Make the necessary amendments and corrections of the following through the journal:

(a) An amount of £22.50 entered in the sales day book has been charged to the account of Robina Lisle as £22.15

(b) The purchases day book total for the month of May was added correctly to £987.20, but was posted to purchases account as £978.20

(c) Motor expenses account has been credited with the sale of an old van (a cheque for £450 was received)

(d) A £28 cheque received from Donald Brown has been credited to the account of his cousin Ronald Brown

(e) A new typewriter which has cost £150 has been debited to general expenses account

(f) The proprietor's drawings of £180 for the month have been debited to staff salaries account

(g) An amount of £50 received from a sub-tenant for rent has been debited to rent account

(h) Goods received from a supplier £130 were taken into stock at 31 December, but the invoice was not received or recorded until 5 January in the new financial year.

5 Ascertain the capitals of the two separate businesses shown below by journal entry, and then draft a proper balance sheet for each business.

Account balances in the books at 30 June
R.A.S.

Cash	£50	Bank	£500
Van	£480	Stock	£360
Fittings	£220	Debtors	£710
Trade creditors	£620		

Account balances in the books at 30 June
D.R.S.

Premises at cost	£4000	Fittings	£250
Truck	£820	Bank overdraft	£450
Stock	£1800	Machinery	£2000
Trade debtors	£1320	Cash	£40
Loan creditor	£3000	Trade creditors	£970
Expense creditors	£60	P & L credit balance	£2880
Drawings for year	£2200		

6   George Lynch's assets and liabilities at the beginning and at the end of June are listed below:

	June 1 £	June 30 £
Cash	25	35
Bank	450	280
Fittings at cost	330	420
Stock of goods	610	820
Machinery at cost	1200	1450
Trade debtors	530	680
Trade creditors	440	490

Lynch had withdrawn £100 in anticipation of profit during the month of June.

You are invited to try to ascertain his trading net profit by the comparison of the proprietor's net worth or capitals at the beginning and the end of June, and to make up his final balance sheet showing his capital account at 30 June in full detail.

Exercises on Chapter 23

1   What do you understand by the term *depreciation*?
What are the three main methods generally adopted by small trading organisations? Illustrate your answer in the instance of wasting assets such as:

(a)   a ten-year lease which has cost £8000,
(b)   a new motor vehicle bought for £3200, and
(c)   the equipment and props of a repertory company where the reduction in value in one particular year was estimated to have fallen from £3500 to £2800.

2   A small delivery van was bought on 1 January for £2700 and sold on 30 June for £2100, being replaced by a larger van costing £3600.
Show the asset account at the end of the first year, charging depreciation at 20% per annum, and give the balance details at the end of the year.

3   The van bought on 30 June (in the previous question) was kept for one and a half years, being depreciated at 20% on the reducing balance basis. It was then taken in part-exchange for £2600 against a new van now costing £3800.
Show the asset account for two years, with the depreciation written off each year and bringing down the new valuations. Also show how the asset account will appear in the balance sheet each year.

4   Make up the machinery (asset) account of Caprice Taylor from the details now given. Provide depreciation at 25% on cost.

Jan. 1	Two machines were bought for £1000 each	£
	(the cost including erection)	2000
March 31	A smaller machine bought for	400
June 30	One of the original machines	
	was sold for	800
Oct. 1	A smaller replacement machine	
	bought for	600
	Wages paid to own workmen in	
	erecting this machine on 1 October	200

Bring down the balance of the machine account on 31 December.

5   From the information given below, make up each ledger account in the general ledger showing the individual debits (or credits) on account of depreciation at the end of the financial year, and also show the fixed assets section of the balance sheet:

   (*a*)   a ten-year lease on adjoining land bought five years ago for £4000 and depreciated at the appropriate charge each year;
   (*b*)   machinery shown on the last balance sheet at £8500 being depreciated on the reducing balance basis at 20% per annum;
   (*c*)   loose tools valued at £400 on the last balance sheet are now estimated to be worth £550 because the firm's apprentices make their own tools with material supplied by the company.

6   Amanda Jane is a hairdresser. She rents a room from her parents at £2 a week and borrows £500 from her brother David on 1 January to buy the equipment and the supplies she needs.
   During the next twelve months she manages to reduce the loan by £200.
   The following balances were extracted from her books on 31 December.

	£	£
Cash	20	
Bank overdraft		184
Supplies bought	150	
Advertising	42	
Sundry expenses	15	
Rent	104	
Equipment	600	
Loan account		300
Drawings	1100	
Cash takings		1230
Credit sales		390
Accounts owing	125	52

You are required to draw up a profit and loss account and a balance sheet as at 31 December, depreciating equipment account by 25% per annum. The stock of supplies on hand was valued by Amanda Jane at £86.

Exercises on Chapter 24

1 Explain the difference between 'writing off a bad debt' of a credit customer and the creation of a reserve or provision for bad debts.

2 Last year the net total debtors amounted to £4400. This year the total of the debtors' balances was only £3500.

Last year the actual bad debts written off was £28. This year the actual bad debts written off was £35, but an amount of £15 previously written off (two years ago) has now been recovered.

The bad debts provision of 5% has been in force for only the past two years.

Show the bad debts account and the provision for bad debts account, and also how the entries will appear on the profit and loss account and in the balance sheet for these last two years.

3 Prepare the trading and profit and loss account and a balance sheet from the following balances, taking into account the adjustments for depreciation and the bad debts provision which are shown as footnotes underneath the trial balance:

Trial Balance   30 June

	£	£
Capital 1 July		7000
Drawings for year	2000	
Premises at cost	4000	
Machinery and plant (balance of account)	2500	
Vans (account balance)	800	
Bank	500	
Cash	25	
Trade debtors/creditors	1600	1250
Purchases/Sales	4890	13630
Returns inwards/outwards	75	60
Discounts all'd/rec'd	30	25
Wages	2330	
Salaries	1870	
General expenses	360	
Stock 1 July	920	
Postages/stationery	45	
Bad debts	35	
Provision for bad debts		65
Carriage inwards	50	
	22030	22030

(*a*) Stock at 30 June £1250
(*b*) Depreciate machinery and plant by 20% and vans by 25% per annum.
(*c*) Maintain the provision for bad debts at 5% of net debtors' balances.

Exercises on Chapter 25

1 What do you understand by the term *year-end adjustment*? Why is it necessary to amend certain expense totals such as wages, rates and insurance at the end of the financial year?

2 A small garage pays employees' wages every Friday, made up to Thursday, the day before. The financial year ends on 30 June, which, in this particular year, falls on a Wednesday.

   If the normal weekly pay sheet averages £420 per five-day week, and the total debit for the year on wages account is £24 400 for payments already made, you are asked to complete the wages account, showing the correct amount to be charged to revenue for the year.

3 Explain the nominal ledger account below in every detail.

Rent and Rates Account
(rent £360 p.a., rates £200 p.a.)

			£				£
Jan. 1	Balance b/f		50	Jan. 1	Balance b/f		90
Jan. 3	Cheque	CB	90	Dec. 31	Profit & Loss a/c		560
Mar. 31	Cheque	CB	90	Dec. 31	Rates in advance		
Jul. 2	Cheque	CB	90		carried down		50
Jul. 8	Cheque	CB	100				
Oct. 5	Cheque	CB	90				
Oct. 31	Cheque	CB	100				
Dec. 31	Rent owing c/d		90				
			700				700
Jan. 1	Balance b/d		50	Jan. 1	Balance b/d		90

4 A retailer negotiated a loan for £2000 on the security of his premises. The terms of the loan agreement stated that capital repayments of £500 would be made every six months, and interest at 12% would be charged on the outstanding balance at the end of each year.

   Show the loan account for the two years, including the interest charges which may be assumed to be payable as they fall due.

5 At the beginning of the year the electricity account of Charlie Gravel showed an amount of £14.50 owing to the Midlands Electricity Board. This was on account of the October/December quarter of the previous year.

   Payments made in the current year were as follows:

	£		£
January 4	14.50	April 15	16.80
July 16	12.20	October 8	8.70

   The bill for the last quarter of the year £15.40 was not paid until 8 January in the next financial year.

   Write up the electricity account for the year, showing the net debit to profit and loss account, and how the item 'creditors for electricity' will appear on the balance sheet of Mr Gravel at 31 December.

6 A fire insurance policy was taken out by Fay Pitt on 1 April and an annual premium of £32 paid on this date. Her financial year ended on 31 December. Show the debit to revenue for the first two years on her insurance account, and how the item 'insurance in advance' will appear on her balance sheet.

7 The following list of balances is extracted from the books of James White on 30 June. You are required to make up his trial balance, after taking into account certain errors (noted under these balances) and making the necessary amendments to the figures in the books in preparation for the drawing up of Mr White's final accounts.

	£		£
Stock 1 July	750	Capital account	3400
Net purchases	6820	Net sales	12600
Trade debtors	1850	Trade creditors	1230
Machinery 1 July	4500	Bank overdraft	210
Motor van 1 July	450	Salaries	3600
Carriage inwards	120	Commissions received	1000
Equipment account 1 July	270	General expenses	80

(a) A filing cabinet, recently bought for £60, has been included in the general purchases.

(b) An amount of £50 for van repairs has been debited to motor van (asset) account.

(c) The drawings of Mr White £1400 have been charged to salaries account.

8 Make up the final accounts of James White, including a balance sheet as at 30 June, from the amended trial balance in the previous question, taking into account these year-end adjustments:

(a) Stock valuation at 30 June £600

(b) Depreciation of machinery is to be 20%; of the motor van 25%; and the equipment 10%, all based upon the balances of these asset accounts at the year-end.

(c) Create and bring into the books a new provision account for bad and doubtful debts at 4% of the total of the trade debtors at 30 June.

9 You are required to identify the 'odd one out' in each of the four groups shown below, and to place your selection within its correct group.

A	Bank Cash Wages Debtors	B	Advertising Drawings Van repairs Rates
C	Premises Capital Net profit Net loss	D	Machinery Fixtures Stock Motor van

10 Frank Rositer's financial position at 1 July was as follows:

	£		£
Fittings at cost	240	Motor van account balance 1 July	480
Cash at bank	680	Stock on hand 1 July	500
Cash in hand	20		

		£
Owing by credit customers:	Isobel Crowe	60
	Rex Hislop	20
	Fanny Purves	100
Owing to suppliers:	Valerie Veal	£300
	Pam Richards	200

After ascertaining Rositer's commencing capital, open up all relevant ledger accounts and post up the following transactions for the month of July:

July
2 Bought office desk £80
   Cash sales £32
5 Paid salary to part-timer £28 by cheque
8 Bought £46 of goods from Miss Veal and paid her June account less 4% cash discount
12 Paid salary £28 out of cash sales of £45 and also advertising bill for £8 in cash.
15 Isobel Crowe paid her June account less 5% cash discount. She bought another £30 of goods.
18 Cash purchases £10
    Paid salary £28 and also miscellaneous office expenses £6 in cash
    Paid half year's rates £48 by cheque
20 Heard Hislop had been made bankrupt and decided to write his sales ledger account off as a bad debt.
24 Sold £40 of merchandise to Fanny Purves. She paid £50 off her outstanding account
    Cash sales £42
25 Paid salary £28
26 Received debit note from garage for £16 for short service.
    Sent a cheque by hand.
    Bought £80 more goods from Pam Richards and paid her June account, deducting 4% as agreed.
31 Drew £60 for own use.

Balance up all ledger accounts and extract a trial balance on 31 July. Prepare a trading and profit and loss account for the month of July and a balance sheet as at 31 July for your client, taking into account the following adjustments on the revenue accounts:

(*a*) Stock on hand 31 July, as per Mr Rositer's valuation £625.
(*b*) Salary owing at 31 July £25.
(*c*) Rates paid in advance are to be carried forward.
(*d*) Depreciate the motor van by 20% per annum.
(*e*) Create a new provision for bad debts of 5% of the total of the trade debtors' balances at 31 July.

Exercises on Chapter 26

1   Freda Flitcroft summarises her rough cash book in total for the month of December:

		£			£
Balance 1 Dec.		300	Payments to suppliers		330
Cash takings		1065	Wages to part-timer		250
Loan from Uncle Jim		500	Equipment purchased		130
			Rent paid (3 months)		150
			General expenses		85
			Drawings for 'self'		160

On 31 December she owed £64 to her supplier, and £22 for printing.
The stock unsold had cost her £95.
Draft her revenue account and balance sheet at 31 December.

2   From the information below, make up the trading and profit and loss account of Areca Nutt, who made a small fortune on a coconut plantation in Sri Lanka, and started a retail hardware store in Port Erin on 30 June, one year ago. Also make up her balance sheet as at the year end.

Assets and liabilities six months ago:

	£		£
Fixtures and fittings	4000	Trade debtors	800
Stock 1 Jan.	1500	Trade creditors	500
Bank	700		

Details from cash summary during the last six months:

		£			£
Cash takings		2786	Payments from credit customers		8080
Cash purchases		1800	Payments to suppliers		6525
Office expenses		830	Drawings of owner		2470
Additional capital		1000			

Miss Nutt paid an additional £1000 into the business from a private investment account on 29 February. Her current assets and liabilities on 30 June, the end of the year, were:

Stock   £1750   Debtors   £1200   Creditors   £950.

3   Marian Moore has a small private secretarial agency. She works from her parents' home. A balance sheet was drafted roughly by her brother on these lines on 1 January.

		£			£
Capital 1 Jan.		180	Office equipment		450
Loan from J. Moore		500	Stock of stationery		38
Creditors for printing		20	Debtors		52
			Bank and cash		160
		700			700

On 5 January Miss Moore bought a second-hand duplicator for £110, being allowed £30 on a much older machine (included in the fixed assets at £35). She paid the balance by cheque.

Her charges for typing services during January totalled £132, and her cash book details showed these entries in total form:

Jan.			£	Jan.			£
1	Balance		160	31	New duplicator		80
31	Cash customers		112		Drawings		100
31	Cheques from				Wages p-timer		64
	credit customers		74		Office expenses		22
					Printing account		15

Draw up Miss Moore's profit and loss account for January and a balance sheet at 31 January. Value of stationery at 31 January was £30.

4   Colin Redfern has these assets and liabilities on 1 July:

	£		£
Furniture	120	Bank overdraft	150
Stock of goods	700	Mortgage on premises	2000
Premises	3500	Cash in office	10
Money owing by customers	£470	Money owing to suppliers	£350

During the first week of July Redfern received £96 from cash customers and banked £50 from his receipts.

He paid £120 off his creditors' accounts.

The bank manager allowed him to increase his overdraft to £400.

Money paid by credit customers during the following week amounted to £150. All this money was paid into the bank.

Redfern's cash sales had absorbed £70 of his original stock. He bought £100 additional stock on credit from his wholesaler.

He also bought some new shelves for £15 and a small safe from a secondhand shop for £30. He paid for both by cheque.

Various cash expenses (including wages to a part-timer) amounted to £38 and he withdrew £10 for a few drinks and an evening meal.

You are asked to find out if Mr Redfern has made a profit or sustained a loss during the first two weeks of July. Make up his statement of affairs as at 15 July.

Exercises on Chapter 27

1   Distinguish between a receipts and payments account and an income and expenditure account. What sort of organisations make use of these kinds of revenue accounts?

2 Make up a receipts and payments account of a social club from the details listed below, covering the year ended 30 September:

	£
Opening cash balance (combined with bank)	150.42
Total of annual subscriptions actually received during the year	420.00
Arrears of subscriptions paid for previous year	30.00
Donations received	35.00
Rent of local hall	250.00
Heating and lighting accounts paid	145.60
Refreshments bought for social evenings	188.80
Receipts taken on social evenings	168.50
Ticket sales for whist drives	226.00
Prizes bought for whist drives	184.40
Stationery and stamps	26.30
Magazines and reading material for members	54.60
Honorarium to Treasurer	25.00

3 Make up a subscriptions account from the information below to show the correct amount to be credited to the revenue account of a Somerset tennis club for the year ended 31 December:

January 1 (beginning of year)		December 31 (end of year)
£60	Debtors for subscriptions	£50
£35	Creditors for subscriptions	£30

Extract from cash summary

Jan. 1	Balance in hand	£ 240.85	June 5	Refund to member leaving district	£ 5.00
Dec. 31	Total subs. received during the year	620.00			

Note: The total subscriptions received during the year (£620.00) includes £30 paid in advance for the following year.

4 The Luna Club was formed on 1 April with a membership of one hundred at the annual subscription of £6.

Details of receipts and payments for the first six months are now given:

Subscriptions from 92 members received. The defaulting members were warned that their subscriptions must be paid before 31 October.

Profit from dances £135.40: net receipts from raffle £76.60: Sundry donations to the club £40.00.

Hire of room £120: Purchase of table and chairs £280: Cleaning £30 paid: Stationery bought £18.50: Fees to visiting lecturers £230: Purchase of books and reading material £56.20: Crockery bought £42.80.

From the information above you are required to make up the income and expenditure account and a balance sheet at 30 September, revaluing the furniture at £200, the crockery at £25, and writing off reading material completely. Allow for an invoice for £12.50 received from printer on 1 October.

5 The cash summary of the Teenage Tennis Club is extracted from the club records for the year ended 30 September.

	£		£
Bank balance 1 Oct.	205.60	Loan repayment	200.00
Entrance fees	50.00	Heating/lighting	137.40
Subscriptions	900.00	New nets	360.00
Competition fees	53.00	Catering expenses	176.40
Donations	30.00	Stationery, etc.	45.60
Receipts from dances	296.80	General expenses	66.60
		New crockery	47.20
		Part-time groundsman	530.00

The club was founded five years ago, and a loan of £2000 obtained (under guarantee of parents) from the bank. Half of this loan had been repaid within the first four years. A wooden clubhouse was erected two years ago for £3000, now paid in full.

Nets and equipment account stood at £440 on 1 October (the beginning of the current year), and it was decided to write off 20% of the year-end balance. Crockery account stood at £24.40 on the last balance sheet and is to be revalued at £50 (including all new additions). An electricity account for £21.60 was due for the autumn quarter, and £36 was owing to the groundsman. The stock position of tinned drinks at 30 September was £15. Subscriptions are to be adjusted according to these records:

Subs. in arrear			*Subs. in advance*	
1 October	£30	Beginning of year	1 October	£20
30 September	£44	End of year	30 September	£24

You are required to make up the income and expenditure account and a balance sheet for the Teenage Tennis Club at 30 September.

Exercises on Chapter 28

1 From the information below make up a total debtors account to show the net amount due from credit customers at 31 July:

July		£
1	Amount owing by customers	11 440
	Credit balances in sales ledger	42
31	Payments from customers	76 294
	Credit sales to customers	86 750
	Discounts allowed	3 350
	Returns from customers	1 860
	Bad debts written off	220
	Credit balances in sales ledger	56

2 Explain each item in these two control accounts in the general ledger:

Purchase Ledger Control

	£		£
Cash/cheques	18686	Balance b/f	9986
Discount	820	Purchases	20500
Returns outward	340	Carriage	240
Balance c/d	10880		
	30726		30726
		Balance b/d	10880

Sales Ledger Control

	£		£
Balance b/f	15434	Cash/cheques	40803
Sales	42318	Discount	1865
Carriage	380	Bills receivable	208
		Returns	570
		Bad debts	132
		Balance c/d	14554
	58132		58132
Balance b/d	14554		

3 Make up the Purchase Ledger Control and the Sales Ledger Control Accounts as they would appear at the back of their respective ledgers:

Jan.

		£		£
1	Bought ledger balances			£4866
	Sales ledger balances			£6972
31	PDB total for month	18590	SDB total for month	27680
	Payments to suppliers	15232	Receipts from debtors	24654
	Returns inwards	336	Discount allowed	510
	Returns outwards	234	Discount received	380
	Bad debts written off	72	Bills payable	960
	Bills receivable	1170	Carriage charges to customers	110
	Debit balances in sales ledger transferred to bought ledger	115	Customers' cheques dishonoured	85

Exercises on Chapter 29

1 Explain the difference, in partnership accounts, of interest allowed on capital and interest charged upon drawings.

2 J. Bee and B. Jay share profits and losses in the proportions of three-fifths and two-fifths. Details of their capital and current accounts are now given:

	J.B.		B.J.	
Capital accounts, balances 1 Jan.	£8000		£3600	
Current accounts balances 1 Jan.	200	Cr.	100	Dr.
Additional capital paid in (30 Sept.)	2000			
Total drawings of partners	7200		4500	

Interest on capital at 10% is to be credited to the partner's current accounts, and 50% of the goodwill account (standing in the books at £6000) is to be written off against profits this year. The net trading profit is £15 000.

Show the partners' capital and current accounts in full detail.

3 The balance sheet of Batten and Tatton (sharing profits and losses two-thirds and one-third) is shown in brief detail at 30 June:

	£	£		£
Capitals			*Fixed assets*	4700
Batten	5000			
Tatton	2000	7000	*Current assets*	3800
Trade creditors		1500		
		8500		8500

The old established firm of Batten and Tatton admit Yatton, their chief clerk recently qualified, as a partner as from 1 July, to take one-sixth share of the new firm's profits. At the same time a goodwill account is to be created of £6000, to be credited to the old partners' capital accounts in their existing profit-sharing ratios; the goodwill asset account will gradually be written down out of future profits. Yatton is to pay the moderate sum of £1000 as his introductory capital, and the old partners will continue to maintain the same profit-sharing ratios as existing previously.

Draft a balance sheet for the new firm as at 1 July, and state the new profit-sharing ratios for all three partners.

4 Alpha, Beta and Zeta share profits and losses in the proportions 3:2:1. Their first trading year, ended 30 June, shows a net trading profit of £14 000 before charging up a small salary of £800 a year allowed to Zeta for additional duties. Interest on capital is to be credited to the partners' current accounts at 8% per annum. In addition to this information and the extract from the firm's cash book (shown below), you are required to make up the current accounts of each partner.

July 1	Capital accounts		£	Dec. 31	Salary to Z		£ 400
	A		8000	June 30	Drawings	A	6600
	B		5000			B	4500
	Z		2000			Z	2500

5   Black, White and Green share profits and losses in the ratios 4:3:2 and Green has an annual salary of £1000 to compensate him for certain extra duties. Their trial balance for the year ended 31 December is shown below:

	£	£
Capital accounts		
Black		5000
White		4000
Green		2000
Drawings (and current		
accounts at 1 Jan.)		
Black	4800	250
White	3500	180
Green	3300	30
Fittings and fixtures	3400	
Van account } 1 Jan.	3500	
Stock account	2520	
Purchases and returns	8440	40
Sales and returns	120	35120
Trade debtors/creditors	5800	4200
Discounts allowed/received	140	80
Warehousing wages	6350	
Office salaries	5630	
General expenses	360	
Printing/stationery	150	
Petrol, oil and repairs	608	
Partnership salaries	500	
Carriage outwards	60	
Bank overdraft		418
Advertising	220	
Rent and rates	1880	
Cash in hand	40	
	51318	51318

You are required to prepare the final accounts of the partnership for the year ended 31 December, at the same time making due allowance for these adjustments:

(*a*)   Stock on hand 31 Dec. £3600.
(*b*)   Wages owing £130.
(*c*)   Insurance paid in advance £60 (included in general expenses).
(*d*)   Mrs Black has taken goods for family use amounting to £160. This is to be charged to her husband's account.
(*e*)   The van is to be depreciated by 20%, and a provision of 3% of debtors to be created.
(*f*)   Interest on capital at 6%.

6 MacLeod and MacLean make arrangements to amalgamate their separate retail businesses as from 1 May. Their individual balance sheets are now shown in brief detail as at 30 April:

MacLeod's Balance Sheet as at 30 April	£	£
Fixed assets		
Machinery	4500	
Fittings	850	5350
Current assets		
Stock	2400	
Trade debtors	800	
Bank	520	3720
		9070
Financed by		
Capital a/c 30 April		8000
Current liabilities		
Trade creditors		1070
		9070

MacLean's Balance Sheet as at 30 April	£	£
Fixed assets		
Fittings/equipt.	2400	
Van (book value)	1600	4000
Current assets		
Stock	1850	
Trade debtors	650	2500
		6500
Financed by		
Capital a/c 30 April		5500
Current liabilities		
Trade creditors	840	
Bank overdraft	160	1000
		6500

Prior to the amalgamation the two Scots decided to depreciate all fixed assets of each sole trader by 20%, and to create new bad debt provisions of 10% on the listed totals of the trade debtors.

Individual stocks were to be re-valued as follows:

MacLeod's stock £2100: MacLean's stock £1700

MacLeod's bank account was to be taken over by the new firm and MacLean's overdraft was to be settled by him privately.

Make all the necessary amendments outlined above, and then re-draft a new balance sheet for the partnership as at 1 May.

Exercises on Chapter 31
1 List a number of items which you think might form part of the 'cost' of (*a*) a shoe manufacturer, (*b*) a grocer, (*c*) a small garage.

2   The production costs of two factories making a similar product are given below:

	Factory 1 £	Factory 2 £
Raw material consumed	8 820	6 730
Labour costs	5 650	4 290
Overhead expenses	1 080	850

Number of articles manufactured
Factory 1	Factory 2
6500	5800

You are required to (*a*) give the average unit cost per article manufactured by both factories; (*b*) draw two bar charts to contrast the production figures; and (*c*) draft a short report to management explaining which, in your opinion, is the more productive factory.

3   Edward Rose, a manufacturer, extracts the following balances from his books, after the cost of production figure has been ascertained. Draw up his trading and profit and loss account, together with a balance sheet as at 30 June, from this information:

	£		£
Cost of production	25 520	Sales for year	39 686
Selling expenses	1 580	Office salaries	2 400
Warehousing expenses	450	Trade debtors	2 320
Factory wages outstanding	140	Trade creditors	1 840
Provision for bad debts	100	Drawings	3 200
Premises at cost	15 000	Bank overdraft	2 850
Machinery at cost	20 330	Capital 1 July	26 000
Depreciation Account		Fixtures	500
(machinery)	10 000	Purchases of	
		finished goods	1 800

The position with regard to stocks was as follows:

Stock of raw materials at 30 June	£3350	} end of year
Work in progress 30 June	£1290	
Stock of finished goods at the beginning of the year	£2876	
Stock of finished goods and at the end of the year	£3250.	

Two adjustments are to be taken into account:

(*a*)   Fixtures are to be depreciated at 10% on the book balance.
(*b*)   The bad debt provision is to be increased by 20%.

4   The financial year of Ross and Cromarty coincides with the normal calendar year. From the information now given, you are required to prepare accounts showing (*a*) the factory profit, (*b*) raw materials consumed, and (*c*) the cost of sales. In addition, in making up the trading and profit and loss account, show the gross and net profits as a percentage of the turnover.

		£
Stocks { Raw materials	1 Jan.	5300
Raw materials	31 Dec.	5800
Finished goods	1 Jan.	6430
Finished goods	31 Dec.	7580

	£
Net sales for the year	120000
Purchases of raw materials	35600
Manufacturing wages	28500
Administrative expenses	12500
Discounts received	800
Directors fees	6000
Office salaries	8500
General expenses	3920
Factory overheads:	
Rent and rates	4750
Production expenses	2350

Note: Goods manufactured are to be transferred to the trading department at the current market value of £79950.

Exercise on Chapter 32

1 Make up the balance sheet of Nanchad Ltd as at 30 June from the information and balances listed below:

Issued share capital 50000 ordinary shares of £1 each, fully paid. 30000 8% preference shares of £1 fully paid. The authorised share capital consisted of 100000 ordinary shares of £1 and 50000 8% preference shares of £1 each.

	£
Bank balance	18850
Formation expenses	2000
7½% debentures	20000
Trade debtors	8000
Trade creditors	6750
Expense creditors	2200
Fittings at cost	3250
Stock on hand 30 June	24500
Machinery and plant at cost	100000
Aggregate depreciation on plant	15000
General reserve account	10000
Credit balance on profit and loss	5500
Taxation reserve	10000
Provision for bad debts	200
Debenture interest due	750

The directors recommend payment of the final preference dividend of £1200, and the payment of 10% to the ordinary shareholders. (Ignore tax deductions at source on proposed dividends.)

Note that it may be assumed that the profit and loss account and the 'published section' has already been made up, and all that is required is a final balance sheet in vertical form.

Exercises on Chapter 33

1　Draft a balance sheet to comply, as far as possible, with the Companies Acts, from the balances and information given below:

The WHT Company Limited had an authorised share capital of £100000 divided into 50000 10% preference shares of £1 each and 100000 ordinary shares of 50p each.

The preference shares had been fully issued at a premium of 20% and were fully paid. The ordinary shares were also fully issued, but there was still a final call of 25p outstanding on one member's holding of 1000 shares.

The directors have recommended the payment of the second half of the preference dividend, but on account of the poor trading year, make no recommendation for the ordinary shareholders. On 31 December, the close of the trading year, the balance of £3300 is brought forward, as undistributed profit from last year, and after all charges and appropriations have been taken into account, there is a final undistributed profit on the published section of the profit and loss account of £1900 to be carried forward.

The financial book balances are now listed:

	£		£
Goodwill at cost	20000	Trade debtors	13600
Provision for bad debts	750	Stock 31 Dec.	6040
Buildings at cost	85000	Trade creditors	10200
12% Debentures	20000	Bank balance	4520
Debenture interest due	1200	Expense creditors	620
Creditors for audit fee	1800	General reserve	4000
Machinery and plant (cost £75000) book value			23500
Motor vehicles (cost £8500) book value			1300
Office equipment at cost plus additions			3760
Taxation reserve balance in the books			5000

2　R.A.S. Ltd had issued to the public 20000 12% preference shares of £1 each and 30000 ordinary shares of £1 each. The preference shares are fully paid. The ordinary shares are also fully issued but the final call of 20p is still outstanding on 200 shares.

After bringing forward the credit balance on last year's appropriation account of £4500, and allowing for all charges and appropriations for the current year, there remained a balance of undistributed profit of £5775.

From the information above and the balances listed below, prepare the balance sheet of the company, in conformity as far as possible with the Companies Acts, as at 31 December.

	£		£
10% Debentures	10000	Formation expenses	7500
Stock 31 Dec.	5520	Provision for bad debts	340
Preference dividend		Debenture interest due	500
for half year	1200	Trade debtors	6800
Fixtures (at cost)	1880	Trade creditors	6310
		Bank balance	2260
Premises (cost £25000) book balance of account now			£20000
Machinery (cost £65000) book balance of account now			28925
Motor van (cost £6500) book balance of account now			1200

3 D.R.S. Ltd has an authorised capital of £200000 divided into 150000 ordinary shares of £1 and 50000 6% preference shares of £1 each. All the preference shares have been issued and 100000 of the ordinary shares. All are fully paid with the exception of the last call of 20p on the 1000 shareholding of one member.

These balances were extracted from the books of the Company on 30 June:

	£
Premises (cost £100000; additions £25500)	125500
Plant and machinery (cost £50000) aggregate depreciation	
£14800. Book value 30 June	35200
Fixtures at cost	4820
Trade debtors	9180
General reserve account	10000
Taxation reserve	7000
Half year's preference dividend	1500
Rates in advance	800
Trade creditors	6970
Profit and loss credit balance from last year	950
Stock on hand 30 June	5500
Bank and cash on hand 30 June	15050
Provision for bad debts	500
Calls in arrear	200

The turnover of the Company for the current year was £165000.

In the ordinary trading account prepared by the accountant £5000 had been written off plant and machinery account for this year, and after charging £15000 for directors' fees (and another £12000 for directors' salaries and emoluments), there was a trading profit of £22330 before taxation.

You are required to prepare the published section of the profit and loss appropriation account in compliance with the Companies Acts, making due allowance for the payment of the balance of the preference dividend, an increase of £3000 for the Taxation Reserve, £2000 for auditor's fees, and the recommended payment of 8% dividend to the ordinary shareholders.

Answers

Answers to Assignments and Revision Exercises

2.1 £45.56   **3.2** £117.15   **3.3** £316.14   **4.1** £92.30
4.2 £99.97   **5.1** £720   **5.2** CB £48.20; TB £501.50
Revision Exercise 1   CB £269.50; TB £725.84
6.1 COS £4300; GP £3000   **6.2** GP £2130
7.1 GP £1570; NP £1180   **7.2** GP £2570; NP £1920
8.1 Profit £4850   **8.2** TB £6650; GP £1073; NP £510
9 CB £104; TB £2463; GP £477; NP £314; Cap. £1714; BS £1714
10.1 CB £35.42; £477.10   **10.2** £10; £516.50
11.2 Debit balance £22.84   **12.1** PC bal. £13.57; refund £16.43
12.2 PC £7.41; refund £27.59   **13.1** PDB £203.50; creditors £111
13.2 PDB £141.60; cash £123.40, bank £559.05; TB £1462.40
14.2 PDB £86; SDB £93.30; cash £20; bank £558.10; TB £1132.20
15.1 Debit £72.20   **15.2** Net purchases £4255; sales £9524
16.1 £178.20   **16.2** £1040   **17.2** £95 credit   **17.3** £40.90 debit
Revision Exercise 2.1   Cash £30; bank £1990.10; TB £3891.40
18.1 GP £264.40; NP £196.40; cap. £3106.40; BS £3310.40
18.2 TB £11 024; GP £4939; NP £2587; cap. £3787; WC £2607; BS £4007
19.1 GP on sales 40%; NP on sales 30%; stockturn 5 times in month
19.2 £5200: £5440   **19.3** GP £3200; claim £980
Revision Exercise 3   Cash £25; bank £457; TB £10 290; GP £57; net loss
£74; cap. £5826; BS £8956
20.1 GP £3294; NP £1828
21.1 Discounts allowed £6.30; discounts received £5.40; cash £20; bank
£427.59
21.2 £40.36 debit   **22.1** Capital £7500
Revision Exercise 4   TB £10 434; cash £20; bank £421; GP £229; NP £168;
cap. £5768; BS £9902
23.1 £180
23.2 Lease £6400; deprec. £800 p.a.; Machinery £2890; deprec. £600 and
£510

23.3 NP £3814; deprec. £1166; cap. £7314; BS £10 004
24.1 Prov. increase £75; bad debts £8
24.2 Prov. decrease £70; bad debts £54
24.3 Prov. decrease £14; bad debts £30
25.1 In advance £66; revenue £72
25.2 revenue £19 106; creditors for wages £662
25.3 Revenue £218; creditors £38; Revenue £195; in advance £65
Examination Exercise **2** Claim £3510 **3** GP £7442; NP £2903; cap.
  £9923; BS £11 308 **5** Asset balance £612 **6** 20 Main Street
26.1 NP £3792; BS £2995 **26.2** NP £240; BS £7180
26.3 NP £14 070; BS £24 210 **27.1** CB £172.10
27.2 Surplus £411; BS £4435 **28.1** Dr. £40; cr. £44 205
28.2 BL £3267; SL £3939 **29.1** M £790; L £560
29.2 A £1100; B £500; C £100 **29.3** SP £8700; MD £3700; BS £14 150
Revision Exercise 5 **1** CB £744; subs £931; deficit £197; BS £1450
  2 GP £8995; NP £5065; BS £13 215; current accounts JM £390,
  PR £50; WC £3630
31.1 C of P £152 000:£135 700; COS £160 000:£140 000; GP % 33⅓:30;
  stockturn 6.4:5.5 **31.2** £18 320; £33 500; £11 450; £44 880
31.3 £8000; £26 198; £4252; £32 105; £14 447
32.1 Bank £99 600; BS £99 600 **32.2** Bank £279 800; BS £279 800
33.1 P&L £127 890; published section c/f £11 540
33.2 WC £3610; net assets £59 660
Examination Paper **1** Surplus £216; subs £570; acc. fund £1114; BS
  £2358 **2** NP £16 571; cap. a/cs D £2624: H £1107; WC £7381; BS
  £62 286 **3** NP £1882; cap. £3292; BS £3760 **4** £10 500; £23 880;
  £6020; £32 290; £15 270; £7520 **5** £7164 debit **7** Bank £6519;
  P&L c/f £5680; BS £55 480

Answers to Additional Exercises

2.4 Loan £2600

3.1 CB £38.65
3.2 CB £51.60
3.3 CB £151.90

4.1 CB £94.30
4.2 CB £117.90
4.4 CB £218.40
4.5 CB £116.50

5.1 CB £204; TB £313
5.2 CB £346.65; TB £679.72
5.3 CB £96; TB £242
5.4 CB £96.40; TB £464.25

5.5 Cap. £1400; TB £5280
5.6 TB £7850

6.2 A COS £2350, GP £2450;
B COS £1600, GP £900;
C COS £7030, GP £2300
6.3 Stock £1200; GP £1700
6.4 GP £41
6.5 GP £960
6.6 GP £650

7.1 GP £965; NP £680
7.2 GP £185; NP £129
7.3 GP £343; NP £278
7.4 GP £365; NP £207

8.1 TB £488; GP £192; NP £133; BS £273
8.2 NP £2240; BS £3240
8.3 TB £8700; GP £2032; NP £1055; BS £2855
8.4 Cap. £3600; 20%
8.5 A £220, B £1770, C £1200, D £2000

9.1 CB £265; TB £721; GP £195; BS £395
9.2 CB £327; TB £1089; GP £243; NP £105; BS £505
9.3 Caps £5900/6350; NP £1450; BS £6350
9.4 CB £434; TB £810; GP £188; NP £77; BS £547

10.1 Cash £23.85; Bank £368.45
10.2 Cash £10; Bank £236
10.3 CB £115; Cap. £185; BS £185
10.4 CB £63; Cap. £188; BS £188

11.2 Bank statement £317.75
11.3 Amended CB balance £196.42
11.4 Bank £136.80
11.5 Cash £20.00; Bank £303.40

12.1 (*a*) £3.22; (*b*) £11.78
12.2 Bal. £2.19; refund £22.81
12.3 Bal. £5.99; refund £34.01
12.4 Bank £460; TB £600

13.3 PDB £179.40
13.4 £11.36 credit
13.5 TB £547.96; GP £187.36; NP £166.11; Cash £12.16; Bank £194.25; BS £266.41

14.1 SDB £82.00
14.2 £54.60 debit
14.3 Cash £39; Bank £499; TB £1323
14.4 Cash £27; Bank £440; TB £865; GP £110; NP £70; BS £600

15.3 £26.80 debit
15.4 £28.60 debit
15.5 £42.00 credit
15.6 Purchases £5153; Sales £11,238

17.2 £46.80 debit
17.3 £23.60 credit
17.4 Cash £16; Bank £683; TB £2184

18.2 Cap. £7000
18.4 GP £455; NP £395
18.5 Caps £2250/2630; BS £3395; WC £1330
18.6 GP £2200; NP £225; Cap £8685; BS £9935; WC £1745

19.1 £2 cost price
19.2 GP £550
19.3 COS £3700
19.4 Average stock £2000; COS £8800; 33⅓%; 50%
19.5 Average stock £1000; COS £4400; 4.4 times; 50%; 19.3%
19.6 Insurance claim £1250
19.7 X 40%, 17.7%, 25%; Y 33.3%, 13.8%, 22.2%

20.2 GP £6870; NP £4960
20.3 Asset balance £7350; revenue £150
20.4 Van account £3150; revenue £735
20.5 BS £13,720; Capital £8300; WC £880

21.2 Discts all'd £3.95; discts rec'd £6.33
Cash £52.40; Bank £421.48
21.3 Discts all'd £2.60; discts rec'd £4.90
Cash £44.00; Bank £281.80
21.4 £33.00 debit; £111.88 credit
21.5 £49 debit
21.6 £111 credit

22.5 RAS Cap. £1700; DRS Cap. £5750
22.6 BS £2705/3685; NP £590

23.2 Van account £3240; loss on sale £330; deprec. £630
23.3 Deprec. £648; profit on exchange £8
23.4 Deprec. £500; loss on sale £75; balance £1825

23.5 Deprec. net debit £1950
23.6 NP £1245; BS £681; Cap. £145

24.2 Bad debts £28 and £20; Prov. accounts £220 and £175;
Revenue £220 debit and £45 credit
24.3 GP £6675; NP £3645; Cap. £8645; BS £9895

25.2 Trading account £24 736; creditors for wages £336
25.4 Loan interest £210.90
25.5 Revenue £53.10 debit; creditors for electricity £15.40
25.6 Revenue £24.32; insurance in advance £8
25.7 TB £18 440
25.8 GP £5570; NP £3133; Cap. £5133; BS £6573
25.9 (*a*) Wages; (*b*) Drawings; (*c*) Premises; (*d*) Stock
25.10 TB £1935; GP £178; Net loss £14; Cap. £1526; BS £1677

26.1 NP £359; Bank £760; BS £1085
26.2 NP £1911; Bank £941; BS £7891
26.3 NP £145; Bank £65; BS £730
26.4 Net loss £12; BS £4723

27.2 Balance £155.22
27.3 £610
27.4 CB £26.50; surplus £287.00; BS £299.50
27.5 Bank O/D £27.80; subs. £910; surplus £159.60; BS £3749

28.1 £16 480 debit
28.3 BL £6535; SL £7990

29.2 JB £360; BJ £40 both credit
29.3 BS £15 500; ratios 10:5:3
29.4 A £40 Cr.; B £100 Dr.; Z £60 Cr.
29.5 GP £21 360; NP £11 578; BS £15 974;
Current accounts: B £2 debit, W £226 credit, G £446 debit

31.2 (*a*) £2.39; (*b*) £2.05
31.3 GP £12 290; NP £8 240; BS £35 870
31.4 (*a*) £9 250; (*b*) £35 100; (*c*) £78 800;
GP percentage; 34.33 and NP 17.00

32.1 WC £25 250; net assets £93 500; BS £95 500

33.1 Net assets £115 650; WC £2090; BS £115 650
33.2 Net assets £48 235; WC £6230; BS £55 735
33.3 BS £167 160; WC £1640; undistributed profit £7360

Index